# CROSSING BETWEEN WORLDS

## MOVING AND BEING MOVED THROUGH THE TRANSITIONS OF LIFE

### DARYL CHOW

Copyright © Daryl Chow 2025.

All Rights Reserved. No part of this publication may be reproduced, stored in a retrieval system, or transmitted, in any form or by any means without the prior written permission of the publisher, nor be otherwise circulated in any form of binding or cover other than that in which it is published and without a similar condition being imposed on the subsequent purchaser.
The moral right of the author has been asserted.
Cover design by Joel Louie
Illustrations by Daryl Chow.
Author photo by Jeremiah Ang.
ISBN-13: 978-0-6482670-3-4
Ebook ISBN: 978-0-6482670-4-1
VISIT: darylchow.com/cbw

*Disclaimer*

I am a psychologist, but I am not your psychologist. If you are in significant distress, seek help.

Note: Names and identifying details have been changed to protect the privacy of individuals.

*To my wife, for crossing between many worlds with me...*

*&*

*For those in your bedrooms, ready to make a change.*

*To every thing there is a season, and a time to every purpose under the heaven.*
*Ecclesiastes (3:1)*

*A time to tend to the self, and a time to forget about yourself.*
*A time to be in the present, and a time to think of the future.*
*A time to look within, and a time to look outside of yourself.*
*A time for solitude, and a time to be in community.*
*A time to say yes, and a time to say no.*
*A time for full acceptance, and a time for change.*
*A time to approach, and a time to retreat.*
*A time to fight for autonomy, and a time to belong.*
*A time to give care, and a time to receive care.*
*A time to grieve, and a time to love.*
*A time to focus on quality, and a time to create quantity.*
*A time to stress, and a time to recover.*
*A time for stillness, and a time for movement.*
*A time to have more inputs, and a time to create outputs.*
*A time to gain control, and a time to surrender.*

# CONTENTS

## PART I: THE FRAMEWORK

1. Introduction — 3
2. Bridge-Crossing — 9
3. Nurture Your Nature — 14
4. Why Needs? — 21
5. Why Seasons? — 25
6. Why Paradoxical? — 43
7. How to Begin — 46
8. What Not to Do When Crossing Between Worlds — 59
9. Structure of the Book — 63

## PART II: WELL-BEING

Paradox 1: Self-Care/Self-Forgetting — 69
Paradox 2. Present/Future — 86
Paradox 3. Introspection/Outrospection — 96
Paradox 4. Solitude/Community — 104
Paradox 5. Yes/No — 112

## PART III: WELL-BELONGING

Paradox 6. Acceptance/Change — 125
Paradox 7. Approach/Retreat — 145
Paradox 8. Autonomy/Belonging — 156
Paradox 9. Caregiving/Receiving Care — 175
Paradox 10. Grief/Love — 191

## PART III: WELL-DOING

Paradox 11. Quality/Quantity — 209
Paradox 12. Recovery/Stress — 220
Paradox 13. Stillness/Movement — 241
Paradox 14. Input/Output — 261

| | |
|---|---|
| Paradox 15. Control/Surrender | 286 |

## CONCLUSION

| | |
|---|---|
| Personal Paradoxical Profile (P3) Redux | 311 |
| A Call to Become a Gift to Others | 313 |
| | |
| A Gift For You | 319 |
| Acknowledgements | 321 |

## APPENDICES

| | |
|---|---|
| Appendix A: The Personal Paradoxical Profile (P3) | 325 |
| Appendix B: The Big Five Personality Construct | 331 |
| Appendix C: Dailies, Strategies, Skills, and Meals (DSSM) Framework | 335 |
| Appendix D: Reading Non-Fiction | 337 |
| Appendix E: Have You Been Faithful to Your Gifts? | 339 |
| Appendix F: Course of Action | 341 |
| | |
| *Notes* | 345 |
| *Also by Daryl Chow* | 355 |

# PART I: THE FRAMEWORK

"You enter the forest at the darkest point, where there is no path. Where there is a way or a path, it is someone else's path. You are not on your own path.
If you follow someone else's way, you are not going to realise your potential."

*— Joseph Campbell*[i]

# 1. INTRODUCTION

This book is for people who are Crossing Between Worlds.

People who have been struck by losses, changes, realisations, significant hurts, or a "waking up" to the reality of this mortal coil, people who would leave an old world behind, even though the new world is fraught with uncertainty and there's no guarantee that it will all work out. You could be in your mid-forties, facing your third life-transition after losing a parent and experiencing a career change; or you could be in your second year of university, facing your first legitimate crossroads in love, experiencing betrayal, and asking "what the heck do I do with my life?" type of question.

In other words, this book is for people who are making changes on the outside and on the inside, inching into a new season of life.

The impetus for embarking on a path of Crossing Between Worlds might stem from one of the following: Losing a job, the death of a loved one, being struck by an illness, an intractable addiction, a relationship breakup, burnout from a lifeless career, a betrayal, mustering the courage to leave an abusive relationship, a divorce. Sometimes, life just likes to throw a bunch of these challenges at us all at once. And it's not just negative stuff. The urge to create a new life can come from stepping out of high school, getting married, the birth of your first child, moving countries, a new career opportunity, beginning a new life project after a reexamination of core existential priorities.

For some, the motivation for change could be the painful realisation that they have been an asshole for a long time. They have had enough of their own attitude. Their conscience is banging on their door. For others, a repeated pattern of others taking advantage of their kindness makes them realise they can no longer be conflict-avoidant. Resentment is eating them from the inside out.

**How Tech Is Trapping Us Between Worlds**

And then there are those who realise they're currently wasting their life, even though they didn't start off that way. Our technological devices—especially the mobile phone—have insidiously not only messed up our attention span, but have also strayed from our original intentions for them. They're more than just distractions. Tech companies call us "Users" for a reason: We are all addicts in our dopamine-drenched culture.

Our youth are paying an especially high price. Anxiety, depression, self-harm, and suicide rates among the young, especially girls, have increased dramatically since the period of 2010–2015. Social psychologist Jonathan Haidt notes in his 2024 book, *Anxious Generation*, that this was the period of the great rewiring of our children that we never consented to.

But what in the world happened between 2010 and 2015 that led to a proliferation of mental health concerns?

In 2010, Apple introduced the iPhone 4, the first smartphone with a front-facing camera. Promptly, Samsung followed suit. "That same year, Instagram was created as an app that could be used only on smartphones," says Haidt. He adds,

For the first few years, there was no way to use it on a desktop or laptop. Instagram had a small user base until 2012, when it was purchased by Facebook. Its user base then grew rapidly (from 10 million near the end of 2011 to 90 million by early 2013). We might therefore say that the smartphone and selfie-based social media ecosystem that we know today emerged in 2012, with Facebook's purchase of Instagram following the introduction of the front-facing camera. By 2012, many teen girls would have felt that 'everyone' was getting a smartphone and an Instagram account, and everyone was comparing themselves with everyone else. Over the next few years the social media ecosystem became even more enticing with the introduction of ever more powerful "filters" and editing software within Instagram and via external apps such as Facetune. Whether she used filters or not, the reflection each girl saw in the mirror got less and less attractive relative to the girls she saw on her phone. While girls' social lives moved onto social media platforms, boys burrowed deeper into the virtual world as they engaged in a variety of digital activities, particularly immersive online multiplayer video games, YouTube, Reddit, and hardcore pornography—all of which became available anytime, anywhere, for free, right on their smartphones.

Essentially, **a play-based childhood has been replaced by a phone-based childhood.** Social media is the new toy that everyone seems to love and hate at the same time. No other theories seem to explain this decline in mental health among the young (especially given the timing), including economic crises, climate change, academic pressure, an increase in self-reporting, and the age-old admonition of the proverbial statistics professor who says "correlation is not causation."[1]

Just to be clear, this is not a Luddite-attack on every form of

---

1. For more on why other competing explanations like "people are more willing

modern technology. I'm a fan of great inventions, and we are beneficiaries of these tools in so many ways. The discovery of fire marked a significant turning point that shaped human evolution. But like fire, if we do not learn to control technology we risk being consumed by its power. If we continue to be passive users and don't actively discern what's best for us all, we might burn the house down.

We have to ask ourselves: What is the ultimate price we are willing to pay for a culture of junkies on their phones, waiting for the next dopamine hit?

Vietnamese philosopher C. Thi Nyugen rightly names the issue that is happening in our culture "Value Capture." In his paper of the same title, he notes, "...It is rather difficult to say, in a principled way, exactly why value capture is so horrifying. For one thing, value capture is often consensual." Nyugen adds, "In value capture, we outsource the process of value deliberation." In other words, we allow our core values to be overruled by quantifiable metrics. We might have begun by caring about things like good health, developing skills and expertise, or a job we love. But increasingly, with the nudge of technology, our values and goals become co-opted by what the machine values. Think FitBit. Nyugen says,

> Even if fitness was your main goal, the FitBit can exert a narrowing influence. Exercise can be valuable in all sorts of ways that aren't measured by a FitBit. A FitBit doesn't capture the ecstasy of complex skillful motion. It doesn't capture the camaraderie of team sports, the meditative calm of paddling a canoe across a quiet lake, or the aesthetic loveliness of a delicate rock climbing move. A FitBit measures exactly one thing: Steps.

---

to seek help," or "kids have less independence" fall short, read Jean Twenge's article: afterbabel.com/p/13-explanations-mental-health-crisis.

Nyugen, an avid gamer himself, had a lightbulb moment when he heard a well-known speaker give a talk at a conference. The German game-designer made the following remark: "The most important thing in my toolbox is the point system... [because] it tells the person *what* to desire." Nyugen told an interviewer, "This is what I'm worried about. It changes *what* we desire."

What has all of this got to do with making transitions in your life? My hope through this book is to advocate for you to follow your deep desires, and not let your progress be stymied by meaningless, shallow desires. I think you and I can agree that there are *many* distractions going around.[2] Think about the last time you were about to do something useful for yourself and got sucked into the ether on your little device. When your attention gets co-opted, it messes with your intentions. The last thing I want for you is to give up on your deep desires because you got lost in the infinite scroll of TikTok.

Desire is a life-force that has the potential to bring more life. Desire is a seed planted within you, and it's your job to not only nourish and raise it to life, but also protect it from Value Capture.

**You Might Not Need This Book**

Though it is not a good marketing strategy for me to say this, I thought I should make it clear: you can do without this book. People have been navigating and adapting to changes in their lives long before the printing press was invented. They seemed to do just fine with all the resources they had. In fact, many people go through transitions in life without any kind of guidance. In Chinese, the word "crisis" (*Wéi Jī*) means a time of both danger

---

2. One of my challenges writing this book for about three years has been wrestling with endless distractions. Maybe I should use a typewriter for my next project.

and opportunity. The one reason this book exists is to help you see and seize the opportunity in a time of shake-ups, to take heed of your deep desires and fan the amber within you, so that you get a fighting chance to experience deep joy in this one life.

Wéi Jī *(Crisis)*

Flip through the pages of this book. You will notice that *Crossing Between Worlds* serves as a vast map of possibilities. This book is not about having more information or catchphrases; it acts as a catalyst for change. It is designed to help you experience life. It is not just about having more ideas; it's about *becoming* who you really are. In other words, **this book will ask of you more than you would ask of yourself on your own.**

I hope that this all will help you deliberate the types of games you are going to play—and enjoy playing them, even when the road gets rough.

## 2. BRIDGE-CROSSING

Over the past 20 years in my clinical practice as a psychologist, this is where I meet and walk alongside fellow travellers: on a bridge.

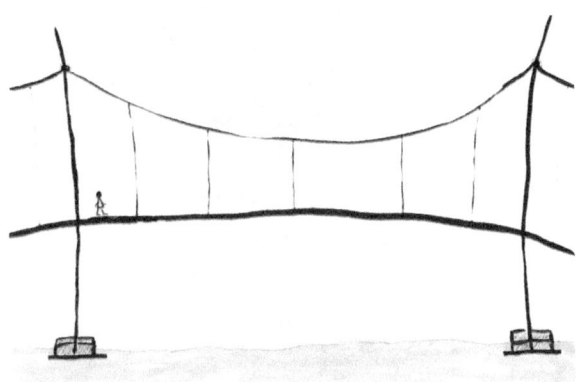

The journey of Crossing Between Worlds is a defining period in one's life. Give or take, you'll probably experience only a handful of such transitions in your lifetime. These periods are often coloured with darkness, uncertainty, ambiguity, fear, suffering, and grief. It's unfortunate that we have a proclivity to reduce our experience to diagnostic labels and reach for the nearest medical or psychological explanation, thereby leading us to water down this liminal state as a "mental health" issue.

In our attempts to make sense of it all, we use various clinical terms, from depression and anxiety to ADHD, trauma, and others. But when you become too quick to name things,[1] you fail to follow the calling path in front of you, the new world that is beckoning you to inhabit it. While the embodied experience and symptoms of such a period can be discomforting and distressful, they are *signals*, and not the issue in and of themselves. Sometimes, all it takes to shift our state is to ask ourselves, *What's making me depressed? What has happened that led me to feel this way?* Not everything has a clear cause and effect, but it would do us good to have a better understanding of our nature, how we nurture ourselves through the emotional needs that we have (more on that later, in "Nurture Our Nature"). By viewing our emotional pains solely from a medical perspective, we run the risk of treating only the symptom and not the problem.

Moving from an old story to a new one is akin to crossing a bridge. This bridge is often wobbly. Your footing is unsteady, your mind is racing, and your heart is riddled with anxiety as you take each step.

And yet, at the brink of it all, the opportunity arises for us to see things differently. As you move along—and you might not fully grasp this while you are doing it—the seasons are changing. Your needs are no longer the same as they once were; what's

---

[1]. To be clear, at times, having a label to define the problem that we have can bring a huge sense of relief. For instance, to be formally diagnosed as autistic in adulthood can bring great comfort to some, since this helps the individual not only to make sense of their challenges as a child, but also helps them navigate the world ahead of them, i.e., learning social skills systemically or learning that it's ok to retreat when they has been in a noisy environment for longer than they can manage due to sensory overload.

required of you previously no longer applies in this upcoming fresh territory.

But the movement between worlds is not exactly new. Like the seasons, we move in circles. Periods of crises might vary, but the inner-challenges that surface have similar patterns and schemas. Most of us will face at least three to five major life disruptions, or as author Bruce Feiler calls them, "Lifequakes."[i] Hence, it makes perfect sense to learn deeply from past reckonings when you are at the fork in the road.

This book is about listening to the **needs and seasons that arise in times of change and crisis.** It is about **moving and *being moved*.** "Moving" implies acting upon our intentions and tilting the sails to help us move in accordance. "Being moved," on the other hand, is to allow ourselves to be touched and inspired by what unfolds in front of us, even when—or rather, *especially* when—it is not our choice.

"To move" is to resist becoming the victims of our circumstances. "To move" is an act of will and responsibility. "To be moved" is to allow ourselves to be touched by what's in front of us, and to utilise that as a mobilising force (See Paradox 15. "Control and Surrender").

Researchers in human emotions offer a fascinating insight. A review article by Janis Zickfeld and colleagues suggested that being 'moved' should be treated as a "distinct emotion."[ii] Sensations of being moved include tears, chills, a lump in the throat, goosebumps, and warmth in the chest. When seen in this light, it's easy to understand why the experience of being moved is often considered a passive one, i.e., not something we can actively control. Let me do my Chinese teacher proud and point out that in Mandarin, "being moved," Gǎn Dòng [感动], literally translates as "to feel movement."[2]

Here's another interesting point to note. The lexeme *being moved* not only implies approach and prosocial tendencies, but it also suggests "insight, meaning, and personal growth."

This book does not offer a fixed path. Nor should you simply take someone else's path. Artist Austin Kleon says, "Some advice can be a vice."[iii]

You must ultimately forge your own path. There is no formula, only a form, a structure that can guide you. Treat this book as a structural scaffold. You pull it down once you are done.

---

2. I failed at Chinese at my GCE O Levels exams, twice. I couldn't read 80% of the text, so I did my Chinese oral exams in English, much to the amazement of my classmates.

## Main Idea

This is the central idea of the book:

**Our nature is designed to be nurtured, informed by our needs and the season we are in.**

We are going to unpack, one at a time, each of the four factors (nature, nurture, need, and season) embedded in this single sentence, and then develop a personalised map for the way forward using the Personalised Paradoxical Profile (P3), which will help you as you are Crossing Between Worlds.

Nature → Nurture → Needs → Naming the Season → Complete the P3 → Read the 15 Paradoxes → Revisit Your P3 → Course of Action

# 3. NURTURE YOUR NATURE

"The major problems in the world are the result of the difference between how nature works and the way people think."

— *Gregory Bateson.*

**What Is Your Nature?**

One of the most beneficial things you can do for yourself is to figure out your nature. The Latin *natura*, or Nature, means both birth and character. Let's unpack each of the two.

*By Birth*

*By Birth,* we are predisposed to a certain temperament, and somewhat bound by our genetic underpinnings. Differences in temperament from an early age becomes apparent when you observe your children. One might be easy going and leap non-hesitantly into the playground with other kids, and the other might be very sensitive to the external environment and needs time to observe others on the playground before they set foot in the sand.

The different shades of temperaments shape our personality. Personality is a set of enduring patterns of thoughts, feelings, and behaviours that make an individual unique. Our personality colours how we see the world. Not only does it cause us to perceive things differently from others, but our unique personalities also lead us to consider different facts. For instance, when dealing with conflict at work, a highly empathetic individual is more likely to consider the feelings and perspectives of others involved, while a logical person is more likely to prioritise effectiveness and efficiency towards the end result. Likewise, individuals higher in Openness to Experience—one of the Big Five personality constructs that we will talk about later—are less likely to conform to pre-existing beliefs and are more willing to consider information that contradicts their existing views.

Why is understanding personality constructs so important? In an in-depth course on personality, Jordan Peterson argues it's because you are a person who is situated in a social world, and you have a personality and must contend with other personalities.[1] Different personalities have different proclivities in their moral and political ideologies. One would imagine that our moral and political beliefs are primarily based on reasoned judgements, but in his book *The Righteous Mind*, Jonathan Haidt notes that our moral foundation and political ideology are shaped by our temperaments, more so than we imagine. For example, individuals high in Conscientiousness, characterised by traits such as self-discipline and adherence to rules, may place a strong emphasis on moral values related to loyalty and authority, which are key aspects of conservative moral foundations. On the other hand, individuals who are high in Agreeableness, charac-

---

[1]. If you are interested in taking an in-depth understanding on Personality, I highly recommend Jordan Peterson's course *Discovering Personality* courses. jordanbpeterson.com/personality. I've learned more from this than any other personality course or books that I've read combined. The Big Five Personality questionnaire comes free with this course.

by traits such as compassion and cooperation, may prioritise moral values related to care and fairness, which are central to liberal moral foundations.

Given the above, and based on the current empirical understanding, what is a useful framework that can help us understand our nature a little better? What are the "givens" in our temperaments from birth? I would argue that the Five Factor Model (FFM), commonly referred to as the Big Five Personality Traits, is one of the most practical tools for understanding ourselves.

An easy way to remember these five factors is to use the acronym **OCEAN**. It stands for *Openness to Experience, Conscientiousness, Extraversion, Agreeableness, and Neuroticism*. See the following table for an elaboration of each trait, along with its corresponding advantages and disadvantages when pushed to the edges.

### Table 1. The Big Five Personality Construct

| Factors | Overview | Subsets | Type | Advantages | Disadvantages |
|---|---|---|---|---|---|
| Openness to Experience | Describes how open-minded, imaginative, and curious a person is. | **Intellect**: Interests in ideas and abstract thinking, ability to handle complex ideas and problems. **Aesthetics**: Creativity, artistic interests, interest in aesthetics (nature, various art forms), appreciation of beauty. | A person who is high in openness to experience is often imaginative and curious, and has broad interests. A person low in openness to experience is more conventional, concrete, and uncreative and has narrow interests. | High Openness to Experience: Creative and intellectually curious. Low Openness to Experience: Pragmatic and likely more focused (especially if high in Conscientiousness). | High Openness to Experience: Prone to overthinking and less practical. Low Openness to Experience: Less imaginative, less open to change. |
| Conscientious-ness | Reflects how organised, responsible, and goal-oriented an individual tends to be. | **Industrious**: Carries out plans, completes tasks, avoids wasting time. **Orderly**: Tidy, keeps a routine and schedule, attends to details, organised and clean. | A person who is high in conscientiousness is self-disciplined and hardworking, and keeps things in order. A person who is low in conscientiousness is disorganised, messy, and easily distracted. | High Conscientiousness: Goal-oriented, organised, and reliable. Low Conscientiousness: Less rigid, more flexible, and spontaneous. | High Conscientiousness: Rigid, perfectionistic, and overly cautious. Low Conscientiousness: Disorganised, unreliable, has no clear goals. |

## 3. Nurture Your Nature | 17

| Factors | Overview | Subsets | Type | Advantages | Disadvantages |
|---|---|---|---|---|---|
| Extraversion | Indicates how outgoing, sociable, and energetic one is. Experiences positive emotions. | **Enthusiasm**: Makes friends easily, quick to warm up to others. **Assertiveness**: Strong personality, takes charge, influential. | A person who is high in extraversion is sociable, spontaneous, and persuasive. A person who is low in extraversion (introversion), is more held back, doesn't show their feelings easily, and doesn't like taking the limelight. | High Extraversion: Assertive, sociable, outgoing, and energetic. Values the present. Low Extraversion: Independent and reflective. Thrives in solitude. Values the future. | High Extraversion: Impulsive, prone to risk-taking. Low Extraversion: Socially withdrawn and less communicative. |
| Agreeableness | Refers to how cooperative, kind, considerate and warm a person is towards others. | **Politeness**: Not pushy, respects authority, doesn't take advantage of others, conflict avoidant, and not focused on personal gain. **Compassion**: Feels others' emotions, has a soft side, focused on doing things for others, interested in other people's lives and problems. | A person who is high in agreeableness is more self-sacrificial, since they place the interest of others over their own. A person who is low in agreeableness is disagreeable, more assertive, competitive, and blunt in their points of view. | High Agreeableness: Empathic, trusting of others, warm and polite. Low Agreeableness: Competitive, critical in decision making, speaks directly to the point. | High Agreeableness: Overly submissive, conflict avoidant. Low Agreeableness: Less cooperative, may come across as argumentative. |
| Neuroticism | Emotional stability. The tendency to experience a wide range of negative emotions (e.g., anxiety, depression, rumination, disappointment, frustration, rejection). | **Volatility**: Easily irritated, unstable. **Withdrawal**: Easily overwhelmed, anxiety-prone. | A person who is high in neuroticism is more sensitive to hurt. Conversely, a person who is low in neuroticism is more calm and reasonable. | High Neuroticism: Emotionally sensitive. Internally focused. Low Neuroticism: Calm and emotionally stable. | High Neuroticism: Prone to emotional instability. Low Neuroticism: Less emotionally aware. May come across as insensitive. |

You might be interested in understanding more about yourself through the lens of the Big Five Personality Construct. I suggest three options for doing so in Appendix B.

Whichever version you decide to explore with, treat the Big Five as a "vocabulary" you can use to recognise your nature, as well as a way to see others as they are. However, do not treat your temperament as fixed. You can broaden your nature based on where you are going—especially as you are Crossing between Worlds. You'll discover and unravel more about yourself than you would expect. (In each of 15 Paradoxes, I provide specific suggestions for certain personality factors, under "Broaden Your Nature").

### By Character

If one facet of our nature is *By Birth*, the other is *By Character*, which comes from the Greek word, *kharakter*, or chisel. In a sense, when we move towards our intentions and face the inherent challenges along the way, our character is formed and "chiselled" into being.

Our temperament is not destiny. Dan Gilbert says, "Human beings are works in progress that mistakenly think they're finished." Tempting as it seems, and as useful as they can be, we should not completely outsource the process of understanding ourselves to a personality test. This might seem contradictory to what was mentioned earlier regarding the Big Five Personality construct, but the key is to have a clear and balanced view about how we can understand who we are.

In Annie Murphy Paul's book *The Cult of Personality Testing*, she points out that these personality tests contribute to oversimplified categorisations of complex human beings, potentially leading to discrimination, biases, and misguided decision-making. For instance, there is still a prolific use of personality tests by one in five Fortune 1,000 companies to assess candidates for executive roles, expending an estimated $2 billion on such assessments.[i] Yet the evidence is poor on the use of personality tests to predict job performance.[ii]

The obsession with "personality" had become so crazy in 2019 that Facebook had to ban such quizzes, because more than 87 million people had given away their personal information in exchange for the answer to a quiz.[iii] I have noticed people in my clinical practice who pigeon-hole themselves prematurely after taking a personality test, like the Myers-Briggs Type Indicator (MBTI)—often dished out to them in a corporate setting—or an Enneagram test they found online. Notice the language that they would use to describe themselves thereafter: "I am an INTJ"

(Introverted, Intuitive, Thinking, Judging) or "I am a Type 3" (The Achiever). To be sure, this can be useful as a springboard for self-awareness. But we must take caution not to over-identify and transfix ourselves with these constructs.[iv] You are not an INTJ, an ENFJ, or whatever Type 1, 2, 3... These are rough clues that give you hints of who you are based on the past projected onto the present. These are not maps for where you are going and who you are to become. As Derek Sivers notes,

> Putting a label on a person is like putting a label on the water in a river. It's ignoring the flow of time... "I'm an introvert, so that's why I can't." No. **Definitions are not reasons** [emphasis mine]. Definitions are just your old responses to past situations. What you call your personality is just a past tendency. New situations need a new response... Nature changes seasons at regular intervals. So should you.[v]

We are, however, about to create the map for the territory ahead of you.

**Nurture Our Nature**

We needn't get caught up in the debate about "nature vs. nurture." Our nature is *designed* to be nurtured. Each of us has a unique predisposition and proclivity. Our task in this lifetime is to cultivate what's inside of us. This is our responsibility. As the great jazz musician Miles Davis put it, "Man, sometimes it takes a long time to sound like yourself."

Why would it take a long time to figure out a way to fully express who we really are? Perhaps because there is so much noise to cut through and so many competing voices inside of us to wrestle with.

There's also a big difference between what's right and *what's right for you*. It's easier than you think to get caught up in the former—and take for granted the latter. Why is this so? Because of the allure of the competing voices outside of ourselves, from those who try to peddle us snakeoil, telling us stories about what we should want, what we should need. It's much easier to follow the pack than it is to heed the small voice that speaks from our nature.

Nurture your nature. You can tilt the direction and push towards the edges of your development. You can identify aspects of your personality and stretch towards where you want to go. The goal is not to fixate on what you've been given. Rather, it is what you do with what you have that matters. Ultimately, the journey in *Crossing Between Worlds* is to broaden your personality.

Our job is to mother our nature. Like a gardener, we plant the seeds, and we give them water, we give them light—perhaps not too much for some types—and make sure they are rooted in good soil, nourished by good fertiliser. After all, good things grow from shit.

---

Here's where we are so far:

**Nature** → **Nurture** → Needs → Naming the Season → Complete the P3 → Read the 15 Paradoxes → Revisit Your P3 → Course of Action

## 4. WHY NEEDS?

Most of us know more about "shoulds" and less about "needs."

As I write this at a cafe, I'm looking at two toddlers with their grandparents. Sitting in their high-chairs, I don't think they can make the distinction between shoulds, wants, or needs. Their moment-by-moment wants and needs are met by their caregiver. Maybe they are hungry; maybe they are thirsty. Maybe the younger brother just did a number two in his diaper. Or maybe as the grandma says to them now, "Nap-nap time."

Physical needs are obvious. Emotional needs are less so.

Emotional needs remind us of a distant truth that we deny. We don't like to feel needy. We feel too "dependent," overly reliant, and disempowered from being a fully autonomous creature. But that is how we come into this world: needy, crying and utterly dependent on our caregivers.

Needs are like beacon lights, flashing signals to tell you, "Hey, look here!"

Emotional needs are **universally non-negotiable.** This is a strong statement. This means that everyone has needs hidden in plain sight, and no one is exempt from them.

What are these non-negotiable emotional needs?

Most of us are familiar with Maslow's Hierarchy of Needs, with self-actualisation at the top of the pyramid. Personally, I don't find that pyramid useful. Turns out, Abraham Maslow never put the "hierarchy of needs" on a triangle. Some management consultancy firm in the 1960s did that.[i]

Early in my career as a youth worker, I was exposed to the teachings of the late William Glasser. He was quite a non-conformist, vocal about his belief that his profession of psychiatry was over-medicating people. One of Glasser's theories provides a useful framework for me. Glasser defined five Basic Needs:

1. Survival
2. Love and Belonging
3. Autonomy
4. Freedom
5. Fun

You'll notice that only one of these needs is physical. The other four belong to the emotional domain of our inner lives.

As I will elaborate later, our needs change at different times and may even be contradictory, especially when we approach critical junctures that impose significant changes around us. But just take a moment and contemplate these questions:

> *What are some of your unmet needs right now?*
> *Where is the pain?*
> *What's missing at this point in your life?*

Allow yourself the spaciousness of contemplation during times of transitions. In my clinical practice, after we've explored what has led the client to make an appointment with me, asking variations of the above questions seems to evoke a visceral response for many people. Most clients unconsciously let out a sigh as they reflect on them, as if someone is gently pressing on an aching point on their body.

When I asked Josephine, who was in her mid-50s dealing with a bout of anxiety, "What's missing in your life? What do you need?," she couldn't come up with a response.

"I have no idea," she replied.

Given that she wished to be able to get out of her house and go to the shops without fear and anxiety crippling her, I initially thought she might talk about the need to be more in control or to have more personal agency. After I walked her through the menu of five basic needs, she jumped in. "You know what? I'm really lacking fun in my life."

This took me by surprise. Since her children had moved out and she'd had a health scare a few years ago, she'd found herself more and more redrawn into her shell and disconnected from her long-time friends.

Isn't it interesting that "Fun" is on that list? Quite often, we neglect a sense of playfulness. We think we need to double down on earnestness when we are going through troubled times. Yet play is a potent antidote to depression. Improv teacher Keith Johnstone says, "Many teachers think of children as immature adults. It might lead to better and more 'respectful' teaching if we thought of adults as atrophied children."[ii]

When we neglect or ignore our emotional needs, psychological symptoms present themselves. Like a fire alarm going off when something's burning, these symptoms are signals. If you treat only the symptoms, it is like flicking off the annoying siren without actually putting out the fire.

In short, needs are your guiding light. They point to a direction, and consequently, a set of actions is asked of you.

Our task is to nurture our nature, informed by our needs.

. . .

Here's where we are so far:

**Nature** → **Nurture** → **Needs** → Naming the Season → Complete the P3 → Read the 15 Paradoxes → Revisit Your P3 → Course of Action

## 5. WHY SEASONS?

Now that we have talked about Nature, Nurture, and Needs, let's take the next step and discuss Seasons.
Different seasons have different needs.
This is why figuring out the season that we are in helps us attend to the accompanying emotional needs.

Don't let the obviousness of this point trivialise it. Without a deep appreciation of the seasonality of our lives, our super-charged, hyper-efficient pursuit of productivity begins to mimic industrial farming's relentless quest for hyper-growth. To treat sick animals, prevent illness in healthy livestock, and boost animal growth, industrial farming accounts for about 80% of the world's antibiotic consumption. In turn, this misuse of antibiotics has led to a global rise of antibiotic resistance.[i]

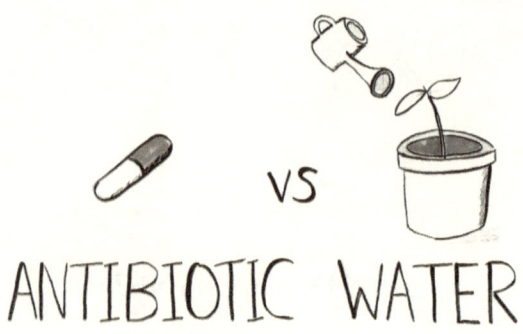

# ANTIBIOTIC WATER

Buddhist tradition has something useful to teach us here: The pursuit of happiness is a source of suffering. We are prone to become "happiness-chasers." Researchers Brett Ford and colleagues state, "People who value happiness to an extreme tend to have worse psychological health, including more depression."[ii] What's more, an over-valuation of happiness can lead to an increased risk of bipolar disorder. Ford and colleagues add, "... Extreme valuing of happiness may be a risk factor for the onset and maintenance of bipolar, and not simply a consequence of bipolar disorder."

I'm not saying that we should de-value happiness so as to inoculate ourselves from manic episodes, but if happiness is all that we are trying to pursue, we are not going to find it. As Viktor Frankl puts it, "Happiness cannot be pursued, but ensued."

Our fixation on hyper-growth is evident elsewhere. We leave the city lights on all year round. Are we really that afraid of the dark? We are unaccustomed to natural changes because we insulate ourselves from the planet's *rhythmic* changes. We become season-blind. Nature unfolds in its own rhythm, and we resist it.

Instead of *inflating* growth, we need to *cultivate* growth. How? We first need to be "season-minded."

## Season Blindness

At any given point in time, we live in two worlds, not one. One on the outside, the other on the inside. Our outer-life is less abstract and more obvious, but our inner-life is often more abstract and hidden from plain sight. If you stop to think about it, you are the only one privy to what's going on on the inside. In addition, some of the most important things that we experience in our inner-life are things that cannot be seen, like love, friendship, and transcendence.

While we can appreciate differences between contrasting life-stages such as childhood and adulthood, we are less observant of the change of seasons in our inner-lives.

Consider Hong Wen, a newly minted father in his 30s. From the outside looking in, we take for granted the degree of change that occurs when a child enters our lives. Some friends might say to you, "Go and enjoy your freedom before the kids come on board!" Not exactly the most helpful frame of mind to have.

In actuality, such a period of Crossing Between Worlds is filled with change and loss. Hong Wen was all geared up for the season of fatherhood, but he did not expect the level of change that it asked of him. Specifically, he was less and less able to keep up with the demands of the twice-a-week basketball team that he and his mates had been in for several years. For his sake, his wife would encourage him to continue his sports. After all, it was his outlet and time to hang out with his mates. On top of that, he was meticulous and hardworking at his job as a data engineer, often putting in extra hours each day to make sure the project at hand was done well. On off days, he would unwittingly be thinking about his work on how to improve certain analytic strategies and processes at play. Trying to keep up with his job, and his promise to himself to do a better job at fathering than his own father had, while also taking turns for the night duties to look after the newborn, was taking its toll.

Obviously, he missed parts of his old life. But one truth that he hadn't really taken into consideration is that change *is* loss. He had the expectation that he was going to be able to keep up with everything from his old life, even with a newborn baby in the household.

We want things to continue as they were, even when the seasons change. Even if we dig our heels and insist on what we want, different seasons will demand different things out of us. We can be willfully season-blind to the changes within and without, and the cost can be high. Not only was Hong Wen's wife realising that he was out of sorts, which made her further insist on him continuing with his sport as per usual, but he started to feel depressed and develop anxiety symptoms. In our initial sessions, he revealed that, much to his surprise, he was totally unprepared for fatherhood. The changes blindsided him. Thus, the process of our therapy sessions was to slow things down and return to the heart of his intentions, which was to not screw up like his father had. Keeping fit was still going to be a necessary activity he included in his life, but not at the expense of sacrificing his new-found role of being a present parent. In turn, his obsession with work had to be consciously dialled down, so as to make room each day for care and play with his baby (see #3. Give 80, not 100, in Paradox 12. Stress).

Paying attention to the seasonality within is like listening to the earth's four seasons. Growing up in a tropical country like Singapore, seasonality was somewhat foreign to me. Before my wife and I moved to Australia more than a decade ago, we hardly ever checked a weather app. Back then, we could predict what the day was going to be like: Hot. As the months rolled by each year, we didn't have to be season-minded. We had the same wardrobe and roughly the same expectation of the humid (and draining) weather.

From the trees to the flowers and the birds, nature is not season-blind. Nature is *season-adaptive*. It responds to it.

To be season-blind is to deny the evolving needs of oneself. What is the price we pay when we are season-blind? We end up modelling ourselves to the industrial complex of hyper-productivity. And, should we really be surprised if artificial intelligence is edging out our mechanistic work? If we keep this up, we end up behaving more like robots, and less like humans.

## Examples of Seasons

Over the years in my clinical practice, I found myself asking clients the following question:

*What would you call this season of your life?*

Another way to ask this. "If this was a chapter in a book, what would you call it?"

There is an old story about a priest walking down the road during the Russian revolution. A passing soldier says, "Halt. Who are you? Where are you going? Why are you going there?" The priest pauses, reflects, and then asks the soldier, "How much do you get paid a month?"

"Ten rubles," replies the soldier.

The priest says, "I will pay you twenty rubles a month if, everyday, you stop me and ask me those same questions: Who are you? Where are you going? And why are you going there?"

**Where Are You?**

In the Biblical story of Adam and Eve, God was walking in the garden in the cool of the day. His first question to Adam was not "How are you?" or "How are things?" Instead, He asked, "Where are you?"[iii]

This is an important question to ask ourselves:

*"Where am I in my life?"*

Following her decision to leave her undergraduate program in Business Administration midway, Josephine faced considerable criticism from her parents and relatives. She wanted to go into the arts instead. It looked impulsive from the outside, because no one had the faintest idea that this desire had been brewing since her last year of high school, three years ago. Going to college had made her family proud, but she couldn't continue to ignore the gnawing feeling that was festering inside, telling her she should be doing something else. In one of our conversations, Josephine said, "I feel like I'm crossing a bridge." Even though a part of her felt like she wanted to "retreat" and give in to her family's desires, she also knew she needed to keep moving, because ahead of her was a figurative new country.

There are lots of unknowns. But this is what's exciting about this bridge-crossing phase. Getting to somewhere foreign, and being open to explore, to learn new things about the world and about yourself—sounds like tourism, doesn't it? Viewed in this light, Josephine could see that the choices that she makes will not be wasted. There was no failure in quitting the Business Administration program and pursuing a course in Fine Arts. Now she simply sees it as a different path to explore, and whatever the outcome, she's committed to learn from her experience. (See #3. Grit and Quit Quadrant, in Paradox 1. Self-Care)

I've noticed that asking "Where are you?" can lead some of my clients to become quiet and pensive for a moment. If it does the same for you, do not pressure yourself for a quick response. Worry less about "naming" where you are. First, take the time to richly describe what is happening in your life, the world around you, and inside you. Next, take all the time you need to reflect on this. Write it down. Let it sit at the back of your mind as you go about your day; let it percolate as you take a walk and come back to it later.

Some people answer the question based on where they like to be, and not where they are currently. While it may be useful to think about what the next chapter will look like, it's often more prudent to tune in to the present signs of our times. It's hard to predict the future, but we *can* shape our responses to the current season so that we can be prepared for what's ahead.

**The Fourth Turning**

To gain further insights into how to make sense of how to look at our inner-seasons through the wheels of time, let us briefly turn to two historians.

William Strauss and Neil Howe's historical analysis provides a fascinating read of our generational and social patterns. They have found that Anglo-American society enters a new era—a new "turning"—about every two decades. The span of four of these turnings is roughly the length of a human's existence (80 to a 100 years), which they call a *saeculum*. Strauss and Howe notes that "at the start of each turning, people change how they feel about themselves, the culture, the nation, and the future."[iv]

According to Strauss and Howe, the four cycles in a saeculum are

1. **High**

"The First Turning is… an upbeat era of strengthening institutions and weakening individualism, when a new civic order implants and the old values regime decays."

2. **Awakening**

"The Second Turning is… a passionate era of spiritual upheaval, when the civic order comes under attack from a new values regime."

3. **Unravelling**

"The Third Turning is…a downcast era of strengthening individualism and weakening institutions, when the old civic order decays and the new values regime implants."

4. **Crisis**

"The Fourth Turning is…a decisive era of secular upheaval,

when the values regime propels the replacement of the old civic order with a new one."[1]

While Straus and Howe was speaking largely of societal and political cycles, I find it useful to apply each of the four turnings to the seasons of life as well:

SEASONS OF LIFE
   1. **RENEWAL**
   - Revitalisation
   - New life
   - Growth
   2. **COME OF AGE**
   - Gains of love
   - Self-discovery
   - Maturation
   3. **GRIEF**
   - Closure
   - Loss
   - Endings
   4. **CRITICAL POINT**

---

[1]. From a global viewpoint, it appears that we are presently in the fourth turning as of this writing.

- Bridge-crossing
- Changes
- Cross-roads

In my clinical practice, I commonly meet people either at the third turning (i.e., season of Grief) or at the fourth turning (i.e., season of Critical Point). If our work were to be fruitful, they typically move towards the first (i.e., season of Renewal) and second cycle (i.e., season of Come of Age).

Return to the question posed in the previous section: **What season of life are you in right now?**

## My Seasons

Throughout this book, along with anecdotes from my clinical practice, I've also shared various seasons that I've been through so that you get a sense of what I am referring to when I talk about Seasons.

Below are four different seasons I've experienced during the process of writing this book between 2021 to 2024. I've named them:

1. **Soften** (Renewal)
2. **Creating a Home** (Come of Age)
3. **Longing for Community** (Grief)
4. **Risk-Write** (Critical Point)

### 1. Soften

After leaving my job in Singapore, I have become my own boss. This was an unusual space to be. I no longer had the security of a monthly salary, my wife and I had our first child, and I was the sole breadwinner.

I became a hyper-focused individual. My Asian work ethic has served me well. I spent time writing, I took extra time and effort with my clinical cases; I was highly motivated to do a good job for everyone who sought my help in therapy. On top of that, I was involved in several research studies, even though I was not an academic, took part in multiple book projects, and spent hundreds of hours listening to therapy recordings outside of consultation hours, trying to help other clinicians I supervise improve at their work.

I became a workaholic. The irony was that I left Singapore because I didn't want to be a slave to work. Yet I was trapped by my own doing.

I had to put on the brakes. The cost was too high. I wanted to be there for my family. I soon realised that I needed to "soften." This meant that I needed to figuratively and literally ease myself into the present, so that I could be open and available to those I love (See related: Rest for Rest's Sake, in <u>Paradox 1. Self-Care</u>).

This felt like a season of Renewal.

### 2. Creating a Home

When I started this book, I was just passing the fourth turning of Critical Point and, perhaps, at the beginning of the first turning of Renewal. I called this season of my life "Creating a Home."

This season has layers of meaning for me. My family and I have moved away from rental properties since moving from Australia to Singapore eleven years ago. We had just completed our new build. I felt like a nomad for a long time. When my wife and I got married a decade ago, we made the decision to take up a scholarship to pursue my doctorate. This meant that I would leave my full-time employment as a psychologist and subject myself to a cap of working less than sixteen hours a week due to student visa working restrictions. Completing my research took nearly double the two years we'd planned. This posed its own challenges. While my peers progressed with their careers and developed their own families, I took a different turn.

We moved back to Singapore, had our first child, and then made the decision to move back Down Under. Then child number two came along. When things got overwhelming, we wondered what in the world we'd been thinking, moving away from support networks that could have helped us care for our children.

After more than a decade, for the first time, I felt a strong impulse to put roots down. Not only in the form of a house to call a home, but also to be much more deeply rooted in myself with people, place, and purpose.

This felt like a natural evolution, a Come of Age season.

**3. Longing for Community**

A few years ago, during a consultation with my friend and mentor Juliana, she asked me if I was homesick.

I wasn't. But she was on to something that led me to an unexpected place.

By that time, I had been living in Australia for twelve years, and I hadn't seen my folks since the pandemic rained down on us. Even though I wasn't homesick, Juliana saw that I was yearning deeply for something I hadn't realised: a true community.

I found myself unexpectedly in tears.

This wasn't because I was an Asian minority living in Western lands, nor was it about having friends and colleagues. I had a few good friends here, and I was part of a group private practice with wonderful colleagues.

I'd been asked to join this or that committee. But because there's often an agenda to these professional clubhouses, I found myself reluctant to say yes to their kind invitations.

I longed to be part of a community with no goals, no agenda, no aims to pursue. No one to impress. A community that existed for its own sake, to invite an exchange of the soulful parts of ourselves with each other.

I recently realised that this ache to be part of a community, a tribe of like-minded people, ran deeper than I had thought. Even though I was an introvert, I'd been lucky enough to belong to a music group, a band of brothers, from my teens until my early 30s. Moving to another country had brought a natural close to that musical journey. I hadn't realised how much I missed it.

This felt like a season of Grief.

### 4. Risk-Write

Through the process of my higher education, I feel like the word "I" has been beaten out of me. "Never start a sentence with 'I'"—so I was advised by countless academic supervisors and editors of peer-reviewed journals. Using the word "I" suggests a personal and subjective opinion. This dictum never really sat well with me, though. Although the intention of this advice is to be more "objective", I felt it was an uncouraging way to present ideas.

A few years ago, I came across a video by award-winning poet, playwright, and editor Jack Grapes. His instruction was straightforward, yet profound: "Say something with 'I' in it. The rest is birthday cake."[v] Using "I" helps the author get to a deeper truth. "Put yourself in danger," he said. Even though I'd written a handful of books before this one, it felt like the time had come to dig deeper and put myself out there in service of a deeper truth that might touch, move, and inspire others. In other words, Risk-Write, for me, was not about me. It was ultimately about gift-giving. I believe that if we dig deep, each of us has something to offer others.

This season feels like a Critical Point.

## Figure out Where You Are in Order to Know Where You Need to Go

Paying attention to the current season you are in is instructive not only of where you are, but also where you need to go. It provides you a navigational guide as to where you need to **nurture your nature**. Understanding the wheels of time makes you appreciate the cycles we go through and see them not as a regression or slipping back, but as part of a winding mountain road; it might not seem like the view is changing, but you are at different points on the journey.

But what if your desires take you in the wrong direction? The road of Crossing Between Worlds is fraught not only with obstacles, but also the possible derailment of wrong turns. If your desire is driven by ego alone—a fulfilment of your self-serving illusions—you cannot express the original goodness in your nature. C.S. Lewis said,

> Pleasure, money, power, and safety are all, so far as they go, good things. The badness consists in pursuing them by the wrong method, or in the wrong way, or too much…Goodness is, so to speak, itself: badness is only spoiled goodness.[vi]

Early in my psychology internship, as we were discussing a difficult case, my clinical supervisor Thomas Lee asked me, "Do you believe that, fundamentally, everyone is good inside?" Up until that point, I hadn't given this assumption much thought. "Yes, actually," I replied.

"Really?" He seemed genuinely sceptical of my response. "So you think that *everyone* is inherently good—even Ted Bundy?"

Twenty years on, I still think about my conversation with Thomas Lee. I believe that each of us, originally, holds goodness. We get to shape this goodness within us and with others. If we are to truly understand the interrelationship we have with other people, we are what Thich Nhat Hanh and Charles Eisenstein calls "Interbeing." In other words, the Self is not just you. If we allow ourselves to expand our consciousness by zooming out just a little, we can see that we are ecologically linked by our relationships, and that we are highly dependent on one another. At some point in most therapy conversations, I will ask about significant people in a client's life. I will ask some variant of "Who has loved you into being?" And I will often hear moving stories of people who have profoundly shaped and influenced them. People often have visceral reactions to recalling this person in their lives.

We are moved by love from others, and we move others with our love for them. We lose our "original goodness" if we deny how much of an "interbeing" we are. This is an important time to come to terms with this. As you are reading this book, you may be in a period of awakening. Maybe the cause is a crisis, maybe it's the passing of a loved one, or maybe it's a different loss of some kind, i.e., a mourning of an old world of what used to be. All of the old roads may have led you here, to a time of "death of the ego." Paradoxically, that "death" inside of you rends open a door to another world, a new life waiting for you to inhabit it. If this is you, don't let this moment slip away. Work through this book. Others have walked through this path before. And others will need your guidance to lead them through in the future.

Ultimately, my hope is that as you are Crossing Between Worlds, the consequence of your actions will lead you to experience **life-givingness**. The opposite of this is life-diminishing. What's life-diminishing robs not only you, but also those around you. On the other hand, what's life-giving begets more life to you and others.

To be life-giving leads to the *good* life.

**Liminality**

I'm not sure why this is the case, but whenever I'm on a plane, something happens to the state of my mind. I seem to develop a heightened sense of awareness of everything in my life. Maybe it's the latitude. Maybe it's being between worlds; I'm neither here nor there. I find myself easily moved by whatever I'm giving my attention to. I could be watching a movie, listening to a song, reading a book, or thinking about my family, and it's not uncommon that I'm moved to tears. It's a little embarrassing to have tears streaming down your cheeks while everyone else is finishing off their cheese crackers and vanilla ice cream cones. Thankfully, most people are looking forward at their screens.

I'm sure there are biological explanations for the cocktail of neurochemistry that is stirring between my ears, but the closest and most meaningful label I can give to this phenomena is that I'm in a liminal space.

The latin word *limen* means "threshold." This liminal space feels like I'm opening a door and about to cross a divide into another space.

Most of us are familiar with this elevated feeling. This liminal space often comes uninvited during periods of loss and change. During periods of grief, we yearn for the people who are no longer physically present, or for the old life that we once had. During a period of change, we become midwives to our hopes, as we are pulled into the frontier of our lives. But in fact, much is not within our control. We are forced to learn the art of surrendering (See Paradox 15. Control and Surrender). The old is replaced with the new. The doors of possibility come knocking.

Richard Rohr calls liminality "a graced time." He adds, "But [it] often does not feel 'graced' in any way. In such space, we are not certain or in control." Paradoxically, even though most of the time we do not ask to be at this threshold of our lives, being in "liminal space" is where we are most teachable, often because we are most humbled. It's no surprise then that we generally avoid liminal space.

Buddhist teacher Roshi Joan Halifax has a similar description of this territory. She calls these liminal spaces "Edge States." There is a heightened quality when you are standing at the edge of a precipice. "Edges are where opposites meet," Halifax notes. "When we are on the edge, [we are] in danger of slipping from health into pathology. There is a bivalent quality to Edge States that can reveal both our fault-lines and failures, as well as uncover possibilities and discoveries of who we really are."[vii]

As we are Crossing Between Worlds, we are in a liminal space. We are standing at the edge between the old world and the new uncharted one. If we are not careful, we may slide into a quicksand of suffering. Being in a liminal space is precious, because it is as if we are awakened from deep sleep. Our conscious awareness is heightened. A new world is inviting us to open that door. Are we willing, or are we willfully stubborn in trying to maintain the old world out of fear and allure of the status quo?

## Willful vs. Willing

Most of us value "self-improvement," and we like to think of ourselves as fully autonomous, high in self-mastery and *always* in the driver's seat of our lives. While psychology has a lot to offer, according to the late author Gerald May, this has made us become "**willful**" people.[viii]

When we are "willful," we might put up a fight in order to make things stay the same as they were and refuse to take the leap of faith to cross to another world. Other times, it's less of a fight and more of a fear. We fear stepping out of our ordinary world because everything in our bones screams discomfort when we are faced with uncertainty. Yet it is a mistake to think that our lives are solely about comfort. Our "comfort" zone, if prolonged, becomes our hell zone (more on this later, in #2. Circle of Development, in Paradox 12. Stress).

Seen in this light, it is no wonder that psychological symptoms of all stripes manifest themselves when we fail to make a proper transition from one world to the next: The young adult who fails to "leave home" into the world of adulthood, stuck in an extended adolescent phase; the mother who is left empty when her children no longer need her constant attentive care; the highly-driven manager who no longer sees any reason whatsoever to continue giving his waking hours to a corporation that is fundamentally at odds with his values.

When we become willful, we become less *willing*.

Being willing is a prerequisite to answering the call of our lives, no matter how "improved" you may be. Stephen Jenkinson notes, "The sign of our times asks of us things we would never ask of ourselves."[ix]

When I look back, many of the seasons I've found myself in situations that were not by choice. They presented themselves without my consent. The truth is, **we are not masters of the wind.**

I think about the people I've loved who have passed away, and how each of their deaths thrusted me into places I wouldn't have chosen for myself. The grieving season has shaped and informed me in so many ways. If I had made a "spiritual bypass" of anaesthetising myself by evading grief, I would have missed the "graced" periods of being in a liminal space.

Even with significant moments that happen because of the choices you make, like getting married and moving countries, try as you may, you cannot dictate how the ensuing chapter will unfold.

We have to confront our fears and take active steps to move forward, as well as allowing all the demands, responsibilities, and changes to move us through. Willingness is a practice of surrender (See Paradox 15. Surrender).

In a liminal space, if we open our eyes and pay attention to the signs of our times, we can answer the call of the season no matter how "self-improved" we may be.

We may not dictate the wind, but we can learn to harness it.

May we be "willing" people.

# 6. WHY PARADOXICAL?

"Do I contradict myself? Very well, then I contradict myself, I am large, I contain multitudes."

— *Walt Whitman*

If you listened to the thousands of conversations I've had with people in therapy over the years, you would probably observe a pattern: I contradict myself.

For Annabelle, she has to learn to say "No." For Joachim, he has to learn to say "Yes."

For Katherine, she has to learn to focus on being "present." For Susan, she has to learn to cast her eyes and make concrete plans for the "future."

The contradiction isn't just between different people, but also *within* each of us. It is intuitive to understand that everyone is different, but it is less so to consider how paradoxical we are to ourselves. As mentioned in the previous section on "Why Seasons", at different times in our lives, we need to move in different directions. As you will experience working through the 15 spectrums in the Personal Paradoxical Profile (P3) to figure out which route to take, you will notice that, in the past, you might have needed to move in an entirely opposite direction. Maybe you needed to be more in community with others, while currently you need to learn to be in solitude a bit more than you are used to (see Paradox 4. Solitude/Community). Or you might have often been in a caregiver role, but now you need to open yourself to receiving care. (See Paradox 9. Caregiving/Receiving Care).

We are walking contradictions. As Lao Tzu would have it, "The words of truth are always paradoxical."

*Leave me alone, but I need to be with people. I need consistency, but I yearn for novelty. I need to be the master of my own life, but I also need to learn to surrender.*

**Equilibrium is Not the Aim...**

This book is not about helping you "strike a balance." Balance is not the aim, or at least not in the typical way we think about what balance means. Take for instance, the so-called "work/life" balance that HR tries to instigate in organisations; it is a losing preposition. Nothing ever happens by living in the middle. Anthropologist Gregory Bateson said, "A man walking is never in balance, but always correcting for imbalance."

This ongoing "correcting for imbalance," which requires us to move, is what keeps us "balanced," or more accurately, counter-balanced.

Sure, on a daily basis, you might need moments of stillness, as well as periods of movement (see Paradox 13. Stillness/Movement). But on a seasonal basis, there might be a more prominent direction to take.

**Balance is not the aim. Direction and motion is.**

## ...Neither Is It "Either/Or"

Before we take the first step in identifying the season that you are in and completing your Personal Paradoxical Profile (P3), I want to stress the point that even as we seek to correct for "imbalance," please be mindful of not falling into "either/or" traps. For example, we don't need to focus only on the self and not on others, or learn to be in solitude and not be active in a community. These are false dichotomies. Instead of a dualistic mindset of "either/or" thinking, we need to learn to embrace a **non-dualistic "both/and" perspective**. This is the paradox we are called to embrace.

This book is for readers who want to not only improve their emotional and relational lives, but to lead a deep, meaningful, and creative life. And in order to achieve that, you will find that many of the ideas in this book are specifically designed to help you take these seemingly contradictory steps.

## 7. HOW TO BEGIN

**W**e want clear-cut answers.

But when someone doesn't know you, well-intended advice may have unintended consequences. This book doesn't tell you what to do, but it will offer you road signs on this inner landscape. Fifteen of them in fact. You get to decide which path to take, based on the season of your life that you are in.

This is tricky business, because we are dealing with what's invisible. Yet, as Antoine de Saint-Exupéry said in *The Little Prince*, "What's essential is invisible to the eye."

Proceed to the next section to get started.

**What Is the Current Season of Your Life?**

Take a moment to answer the following question: **What would you call this season of your life?**

Reflect on this. Examine not only the events surrounding your life of late, but also look inward. How have you been feeling? What has been on your mind? Your response to this can take the form of a word or a sentence, a direct reference to the four seasons, or even a drawing. Feel free to use the space below to write it down, or turn to your notebook. I recommend that you date it. If you prefer, you can download the worksheets (**daryl chow.com/seasons**).

**THE CURRENT SEASON OF MY LIFE IS:**

_____

_____

Here's where we are at so far:

**Nature → Nurture → Needs → Naming the Season → Complete the P3 → Read the 15 Paradoxes → Revisit Your P3 → Course of Action**

## Instructions to Personal Paradoxical Profile (P3)

Now that you've done the "Season of Your Life" exercise, keep your answer to it in mind as you complete the P3. Here are the instructions:

1. Recall the last two weeks of your life. Review your calendar to see what took place and how you felt in those times.
2. There are 15 items across three domains: self (Well-Being), relations (Well-Belonging), and actions (Well-Doing).
3. In the following page, a summary of the P3 is provided. **Mark a '>' , '<' or 'X'** on each of the 15 lines.
4. Where you demarcate on the line is based on **where you are now**, and the symbol you use will depend on **where you need to go**. Each of these three symbols represent a marking of your current situation and the direction you need to take (i.e., > means you feel a need to move more to the right; < means you feel a need to move more to the left; x means you feel a need to maintain where you are at).
5. For example, for the first item, **Self-Care/Self-Forgetting**, if you feel more compelled to attend to your needs as you've been neglecting them, mark a '<' more towards the right.

Self-Care<————————————<————> Self-Forgetting

6. If you feel that you have a good level of self-care and you need to focus more on others around you, mark a '>' more towards the left.

Self-Care<———>————————————> Self-Forgetting

7. If you feel you need to have a good balance in this spectrum, mark an 'X' wherever is appropriate on this line. This could be either in the middle, if you feel you have a good balance of both, or, if you sense that in this season of your life you need to be more on the *Self-Care* end of things on the left. In other words, 'X' represents a match between where you are and where you feel you need to be.

Self-Care<————x——————————> Self-Forgetting

8. After marking each of the 15 lines, read each Paradox in order to make sense of your needs at this stage of your life.
9. At the end of each Paradox, each of the spectrums are presented again for easy reference. Feel free to modify your response as you proceed with the book.

Finally, complete the P3 profile in Appendix A and the Course of Action in <u>Appendix F</u> (or download a copy of the P3. See **A Gift For You**). Make sure you set aside an hour in about a month's time to review what you've planned out to do.

In summary, here's a checklist of what you need to do:

☐ First Pass on the P3 (see Appendix A)
☐ Read the 15 Paradoxes
☐ Revisit the P3
☐ Complete the Course of Action (see Appendix F)

For some, you might find it challenging to complete the P3. Go easy on yourself. As mentioned in the instructions, each of the 15 lines that you demarcate on represents not only where you are, but also where you need to go. You might not be clear what each of the descriptions means, especially if you are doing the P3 for the first time. Feel free to pause and read the relevant Paradoxes to get an idea first.

*Note: The P3 is not designed to be a psychometric tool. It is meant to be an individualised tool to help you navigate direction as you are making changes in your life.*

**Your Personal Paradoxical Profile (P3)**

### Section I. Well-Being

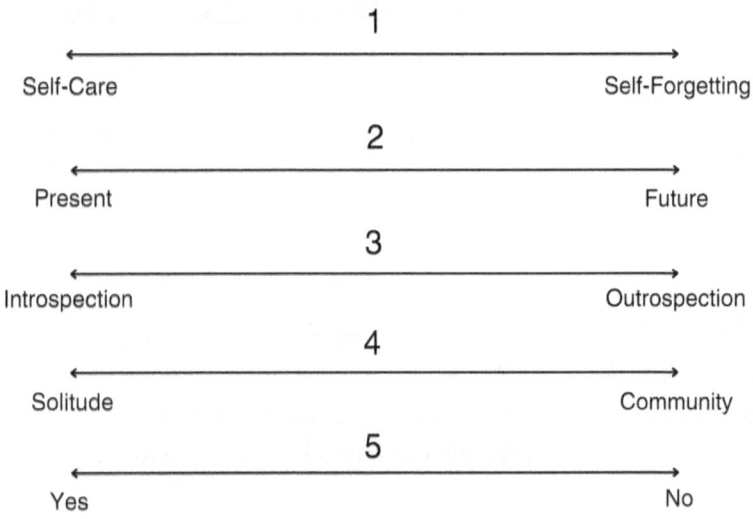

## Section II. Well-Belonging

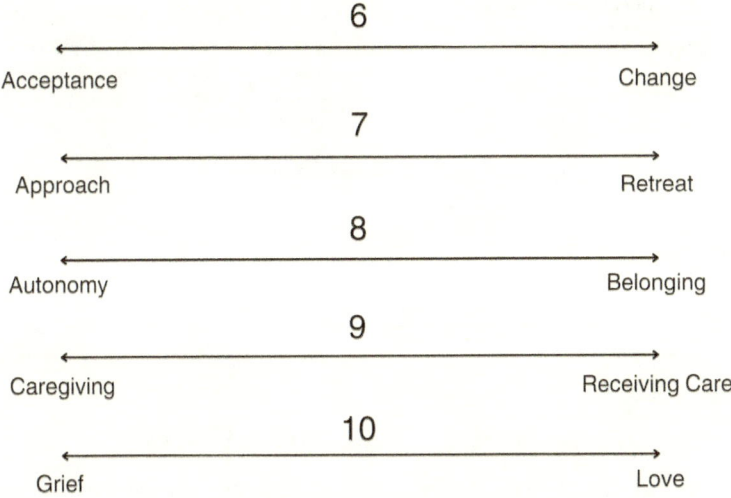

## Section III: Well-Doing

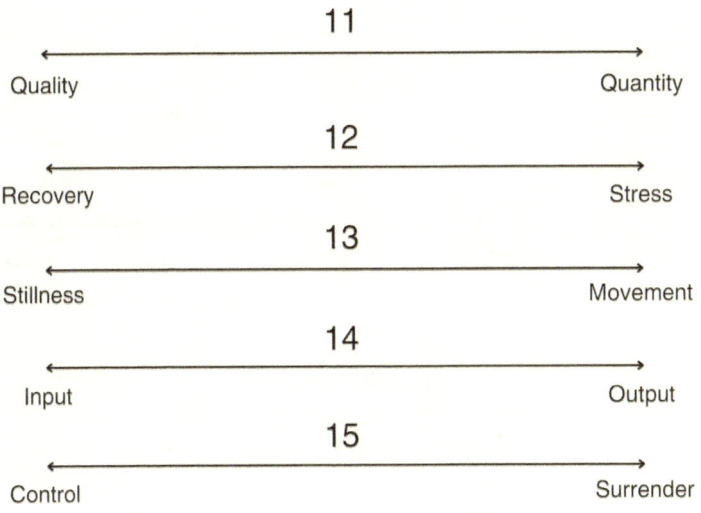

## An Overview of the 15 Paradoxes

To help you with the initial completion of your P3, Here is a quick overview of each of the 15 paradoxes that we will be addressing in this book:

### WELL-BEING

#### Paradox 1

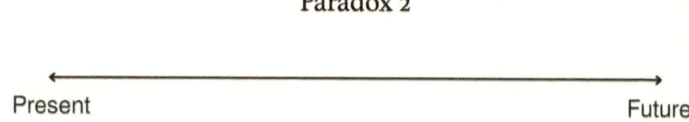

Self-Care                                              Self-Forgetting

The person who is a constant outpouring of love for others needs to attend to their own neglect, while the person who is overly focused on the self needs to focus more on others.

#### Paradox 2

Present                                              Future

Someone who defers life to the future needs to relish in the present moment, and the one who is wholly absorbed in the "now" needs to cast their eyes on the future, because they have no idea what's for tomorrow.

#### Paradox 3

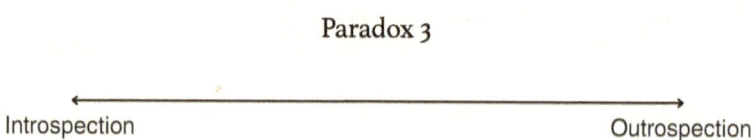

Introspection                                    Outrospection

The inward gaze of introspection is helpful for those who do not take the time to reflect on where life has been instead of where it's going. But an overdose of introspection is like driving with your eyes glued to the rearview mirror.

### Paradox 4

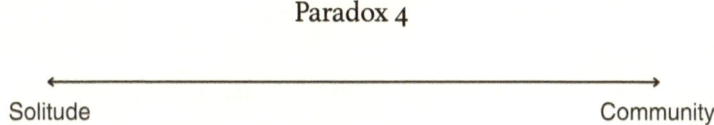

Solitude is necessary for hearing ourselves clearly. Yet we can truly grow only in the company of others.

### Paradox 5

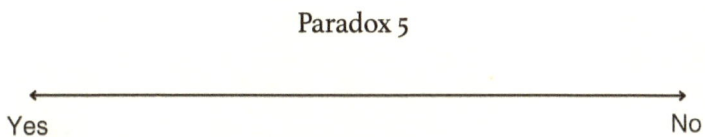

Sometimes we say Yes to the things we want to say No to. Other times, we say No too quickly and close ourselves to the world of possibilities that lie ahead of us.

## WELL-BELONGING

### Paradox 6

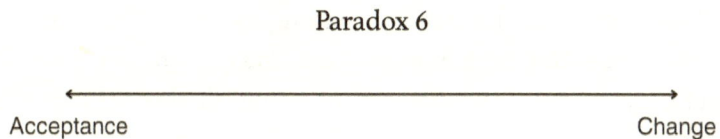

Change happens when we embrace life with full acceptance. Brute-forcing change can cause harm. Yet a fear of change denies our instinct for growth.

### Paradox 7

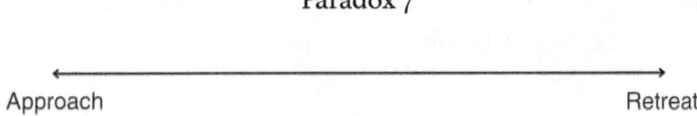

There are seasons where we need to retreat from the world in order to appreciate the reality we live in, and there are seasons where we are called to approach what we fear.

### Paradox 8

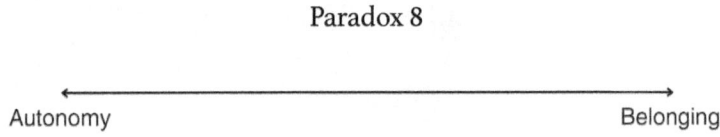

In order to become our own person, we have to learn to belong. In order to be together, we need to learn to be by ourselves.

### Paradox 9

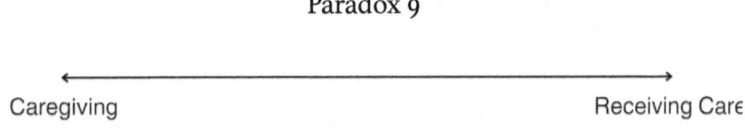

Caregiving can be second nature to some. For others, receiving care can be a foreign experience. And some would benefit immensely from the gift of being allowed to care for others.

### Paradox 10

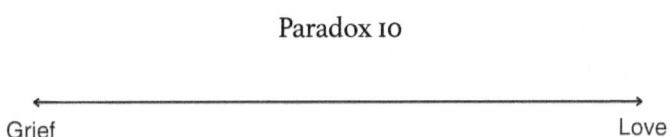

We are called to be practitioners of love and grief. In this time-limited mortal arrangement, if we deny invitations to grieve and do not learn how to love, we might cause grief to others and ourselves.

## WELL-DOING

### Paradox 11

Quality / Quantity

At the beginning, if you aim for quality, you'll miss the mark. Aim for quantity, and you are more likely to get quality. At the later stages of any development, take the opposite approach.

### Paradox 12

Recovery / Stress

We think stress is the issue. But stress is not the problem; a lack of recovery is. In fact, some of us might need to embrace stress in order to stretch ourselves.

### Paradox 13

Stillness / Movement

Stillness is required to see things clearly, while movement is required in order to reach what's ahead of you.

Paradox 14

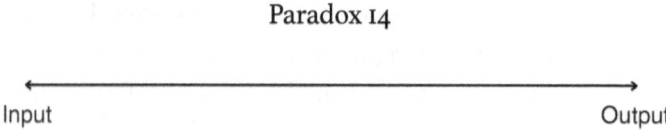

It is easy to get stuck on "feeding" yourself with inputs without taking the risk of putting out your creations. No one is going to take care of the quality of your inputs except you.

Paradox 15

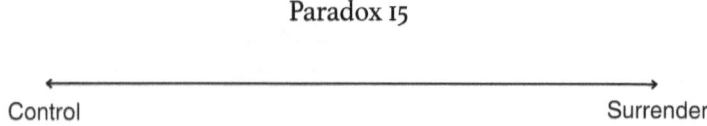

There are many things that we can do to regain a sense of agency in our personal and professional lives. At the same time, modernity tends to over-glorify people with a sense of control and under-value people who know how to surrender.

**More About Your Personal Paradoxical Profile**

Now that you have an overview of the P3, there are a couple more things to say about your P3.

Your P3 is...

- Contextual
- Counterintuitive
- Contradictory over time
- Personal

*Contextual*

Trying to achieve something in a decontextualised manner is like improving your conversational English when you are visiting France. You're spending your energy on the wrong language. This is why your P3 is context-bound by the current seasonality of your life, what it asks of you, where you need to be heading, and where you need to grow.

*Counterintuitive*

As highlighted in the previous section, "Why Paradoxical," many of the tasks ahead of you might seem counterintuitive at first, since learning to go at your leading edge might involve counterintuitive actions that challenge your expectations. However, after you have a handle on the principles behind this book, you'll realise that much of what is described here is common sense, just not common practice.

*Contradictory Over Time*

You'll find that your present and future needs become contradictory to what you needed in the past.

One example is the process of moving from singlehood, to being part of a couple, and then eventually becoming a parent. Not only will your needs evolve, the expansion of your world moves you to expand your sense of self beyond the individual. The Self now encompasses a much larger community of others in your life. And later on, given the trajectories of family development, a different set of needs, actions, and emotional growth is required as your children leave home, moving towards their own frontiers.

Thus, the use of the P3 is not a one-time application. It is repeatedly helpful to get your bearings when you experience significant transitions.

*Personal*

Finally, this book faces a paradox: Though our foundational needs are the same, what's most universal is personal, as each of us requires different things at different times. There is a certain sense of *particularity* in our endeavour that cannot be prescribed as a general course of action that we all must take. Thus, a "formula" will not work. When we can take that journey towards what speaks to each of us, we can then come together in our diversity. As the late Rabbi Jonathan Sacks puts it in his book, *The Dignity of Difference,* "Our particularity is our window on to universality."

The ethics of embracing each other's differences is easy to state, but hard to do. Just take a look at the world around us to see how this has played out in the history of our civilisation. Sacks points out the Hebrew Bible's counterintuitive contribution to ethics: "God creates differences; therefore it is in one-who-is-different that we meet God."[i] Imagine if we were to encounter each other with that level of reverence, especially those who are different from us. Maybe one of the channels towards unity in our diverse society is to encounter and embrace our paradoxical selfs within.

# 8. WHAT NOT TO DO WHEN CROSSING BETWEEN WORLDS

Before we go down the rabbit hole of each of the 15 Paradoxes of this book, let me just spell out what you *shouldn't* be doing when you are making significant transitions or at a crossroads:

### Mistake #1. Acting on impulse

I know you know this, but some of us are more prone to impulsivity than others.

Hold your horses. It's hard to see when you are travelling at the speed of impulse. You see the same street very differently when you are walking through it compared to when you are driving in your sedan.

### Mistake #2. Following someone else's advice

Some advice can be a vice. No matter how well-meaning they are, we can't outsource our decision-making process to someone else.

### Mistake #3. Following someone else's desire

Who in their right mind would follow the desire of another person instead of their own? Turns out, we are all susceptible to what French philosopher René Girard calls **mimetic desires**. Individuals often end up desiring things because they see others desiring them, not because of any intrinsic value or personal preference. We end up wanting what others want.

Mimetic desires are pulled by the need of status. It's not just about cars; it's more about our identity.

Maybe you are leaving a job to launch a startup that's for a good cause. This is laudable. But be brutally honest with yourself. What's behind your motivation? Is it really the common good, or is it more so you can *say* that you are doing something for a good cause because two of your close buddies are also doing something in that space? (See #2. Your Desires—Or is it Mimetic Desires? In Paradox 8, Autonomy).

You are in a bad way if you succeed at something that is not your desire.

### Mistake #4. Numbing yourself

When you are at the crossroads, it's so much easier to numb yourself with Netflix and the infinite scroll of Instagram and TikTok than it is to make a real choice.

Do not anaesthetise yourself during this important period of your life. Don't flood yourself with junk. Nourish yourself (see #1. The Dailies, Strategies, Skills, Meal (DSSM) Framework, in Paradox 6. Change), and learn to feel what you feel, and not "fill" yourself with distraction.

As you are Crossing Between Worlds, your internal compass will serve you more than the external noise that fractures your attention and intentions.

**Mistake #5. Focusing on the *how* and not the *what***

It's easy to fixate on the "How-tos" by learning all sorts of strategies and tactics to sort your life out.

But first, before obsessing over the how-tos, focus on *What* is most essential.

Don't mistake being busy with being productive.

Figuring out the *What* not only gives you leverage, but more importantly, it helps you set your directionality and shape your priority before proceeding.

For many, this will entail periods of self-reflection. I hope to walk you through the process.


**Mistake #6. Isolating yourself**

Our minds need another mind to function well. No other vital organ needs the vital organ of another person in order to survive,[i] but our minds are fundamentally shaped by other minds. If our mind is not stimulated by the engagement of another mind, we atrophy.

Gregory Bateson quipped, "It takes two to know one." This is especially true when you are Crossing Between Worlds.

Sure, you are going to need time to retreat and clarify your own thoughts (see Paradox 7. Retreat). But don't dig yourself a hole, because you are going to need to tap into the minds of others through conversation, brainstorming, teaching, and learning and reading to sharpen your own thinking.


**Mistake #7. Assuming that there is only one right way**

One of the things in the cards when I got married was to move to another country. I'd felt like I'd managed to con a university into giving me a full scholarship to do my doctorate (I had never done well in my early schooling years). So I was thinking I'd get married and then go back to school in another country. I was so worried that I was doing something that was purely for selfish reasons. This would impact not only my life, but that of whoever was crazy enough to marry me, we'd be living a life of student's subsistence for three years.[1]

I disclosed my dilemma to a mentor and friend, a former zookeeper turned Redemptorist priest, Glenn de Cruz, C.S.s.R.. He listened closely as I rambled on about my plans and fears of not going where God and Life were calling me to be. "Am I following the *right* path?" I asked him.

Glenn looked at me. "So your wife-to-be, she's happy with the idea of moving to another country?"

"She's more adventurous than I am. She's game-on," I said.

Glenn smiled. "Daryl, there isn't 'the one' choice that you have to make. He will go with you, wherever you go, since you seek Him."

You don't have to be religious to make sense of his statement. I have to tell you, Glenn's counsel left me both embarrassed and relieved by a simple suggestion I'd overlooked. I was fixated about there being only the one, right choice.

There are many roads open to you. Don't think that there's only a single "right" path to take.

Now, with your P3 completed at hand, let's choose your own adventure.

---

[1]. Our student visa limited both of us to work at most part time during this period.

# 9. STRUCTURE OF THE BOOK

In the upcoming sections, we will discuss each of the 15 Paradoxes in detail. These Paradoxes comprise three main sections: Well-Being, Well-Belonging, and Well-Doing. That is, the relationship with the Self, our relationships with others, and actions that we take related to our place in the world.[i]

Each Paradox is organised into four sections: **Contradiction, Clarity, Counsel,** and **Broaden Your Nature.** The Contradiction section explains the tension that we face in the 15 Paradoxes. In Clarity, we examine each flipside of the 15 domains. In Counsel, I'll give three suggestions for each end of the spectrum, for a total of six suggestions. In order to make things concrete, each of the suggestions ends with specific skills and areas that you can practise. Lastly, we conclude with "Broaden Your Nature". This section provides a brief note about particular aspects of your personality traits that might be noteworthy to pay attention to.

You may want to read the book in its entirety so that you get the breath of its scope. This may not only provide insight into where you need to focus your energy, but also provide you a "lay of the land." This is likely to serve you well in the future when you approach different seasons of your life. Depending on how you completed your P3, you may use the corresponding sections of the book to help illuminate the steps you will need to take going forward. In addition, within each Paradox, other related Paradoxes are suggested, creating a network effect of related ideas.

Don't be surprised to find yourself skipping between pages and revisiting certain Paradoxes. This is to be expected given the nature of the task at hand. Plus, I will not take any offence if this book ends up dogged-eared, highlighted, and marked with scribbles. Go ahead. In fact, I will be extremely pleased.

Remember to keep a copy of the P3 close to you like a compass, as I recommend you refer to it from time to time.

My hope is that this feels like less of a "self-help" book and more like a travel guide. A self-help book typically suggests what you should do. Instead, my aim is to tap you on your shoulder and point out significant things to look at as we move along the 15 Paradoxes.

I've included some personal stories when called for, mostly about the struggles I've encountered in specific areas. My intent is not for this to be a memoir, but to highlight certain points that might help you along the way. I've also related the stories of specific individuals I've known, from friends, family, fellow colleagues, and the thousands of people I've encountered in my clinical practice and professionals I've consulted with. I imagine speaking to each of them and to each of you, dear reader. This is out of necessity, because each of these ideas has its polar opposite. For instance, in the section on Well-Belonging, some people in specific seasons need to learn to *approach* things that they have been avoiding, while others might need to learn to listen more to their body and *retreat,* to pull away from the noise. Don't worry if you feel uncertain about which direction you need to take in specific Paradoxes.[1] We will pull it altogether at the end of the book.

Let's cross this bridge.

---

Here's where we are so far:

**Nature → Nurture → Needs → Naming the Season → Complete the P3 → Read the 15 Paradoxes → Revisit Your P3 → Course of Action**

---

[1]. If you are working with a helping professional, like a counsellor, psychologist, or a therapist, you might want to share your P3 with them.

# PART II: WELL-BEING

"The good life is a *process*, not a state of being. It is a direction, not a destination...
The good life...is the process of movement in a direction which the human organism selects when it is inwardly free to move in any direction, and the general qualities of this selected direction appear to have a certain universality."

— *Carl Rogers, 1961.*[i]

In this first section, we focus on Well-Being. We will look at the tension of opposites between self and others, present and future, reflecting inwardly and outwardly, solitude and community, and our Yeses and Nos.

# PARADOX 1: SELF-CARE/SELF-FORGETTING

## CONTRADICTION

Friends seem to say that I should prioritise self-care and stop neglecting my own needs. But when does that become indulgent?

Should I be moving more towards attending to my own needs or those of others?

## CLARITY

### A. Self-Care

Over the last decade or so, we have gotten really good at levelling the playing field between physical and mental health. We are taking heed of the importance of addressing psychological problems like anxiety and depression. However, our modern hyper-productivity schedule is creating a pattern of behaviour that tips us easily into self-neglect. Self-neglect often leads to psychological strain. As mentioned previously in the Introduction, "Why

Needs?", we mute the signals of the fire, and we soldier through work and family life while the sirens are blazing.

Neglecting our emotions is a form of alarm-bell denial. We fight on as if it's a badge of honour to persist in the face of despair, tearing us apart from the inside out. We fear that we might crumple if we stop to take care of what our feelings are actually telling us.

When we need a dose of self-care, it is often because of self-neglect and burnout caused by the demands of work, caregiving, and the tyranny of staying productive around the clock.

In a sense, we are experiencing a kind of collective amnesia: we have forgotten how to rest.

We think of rest as for the lazy, the inefficient, and the ineffective. And when we do attempt to "rest," our eyes are entranced by the endless scroll of news, click-bait, and social media feeds.

The territory of rest also comes with the neighbouring challenges of learning how to be bored, to incubate, and to retreat (see Paradox 7. Retreat).

In his stirring book *Consolations*, poet David Whyte illuminates the topic of Rest:[i]

*To rest is not self-indulgent, to rest is to prepare to give the best of ourselves, and to perhaps, most importantly, arrive at a place where we are able to understand what we have already been given.*

David Whyte goes on to flesh out five states of Rest:

### 1. Stop

"*In the first state of rest is the sense of stopping, of giving up on what we have been doing or how we have been being.*"

When was the last time you intentionally stopped yourself in your tracks to take a moment to do nothing?

### 2. Return Home

"*In the second is the sense of slowly coming home, the physical journey into the body's **un-coerced** and **un-bullied** [emphasis mine] self, as if trying to remember the way or even the destination itself.*"

If you have trouble stopping, you will have trouble seeing.

This coercion and bullying of time manifests itself as anxious productivity, as if everything at hand is ultra-urgent, pushing us to the brink of exhaustion. We think we are stealing time, but the truth is the real thievery happens *to* us.

### 3. Heal

*"In the third state is a sense of healing and self-forgiveness and of arrival."*

It is a prerequisite of healing that we make the conscious effort of stopping and returning home to the inhabitant of our body "un-coerced and un-bullied." Travelling at the speed of light instead of the speed of life[ii] creates a harsh inner-terrain that is not conducive to repair, rejuvenation, and revitalisation. Travelling at the speed of light makes you irritable and impatient. Your body pays the price for this. Your body needs to heal and recover.

### 4. Breath

*"In the fourth state, deep in the primal exchange of the in-and-out breath, is the give-and-take, the blessing and the being blessed and the ability to delight in both."*

Just notice your breathing the next time you are caught up in a whirlwind of busyness. We all need little moments of catching our breath, to breathe the life that we have.

### 5. Presence

*"The fifth stage is a sense of absolute readiness and presence, a delight in and an anticipation of the world and all its forms; a sense of being the meeting itself between inner and outer, and that receiving and responding occur in one spontaneous movement."*

The call to presence is a gift-exchange between you and life.

Meanwhile, we wrestle with the tension that there's always something more important than now. Yet the existence of any future is contingent on the present. (see Paradox 2. Present).

Presence is a cumulation of our intentional act of stopping, slowing, healing, and breathing. Forcing yourself to be present without practice is like expecting to complete an Ironman triathlon after binge-watching YouTube videos on Ironman triathlons. Yes, it's strange to say it, we do need to practise how to rest.

### Rest for Rest's Sake

In a thriving country like Singapore, where I was born and raised, top performance, hard work, and sleep deprivation are the lifeblood of what it means to be a contributing member of society. In the early years of immigrating to Australia, my wife noticed something about me that strangely hasn't changed. She said that I may have left Singapore, but I don't seem to be able to leave the Singaporean in me.

But I'm discovering—especially as I watch my kids grow—that this side of me needs to be tampered.

The Japanese have a word for un-rest: *karoshi*.[iii] It literally means to work yourself to death. I don't want *karoshi*. Nobody wants *karoshi*. I recently watched a documentary about overworked men in South Korea who died from sheer exhaustion. This made me worry about my friends back home who work 12-hour days, six days a week.

We don't need a reason to take a break. **Rest has goodness in and of itself.**

In periods of rest, we also need to cloister, as judge Raymond Kethledge and CEO Michael Erwin put it, to have "**no inputs from other minds.**"[iv] (See Paradox 4. Solitude).

Curiously, studies show that top performers take more rest than the average person. For example, K. Anders Ericsson and colleagues found that on average, the top violinists took **5.4 hours** more in states of rest than their peers. (The amount of time that top musicians rested was 60 hours a week, compared with the average performer's 54.6 hours a week.) Not only did the top violinists sleep more (8.6 hours vs 7.8 hours), they also took more naps in the afternoon. Our culture places more emphasis on the crude estimate of the 10,000-hour rule instead of the 60-hour rule.[v]

So sleep, take a nap, go for a walk, hop on a bus, lay on the grass in the backyard, go to the park and stare at the clouds, do nothing. Learn how to rest by resting.

Stop being that amateur athlete who just keeps going and doesn't realise that we need both stress and recovery in order to build strength and fitness. Turn pro by behaving like the pros.

Stress is not the problem; a lack of recovery is. (See Paradox II. Recovery).

Rest to recover. Honour Rest the way we give the badge of honour to hard work. Nature has it that we grow when we rest deeply.

When we fail to take heed of our natural rhythms, we set ourselves up for burnout. Burnout is cumulative and amplified stress plus a lack of recovery, multiplied by the unrealistic expectation of time and our biology.

**Burnout = (high and continuous stress – recovery) x unrealistic expectations**

## B. Self-Forgetting

Although it seems counterintuitive, focusing less on the self is the most fundamental shift we can make as we are Crossing between Worlds.

Self-help books focus on the Self. However, **an overemphasis on the self is a wellspring of suffering.** For example: If you are socially anxious, the worst thing you can do is focus on how you think others see you.

The late poet and writer John O'Donohue wrote, "Love begins with paying attention to others, with an act of gracious self-forgetting. This is the condition in which we grow."[vi]

It's 1990, I'm 12 years old. I'm lying in bed, thinking about the big move from primary to secondary school, my terrible grades from my Primary School Leaving Exams that I'll be spending an extra year in an all-boys school, and all the girls that I'm never going to meet because of that.

There is something else on my mind: Even though I know it's still a long way, I know it will eventually arrive. In six years, I will have to go to a place that I do not want to go.

When I turn 18, I will have to enlist. Two and a half years of my life will be lost to the military. I will have to shave my head, don a green uniform, march like an automaton, and do manly things like pick up arms, shoot at targets, crawl in mud, and climb man-made obstacles with sergeants yelling down my back. For some reason, I also have it in my head that I will have to jump out of a plane and paratroop into a snake-infested jungle.

And I'm afraid of heights.

If you are a male living in Singapore, you must be thinking I'm a sissy for worrying about nothing. Other boys my age aren't concerned about it; some are even looking forward to it. But the truth is, I'm totally anxious about this impending doom. Besides the disruption it will make to the prime time of my life at 18, plus my philosophical disagreements with taking up arms, all I can picture is being ordered to jump off a Boeing CH-47 Chinook with a parachute pack that won't open.

My dread of heights is confirmed when I turn 13. I am on top of a tree, at the start of a makeshift zipline. I'm a reluctant boy scout, and Jason, the instructor, is cursing at me to get my butt off the tree and make the leap down the rope. I am terrified, and despite the jeering from my peers in the queue behind me, my height phobia is not about to relent. The cursing from Jason ramps up by three notches, and he begins to threaten. He says I will lose my hands, and he means it. Not because he will cut them off, but because the rope around my wrist is cutting the blood supply to my fingers. Oh shit, he's right. My hands are turning blue; I can barely feel my fingers.

I didn't realise at that time, but more than an hour passed with me standing there. I don't know what happened next, but out of sheer annoyance at my lack of bravery, I—or was it Jason? —must have given myself a nudge down that zipline. I made it down the tree in one piece.

My height phobia is still very much intact. My fear has not gone away. In fact, I am now more afraid of the impending helicopter jump I'm sure I will have to make in five years.

I'm not going to go in unprepared. I start to train before I enter the first three months of Basic Military Training (BMT). I have to, because I am a borderline underweight, scrawny kid who could easily be blown by the wind kicked-up by a landing helicopter.

I have another method of preparation in mind: to "downgrade." When someone is not medically fit, they get a downgrade status. With that comes "privileges." I've heard stories of friends who got downgraded due to things like asthma, allergies to grass, skin reactions to the uniform, and all types of pre-existing medical conditions that exempted them from going outfield. This kept them in the frosty 19.5-degree air-conditioned headquarters throughout their two and a half years of mandatory service.

So what do I do? Two days before the medical exam, I begin my prisoner of war commando-style home-training: I refrain from sleeping. I drink copious amounts of coffee and energy drinks, hoping to raise my blood pressure temporarily, as well as to reduce my psychological tests results to one standard deviation below acceptable. It doesn't work. Oddly, I am still fit as a fiddle, and I have no idea how I fared in those batteries of questionnaires.

I think of my friend Robin. He's twice my weight. Maybe I could get him to sit on me and slide down my leg to dislocate my knee. Robin laughs at my idea. Well, he could laugh, because *he's* downgraded.

I know, this all sounds silly, but this was a very difficult time in my life. Nearing the time of enlistment, I was on the verge of getting kicked out of school from my tertiary education in business administration.[1] I was in a tumultuous relationship that was going nowhere, and the only saving grace was playing music in a band. That was going to be disrupted. Besides, all of my bandmates were already enlisted. One of them was an Army Guard, another was a police officer, and "downgraded" Robin—lucky guy—was a storeman.

To top it off, since the business diploma wasn't my thing, I had no idea what I was going to do with my life.

My head is now shaven; I look like an egg. I'm lined up with the rest of the other eggs, fashioned with green uniforms on an island off Singapore for BMT. My folks are with me. I maintain a brave front. Some boys are crying, not because of leaving their moms and dads, but mostly because someone who looks like a butcher has shorn their locks of hair like a helpless sheep. Any preferred hairstyle request was met with nonchalance by the butcher-barber; some were mocked by the military instructor nearby. Everyone got the same haircut: Egghead.

As we say goodbye to our parents and march as a company for the first time to our bunks, I am filled with dread. I'm cut off from everything else in my world. Cell phones are not yet a common thing. All I have in my possession is a pager, my Discman, and a Bible my friend bought for me a few years back.

Some of the other boys carry a gangster bravado. Some know each other and speak a dialect that I am vaguely familiar with

---

1. I dreaded the course. There was something about how modules like Economics and Marketing that didn't sit well with me, or at least how it was taught.

(Hokkien). Some are solemn like me. I will now have to spend at least three months in BMT with all of them.

As we file in lines of three as a company and march to the beat of swearing instructors, I dissociate. I am physically there, but my mind is elsewhere, in the clouds. My feet are moving, but it's as if I've somehow managed to detach from my own body. I must be hallucinating. I see Mother Mary in the clouds.

I look around. Everything slows down. All of us eggheads are now in the same boat. I'm not sure why, but for the first time in my life, I make the decision to forget about myself.

I didn't realise it then, but this was a pivotal season of my life. It wasn't just about my mandatory enlistment to National Service. That's what it looked like from the outside. But on the inside, an invisible story was unfolding, not of my own choosing. Years later, I came to understand this chapter of my life as **"Leaving myself and focusing on others."**

## Stumbling on Self-Forgetting

Going in with this frame of mind saved my life. I spent the first couple of weeks focusing on my 12 section mates in the platoon. We were housed in one bunk. I learned that the guy on my left, Bob, was not only born on the same day as I was, but also had the National Registration Identity Card that was one digit smaller than mine. In other words, his mother must have been the person in front of my mother in the birth registry queue. The guy on my right—my assigned buddy—was a recluse. He was more timid than I was. Two weeks into BMT, there was a stench in our bunk coming from my buddy's cupboard. We had to confront him about it. Turns out he had been too afraid to go bathe with the other lads. He hadn't taken a proper shower for several days.

I focused my attention on being there for my section mates. To be clear, I was no saint. It was all I could do to not let anxiety crumble me. When we did our endurance run, I did what I could to cheer on the others, even though I was as fast as a turtle. When we did the obstacle courses, I did what I could to push the slower guys up the brick wall climb.

Back in the bunk at night, we talked all kinds of shit. I listened to Bob talk about his girlfriend woes. In exchange, he would lend me his prized possession, his cellphone (a rarity in that era) to call my own girlfriend. A saving grace.

Then there was Edward. We thought he was gay, but he never said so. But Edward was the comic relief we needed. He was the livewire. We became good friends. Levity is most welcomed in an insane environment of screaming instructors.

I didn't know it then, but more than two decades later, I now realise that if we see the movements of our lives, we are moving—and being moved—between different seasons of our lives. Circumstances on the outside may not be our choice, therefore it can feel like we are cajoled into things. But on the inside, we can figure out a way through. We depend on the winds to be moved, but we must also figure out a way to steer.

Oftentimes, as we are Crossing Between Worlds, we don't completely know what the new terrain is like until we get there. But I invite you to embrace the period of bridgecrossing. When crossing bridges, our senses are heightened. When we are at the edge of everything, we see things more acutely. Do not numb yourself in this process. If you keep your eyes open, you might realise what this new season is asking of you.

---

The person who is an outpouring of love for others would need to attend to their own neglect, while the person who is over-focused inwards needs to leave the self and focus on the world outside.

Tending to the self is needed when we are burned out, while a form of gracious self-forgetting is needed in order to be an active participant in life, contributing as a life-giving force to others.

*In this season of your life, where do you need to be on the spectrum of Self-Care and Focusing Less on the Self? (Mark an '<', '>' or 'x' on the line below).*

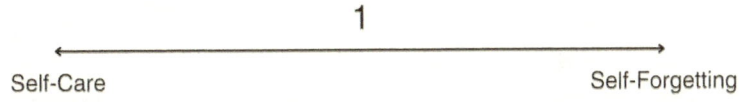

Self-Care                                              Self-Forgetting

## COUNSEL

### A. Self-Care

If you find yourself moving towards the side of needing self-care, take heed of the following suggestions:

**1. Loosen the Trappings of Busyness, One Day at a Time.**

*i. Build "White Space" into your schedule.*

White Space is the opposite of "do something." Build slack into your busy schedule. Treat it like any other event in your calendar. Like driving, create an ample buffer between you and the car in front of you. This allows you to be responsive to anything that might pop up. Refrain from scheduling back-to-back meetings or activities. By incorporating White Space, you give yourself time to think. Moreover, this prevents you from falling prey to a planning fallacy (See the next point).

*ii. Multiply Activity Time by 1.5*

This is one of my biggest mistakes. I tend to believe I can squeeze in more than I can manage. Especially at the beginning of the day, I imagine I can get more done than I really can.

Because of this planning fallacy, I schedule more than I can really handle.

Consider your work activities. Meetings often end later than scheduled, and that causes you to be late for the next meeting. This lateness then snowballs until the end of the day. Even dinner gets delayed.

A good method to inoculate yourself against this bias is to multiply all planned activities by roughly 1.5.[2] In other words, if I have a one-hour meeting scheduled at 9 a.m., instead of locking it in till 10 a.m., I will block out 9 to 10:15 a.m. If the meeting ends on time—a rare treat—take that time to consolidate key points from the meeting, get started on any follow-ups, or even just give yourself a breather. (See #3. Give 80, not 100 in Paradox 12, Recovery).

Practise buffering for more time.

## 2. Lighten the Suck-It-Up Muscles

The older we get, the more "suck-it-up" muscles we develop. Some of us mistakenly think that the ability to grit our teeth and bear the pain is a sign of resilience. Resilience is not about increasing our ability to hustle and keep the economic wheel turning. It is the result of growing through challenges.

Are there things in your work and personal life that you keep "sucking it up" for and, in turn, ignoring the hurts and wounds that you are experiencing on the inside? If so, lighten the strain on your suck-it-up muscles, and attend to what your emotions are saying.

This is not to say that every decision should be dictated by your emotions. Rather, emotions have a form of intelligence. You have to decide based on the intel it provides. It tells you things, if you know how to listen. Even so-called negative emotions, like anger and sadness, tell us something. Anger's intel might speak of

---

2. I first learned about this idea from Cal Newport.

things we care about that have been treated unfairly. Sadness's intel might be about the experience of a loss: the loss of a relationship, the loss of what was, the loss of what was supposed to be.

When you are feeling like you need stronger "suck-it-up" muscles, it's likely that you actually need the help of others. This is one muscle faculty that you want to flex less, and instead call up other faculties, like asking for help. Take a moment to think about this: We come together in times of weakness, less so in times of success. That is why social media's utility as a bonding agent is not what it's touted to be. Sharing our accomplishments and achievements does not bring people closer as much as us sharing our honest vulnerabilities does.

Practise relaxing your suck-it-up muscles.

### 3. The Grit-and-Quit Quadrant

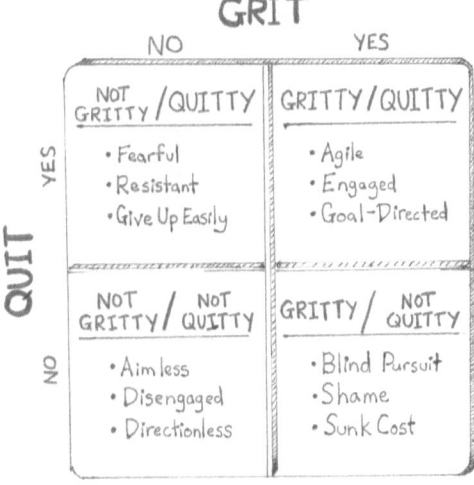

Former professional poker player Annie Duke points out a prevailing viewpoint many of us hold: "While grit is a virtue, quitting is a vice."[vii] Even the 12-item psychological measure of Grit by Angela Duckworth and her team penalises people whose "interests change from year to year" and who "set a goal but later choose to pursue a different one."[viii] In other words, people who quit their original pursuits score lower in Grit and are deemed as "less gritty."

Duke argues that both "Grit" and "Quit" are decision-making tools. Knowing when to persevere and when to walk away are two opposing tools that keep you flexible. If you persist for the sake of it (i.e., the sunk cost fallacy), even though you are not going in the right direction, you are in a bad way. If you think of quitting as not entirely leaving the court, but as a way of changing directions, you are in a good position.

Make a distinction between Grit and Quit. The last place you want to be is in the bottom left quadrant, "quitty" and not gritty. You give up too easily and are consumed by fear of taking the first step in trying anything new. Neither do you want to be not Gritty and unwilling to walk away from things. If this is you, you are disconnected from life.

In the bottom right quadrant, you are Gritty to a fault. You work your butt off, even though the endeavour is not meaningful to you. You hold a false belief that quitting is a sign of weakness. You base your decisions more on the sunk-cost of the past than the future. You don't want to take any risks. Finally, in the top right quadrant, you are Gritty and Quitty. You ask yourself the right questions. You are engaged in the work and prioritise direction over conformity.[ix]

If we know what to prioritise and persevere for, coupled with knowing what to let go of, we will be in a much better place to care for ourselves.

Practise making the distinction between when to be Gritty and when to be Quitty.

## B. Self-Forgetting

If you are moving towards the side of needing to focus less on yourself, here are some suggestions:

### 1. Focus on the Task at Hand

Immerse yourself fully in whatever you are doing—be it exercising, conversing, or working. Being in an immersive "flow" state has a way of changing how we experience time, and we consequently experience more enjoyment.[x] Deep absorption combined with a genuine challenge is beneficial to attaining flow states.

Practise pouring your full attention into the single task at hand.

### 2. Stop Taking Selfies

"Humility is not thinking less of yourself, but thinking of yourself less," said Rick Warren.[xi]

If you experience social anxiety, you are likely caught up in worries about what others are thinking. You might be sensitive to the feelings of others, to the point that it cripples you.

Here is something you can do metaphorically and literally: Point your camera at the world. On your mobile phone, put tape over the front-facing lens (unless you are taking video calls). We come alive when we can get out of our minds, and into the tasks at hand and the relationships that we ultimately care about. Train your attentional muscles to focus on others, not yourself.

A related tip: The next time you are on a video call, once you've checked that you are in frame, turn off the self view. Like walking into an elevator with mirrors, people can't help but look at themselves when their reflection is staring right back at them.

By turning off the self view on a video call, you train your attention to focus on what truly matters: **the other person.**

Caring for others in a deep way shapes our sense of self. Of course, focusing on bringing delight to and helping others feel good about themselves should not be done purely to make oneself feel good, but being generous and others-centred does help you get out of your own mental shell. Though reciprocity can occur, giving others a bucket of water is not done for the purpose of getting something in return or receiving a heavenly reward for being a good person. The act of generosity is the reward in and of itself.

Paying less attention to yourself does not mean neglecting or treating yourself like trash. John O'Donahue said, "There is an uncanny symmetry between the way you are inward with yourself and the way you are outward." The way we treat others on the outside is the way we treat ourselves on the inside.

Practise focusing your attention on the person in front of you.

### 3. Notice Something New Every Day

Look at the world around you. Pay careful attention to the places, buildings, nature and people you encounter. Each day, make a commitment to spot something new in your everyday life. This is a doorway to presence.

This could be an interestingly shaped tree during the walk from the carpark to your office, the beautiful face of a person you meet in a cafe, or the shape of a cloud above you. Or maybe it's even paying attention to the shadows of the trees cast by the morning sun. Alan Jacob notes that "surprise is the great enabler of seeing."[xii]

Learning to draw has helped me see things in a different light.[xiii] I only started doing so about a year ago. I carry a small notebook and a pen. If I am waiting for my kids, or if I pass by an interesting building or a tree, I take a quick reference photo with my phone, and then I sketch. I am no Picasso, but I thoroughly enjoy the process. After a few months of doing so, I realise that I am noticing things that I usually take for granted. Even when I'm not drawing, I now observe people, nature and made-made objects about seven seconds more than I typically would, and this makes me happy.

When you are noticing and seeing something you typically take for granted, you inadvertently forget about yourself. You are now not the subject. You are the observer of a subject (See #1. Sense, in Paradox 2. Present). And when you truly observe, you can be surprised.

Practise noticing something new every day.

## BROADEN YOUR NATURE

If you are high in Agreeableness, this makes you more likely to be empathetic than someone who is low on agreeableness. As such, you might find it a challenge to tend to your own needs, i.e., to practise self-care. Don't mistake struggle for failure.

If you are low in Openness to Experience, you might find the suggestions on Self-Forgetting slightly more challenging than someone who is more open to experience. This is okay. Cultivate a sense of awe and wonder. It helps to fall in love with the everyday world around you.

---

*Related Paradoxes: 3. Introspection/Outrospection, 5. Yes/No, 9. Caregiving/Care Receiving, 12. Recovery/Stress.*

# PARADOX 2. PRESENT/FUTURE

**CONTRADICTION**

Everyone says, "Be in the present."
Do I need to stay focused on the now or actively make plans for the future? How do I reckon with the timeless pull between staying present and time travelling into the future?

**CLARITY**

**A. Present: "The Surfer"**

"Yesterday is history, tomorrow is a mystery, but today is a gift. That is why it is called the present."

— *Master Oogway, Kungfu Panda.*

From the little I know about surfing, the moment you are in the waters, you have no other choice but to be *present* to the waves.

As I watch surfers at Margaret River, I see that they know that the future is *now*. The ocean demands nothing less than their undivided attention.

Being joyfully present is a gift. It is as if our nerve endings are porous to life outside. When we absorb our in-the-moment experiences, we are reflexively led to a place of gratefulness (See #3. Involuntary Gratitude, in Paradox 15. Surrender).

Mindfulness has become such a craze in- and outside of the field of psychotherapy that you can't help but hear whispers of incantations and catchphrases like "let your thoughts be thoughts" and "you are not your thoughts" and breathing exercises from therapy-office hallways.

There is a trade-off for the Surfer. One can live a life of being fully engaged in the moment and suffer tomorrow. At times, "being present" can be a guise, causing us to shy away from thinking about transformative, hard goals. Such avoidance not only impedes the future, but also creates a form of disconnection from self and others. Saving money, setting up life insurance, making goals for your future, or even buying that extra warranty on your latest kitchen appliance requires some form of time travel in your mind. Your future self will be pleased you got that sturdy iPhone case that prevented a cracked screen, or God forbid, a need to completely replace your mobile device for the third time.

### B. Future: "The Futurist"

> "Images of the future are the single most powerful socialising agents that exist in Western culture."
>
> — *Jeremy Rifkin*

Our capacity to imagine a future is such a compelling force.

Without this ability, there wouldn't be efforts to save the planet or make plans for retirement.

In 1955, there was a team of medical researchers who were true Futurists. After a decade of experimentation, Jonas Salk and his team developed the first polio vaccine. However, they didn't patent it, because Salk's mind wasn't focused on financial gain. He said, "The most important question we must ask ourselves is, 'Are we being good ancestors?'"

The Futurist knows that you have to shape a better tomorrow, because that's where you and your "future-cestors" are going to be. "...As we are living longer, we are thinking shorter," says anthropologist Mary Catherine Bateson.[i]

The very act of reading this book is you making plans for the future.

The trade-off for the Futurist is not getting to savour the present. Think of someone who is extremely goal-directed but misses the beauty of the present life: being an absent parent, justifying their work as trying to build a better life for their family, etc. One can be lost to the la-la land of the future.

---

The one who defers life to the future is in need of experiencing the precious moment, and the one who is absorbed in the "now" needs to cast their eyes towards the future because they have no plans for tomorrow.

The Surfer can learn from the Futurist, and the Futurist can take a cue from the Surfer. The Surfer knows how to savour the moment, and the Futurist creates an impact.

*In this season of your life, where do you need to be on the spectrum between* Present and Future focus? (Mark an '<', '>' or 'x' on the line below).

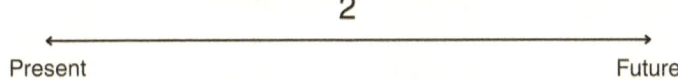

## COUNSEL

### A. Present

If you find yourself moving towards the side of getting overwhelmed by being overly future-oriented, there are four "S"s you can practise to help you be more present: Sense, Savour, Slow, and Sing:

### 1. Sense

Go for a walk. Focus your attention on what you see, not what you think; what you hear, and not the voices in your head. Come to your senses. Pay attention to the sensation on your skin... pay attention to your breath. Leading emotion researcher Lisa Fieldman Barrett argues that our brains are a prediction organism.[ii] The brain is akin to a black box inside our skull, and it's informed by past experiences and the inputs coming in from our senses. When we take in new inputs from the world outside, we are updating our experiences.

Practise taking in the outside world and let it reach you on the inside. This is a great way to get out of your head and into life.

### 2. Savour

The next time you have a meal or a get-together with a friend, be a sponge and soak it all in: the food and the company. Let go of the anticipation of what's next, and hold lightly when the past creeps in. If you get distracted, come back. Maybe when you are looking at nature or a painting, take it all in before trying to make meaning of it. Absorb the multitude of colours and the multi-layered textures that are hitting your retinas.

Practise taking it all in, as *completely* as possible. When you do, you'll notice you can't help but slow down.

**3. Slow**

You can see, feel, and taste things only if you slow down. You can drive past the same street every day and not notice the buildings and the trees around you. But you discover something completely different when you walk that same street. You *notice*.

The next time you are on the road, drive like your superchill Aunt Agatha.[1] Let the other people overtake you. Let them drive faster than you. Let them get to the traffic light first.

Go even further. Wave to the other drivers and let them get ahead of you—simply to be graceful.

There's no need to rush. Rushing might get you to your destination two and a half minutes earlier, but it will cost you a flustered face when you reach your destination.

Do you notice how people drive differently in dense cities compared to less-populated places? Most people aren't assholes. Context affects behaviour more than we realise. We underestimate how different sides within us come out and play depending on where we are and who we are with.[iii]

When you are on the road, you get to be either like the lot of us, driving as if we are late for a job interview every single day, mumbling to ourselves how idiotic others drivers are, or you get to *subvert* the norm. The norm is that everyone is trying to get ahead, in every sense of the word.

Mark Twain said, "The moment you are on the side of the majority, it's time to pause and reflect."

---

1. Not so slow that you get pulled over by the cops.

Be like a grandparent who has all the time in the world for their grandkids. They know how to take their time, how to be present to the little things, and they do not travel at light speed. A grandparent sees things that you might miss. When you speed through life, you miss life.

Practise travelling at the speed of life.

### 4. Sing

This is a bonus tip; it's a fun one.

You don't need to be Freddie Mercury to open up your vocal cords. Renowned improviser Bobby Mcferrin recommends this exercise: Take the courage to open your mouth and sing for ten minutes ... and fight the urge to stop![2] Notice how your critical side creeps in pretty quickly: "I'm out of tune." "Others must think that I'm crazy." "What's the point!?" To sing with disregard of the external world is to let your voice be your guide while letting your inner critic fade into the background without getting into a tassel with it. Sing about your critical side if you have to!

If you are up for an advanced level of being present, you can combine all four tips. For instance, you can pay attention to your senses while you take a bike ride and savour the wind on your face ... while making up new lyrics to Queen's "I want to ride my bicycle..."

Practise opening your mouth, and sing non-stop for two minutes, then five minutes, and then 10 minutes.

### B. Future

If you find yourself moving towards the side of losing yourself in the present, take a moment to contemplate the following, so as to

---

[2]. Yes, Bobby Mcferrin was the one who sang *Don't Worry, Be Happy*. And no, he didn't commit suicide. See snopes.com/fact-check/dont-worry-be-dead/

cast your eyes further into the future, a future that you are likely to inhabit:

## 1. What Do You Want to Create?

The question "What do I want to create?"[iv] is not one of problem-solving or finding alternatives. Creating is independent of the problems you are facing. It's a question of what you want to turn into reality.

A creative life is not only about artistic pursuits.

To lead a creative life is to create things and experiences as a generous act for others.

To lead a creative life, you have to subvert the status quo of being primarily a consumer. Instead, you are called to be a **creator**.

To lead a creative life, you have to be *creating*.

Acts of creativity could include staging a play, making a shoe, writing a book, performing a song, cooking a meal, planning a lesson, or cultivating a safe and engaging environment for your kids to grow up in. Acts of creativity come from a place of love (see Paradox 14. Output).

The act of creating requires *flexibility*, the antithesis of rigidity. By the way, this has positive effects on our well-being too. The late psychiatrist Milton Erickson pointed out that psychological issues are a result of inflexibility. Staying psychologically flexible is a hallmark of a good mind.[v]

The Irish poet Michael Longley was asked in a butcher shop why he does such a useless thing as writing poetry. He replied, "The answer is, 'No use...' It is useless... But it is *valuable*."[vi]

What we choose to create is ultimately valuable when it comes from the depths of our human experience.

Take a moment to ask yourself, "What do I want to create?" Write the answer in your notebook. Return to this at the end of each week and build on it. Don't worry if you don't have immediate answers. Tough questions take contemplation. Ask the tough questions now, and your future self will thank you for the good life it will experience in the future.

Practice responding to the question "What do I want to create?"

## 2. Who Do You Want to Become?

Goals are well and good. Having a sense of purpose is even better. But at the heart of this, one of the most vital questions to reflect on is "Who do I want to become?"

Do not be taken aback if you don't have an immediate answer. Many do not have a quick response to this question. Questions about our identity put us on a *quest* (See #2. Writing, in Paradox 13. Stillness).

To sharpen the resolution in your mind, let's take two steps:

**i. Chronos to Kairos:**

In Greek, there are two different aspects of time. Chronos is the chronological, measurable clock time. Kairos, on the other hand, is often referred to as the immeasurable deep time. View time less as "chronos" and more as "kairos." Stepping into kairos means that we entertain questions of greater depth and meaning.

*What is important to you?*
*What do you care about?*
*Who do you love?*

**ii. Three Dimensions:**

Next, think about life in these three dimensions: relationships, the present, and the future.

*Who do I want to be when I'm with my family?* (Relational)
*Am I the person I would like to be?* (Present-oriented)
*Who do I want to become? Do I have a reference from someone I admire?*

(Future-oriented)

The last thing you want to do is get what you want but become who you do not want to be.

Practise responding to the question, "Who do I want to become?"

**3. Good Ancestors**

"Are we being good ancestors?" As you'll remember, this was a question raised by Jonas Salk, the inventor of the polio vaccine mentioned earlier. We need to think not just of our children's generation, but seven generations down the line and beyond.

What sort of legacy are you leaving behind? Such ultra-long-term thinking focuses less on the self and more on what Roman Krznaric calls "cathedral thinking,"[vii] i.e., planning for things beyond your lifetime. After all, we are the beneficiaries of the people before us. Let us also become *benefactors* to others who are not yet here.

There are many ways to do this. A simple but profound way of doing this is to write personal letters to your loved ones. A letter is unlike a conversation, a text message, or an email. It provides a living legacy of thoughts and feelings, bonds and intimacy that are experienced and can be kept for posterity.

Practise writing letters to people you care about.

## BROADEN YOUR NATURE

If you are high in Extraversion, you are likely to have a tendency to prize the present. Conversely, if you are low in Extraversion, you are more primed to focus on the future. That's because people who are high in Extraversion value positive emotions more, whereas people who are Introverted are more reflective and spend resources to map out a variety of possibilities before execution. Pay attention to what this particular chapter of your life asks of you so that you can take steps to cultivate your nature and attend to the needs of the times.

---

*Related Paradoxes: 6. Acceptance/Change, 13. Stillness/Movement, 15. Control/Surrender.*

# PARADOX 3.
# INTROSPECTION/OUTROSPECTION

## CONTRADICTION

"The unexamined life is surely worth living, but is the unlived life worth examining?" says Adam Philips.[i]

Do I need to become more self-aware? Or do I need to learn to look more outwards?

## CLARITY

### A. Introspection

The ability to introspect is to appreciate that, fundamentally, we live in two worlds: one on the outside and one on the inside. Focusing solely on the external aspects of our home, social, or work life, without tuning in to our deeper inner experiences, can be perilous, not just for ourselves, but for others too. It's like driving a car with no mirrors or dashboard indicators.

Introspecting is not navel-gazing, wallowing in self-indulgence or self-pity. Introspection is an attentional skill, guided by the types of questions you choose to reflect on. Well-formed questions help you take aim toward an inward journey that you undertake to discover more about your nature and what you are capable of.

On the other hand, poorly formed questions put you on a loop, ruminating on a topic that leads to feeling worthless and useless.

You can be guided by a trusted mentor, counsellor, therapist, or spiritual director, but introspection needs to be done by *you*. It would be unrewarding if someone went on a holiday on your behalf. You are the one that needs to do the active soul-searching, because *you are the only one experiencing what you are experiencing on the inside.*

## B. Outrospection

The aim of outrospection is to be able to leave the self and engage with the world outside the self.

In the best-selling book *How to Win Friends and Influence People,* Dale Carnegie argues for an "important formula that will work wonders for you." Carnegie says, "Try honestly to see things from the other person's point of view."

Perspective-taking is often seen as the hallmark of empathy. Except that trying to put yourself in someone else's shoes isn't going to make you more empathic. In fact, it might even make you less accurate in your judgement and exaggerate stereotypes.

Social psychologist David Epley says,

> The weakness of perspective-taking is also obvious: it relies on your ability to imagine, or take, the other person's perspective accurately. If you don't really know what it's like to be poor, in pain, suicidally depressed, at the bottom of your corporate ladder, on the receiving end of waterboarding, in the throes of solitary confinement, or to have your source of income soaked in

oil, then the mental gymnastics of putting yourself in someone else's shoes isn't going to make you any more accurate. In fact, it might even decrease your accuracy.[ii]

Our empathy for others is enhanced when we engage less in perspective-taking and more in **perspective-getting**. To understand another person, ask them questions. Curiosity never killed the cat.[1] Not only does asking questions reduce errors in our judgement and minimise stereotypical views of others, it also builds deeper connections when we use curiosity as a growth agent for relationships.

What's more, understanding someone is different from helping someone *feel understood*. One might comprehend how the other feels, but the other person still might not feel heard by you. It is necessary to understand, but understanding is not sufficient to help them feel understood. It is only through our words, actions, and deep listening that we can truly outrospect.

---

The inward gaze of introspection is helpful for those who do not take the time to reflect and see where life is going. But an overdose of introspection is like driving with your eyes glued to the rearview mirror.

For some, the best form of introspection is outrospection. Others may need to search inside themselves.

*In this season of your life, where do you need to be on the spectrum of Introspection and Outrospection? (Mark an '<', '>' or 'x' on the line below).*

---

1. A less frequently seen rejoinder to "curiosity killed the cat" is "but satisfaction brought it back." See en.wikipedia.org/wiki/Curiosity_killed_the_cat.

## 3

⟵——————————————————⟶
Introspection                              Outrospection

## COUNSEL

### A. Introspection

If you find yourself moving towards the side of needing to understand yourself more, here are a handful of questions to guide your reflection.

**1. Level I:**

> *What has been on my mind?*
> *How is my heart?*
> *How do I feel about how I've spent the last week? What did I do?*

**2. Level II:**

> *What inner struggles am I going through? What inner-strengths am I most proud of?*

**3. Level III:**

> *How am I loving the people around me?*
> *What do I really care about?*
> *Am I spending time on the things that matter to me? (See #1. Do Hard Things, in Paradox 12. Stress).*

These questions are an invitation to contemplation, not just a Q&A exercise. Work through each of the three levels before proceeding further. Each level represents the depths of your inner experience.

Use each of the questions as a springboard. Let them put you on a quest. You will need to create space for this, and you may need to be patient for the waters to calm down before you can see inside.

Write down your responses. Engaging with external material like journaling or even drawing (mindmapping, sketchnoting, abstract drawing) might be helpful to concretise your thinking.

Practise asking yourself reflective questions. This will reveal what's on the inside.

## B. Outrospection

If you find yourself moving towards the side of needing to "get over" yourself, here are some tips to move from perspective-taking to perspective-getting.

### 1. Be a Tourist

Before the COVID-19 pandemic you could often tell who was a local and who was a tourist in a town. The local would be going about her business, while the tourist would be wide-eyed, armed with their smartphone, taking pictures of the buildings and trees that you walked past everyday.

Travelling to a new place creates a sense of novelty. We can intentionally "be a tourist" in familiar places by noticing the details in our surroundings. I take journalist Rob Walker's advice of being a perpetual tourist in my own town, and I try to "spot something new every day."² Sometimes, due to limited parking nearby, I'll find a lot ten minutes away from my practice in Fremantle. As I walk, I make a point of being a "perpetual tourist" as I take in the surroundings. This means that, from time to time, I feel the compulsion to whip out my phone and take a picture of the ocean or the heritage buildings or the interesting reflections in a shop's window. I squint, I put the phone at funny angles, I hunt for fresh perspectives. As a "tourist," everything becomes interesting. Like drawing (see #3. Notice Something New Every Day, Paradox 1. Self-Forgetting), photography trains my eyes to really take notice.

Practise being a tourist.

## 2. Engage Like a Journalist

The next time you're at a party, put on your invisible journalist hat. A journalist's job is to learn about people and the world outside. You are inducing and feeding curiosity, and you become the Curious Monster. The more you get curious, the more interested you are.

Get fascinated about other people. Learn what people like to do, what they've been busy with, what they care about.

Don't just listen to speak, but speak in order to listen. Listen to what others have to say. People are strange when you are a stranger; people are interesting when you are interested.³

Practise being a good journalist.

---

2. Rob Walker's book *The Art of Noticing* is a great delight, packed with 130 other suggestions of noticing your everyday life.
3. For proper attribution, this sentence is a hybrid from The Doors song, *People are Strange*, and a paraphrasing of Dale Carnegie's *How to Win Friends and Influence People*.

### 3. Take Care of Others

This should not be taken as permission to subjugate your own needs, but rather to tend to others who may benefit from your care (See Paradox 9. Caregiving).

Giving your time to people in need can have a positive effect. In my early 20s, I noticed I was indulging in too much navel-gazing and felt I needed to get out of my head. I pushed myself to volunteer every Saturday morning at a psychiatric hospital. Who would have thought that I would later on get a job work there for more than a decade?

An 18-year-old therapy client shared with me a recent self-discovery. He had made a deal with himself: "Even though I'm nervous, I remind myself to stay focused on helping other people feel comfortable in the group. In turn, I feel comfortable about myself!"

When someone appreciates our care, we are gifted with the knowledge that we have something to give. We all have something to give.

Practise taking care of the needs of others.

## BROADEN YOUR NATURE

If you are high in Extraversion, you might find the Introspection suggestions challenging. If this is the direction you need to take, be patient with yourself as you work through the self-reflection, bit by bit.

If you are high in Introversion, the Outrospection activities might not come as second nature to you. Same advice. Play around with the ideas one at a time, and then evaluate how it went—after the fact, not before.

If you are high in Neuroticism (i.e., proneness to negative emotions), and you are working through the Introspection section, make sure you are guided by the specific questions and parking a specific amount of limited time to do so. This will prevent unproductive rumination.

---

*Related Paradoxes: 1. Self-Care/Self-Forgetting, 9. Caregiving/Care-Receiving.*

# PARADOX 4. SOLITUDE/COMMUNITY

## CONTRADICTION

*Leave me alone, but don't leave me... I need to be with people, but I also need to learn to be by myself.*
  *What do I really need?*

## CLARITY

### A. Solitude

While there is an instinct to belong to a tribe, it is also possible to hide from yourself in community.

For many, being in solitude takes practice.

The experience of solitude can be painful, because it is a close cousin to loneliness.

Yet we need solitude like we need water: regularly. You don't realise its importance unless you are dehydrated.

We are experiencing a drought of solitude. Technological attempts to "connect" us have all failed dismally.[i] Thanks largely to our mobile devices and their constant barrage of notifications from shiny apps, our attention has been hooked and hijacked. It is as if every few minutes someone is flailing their arms in the air and screaming, "Hey, look here!" The aggregate experience is a cacophony of digital noise, leaving no space for silence in between the notes to breathe in the music of life.

Thomas Merton defines the relationship of sound and silence:

> Music is pleasing not only because of the sound but [because] of the silence that is in it: without the alternation of the sound and silence there would be no rhythm. If we strive to be happy by filling all the silences of life with sound, and productive by turning all life's leisure into work and all our being into doing, we will succeed only in producing hell on earth.[ii]

## B. Community

Friendships are a diagnosis of our lives.[iii]

Who are your friends? What is the quality of these friendships?

In the presence of true friendship, we find ourselves not needing to prove anything or highlight certain sides of ourselves. When a friendship is well-formed, we find ourselves befriending who we are on the inside.

Friendship shapes a community, but not everyone in the community is your soulmate. Communities are like an extended family: some we bond very well with, and others, not so much.

A community calls us to open our doors. Maybe these are the groups you belong to at your workplace, at your place of worship, or even in your neighbourhood. Deep communities are forged not by the sharing of our successes, but by the willingness to open up our needs. When we feel the emotional safety of friendship cultivated in community, we are more likely to reveal our brokenness and wounds. This is the soil of friendship.

As mentioned earlier in "My Seasons," I experienced a deep longing for community after moving to another country. I'd left my group of close friends, and I felt an ache, one that missed being part of a tribe.

When I lack a strong community, I become acutely sensitive to remarks made by others. My mind goes in circles trying to figure out whether I misread the intentions behind someone's words. I am easily hurt by small remarks. But when I feel stronger ties to people around me, my mind ruminates less. It's as if somewhere in me understands that "It's ok. You don't have to figure this out in your head. You *belong*. You can talk with your friends about this if you want to."

The Solitude/Community paradox runs through the variety of seasons in our lives. As the author Parker Palmer says, we need to "practise the paradox of 'being alone together.'" Palmer cites the theologian Dietrich Bonhoeffer from *Life Together*: "Let [the person] who cannot be alone beware of community. Let [the person] who is not in community beware of being alone."

It is difficult to not fall into a dualistic "either/or" perspective. What's closer to the truth is that we need "both/and." (see Personal Paradoxical Profile Redux). But in certain seasons, we need to slant towards a particular direction based on what's calling out to our unmet inner needs.

At the time of writing, I'm finding this especially challenging. I feel like I'm missing close friendships. Moving away from my home country in Singapore meant that I lost close contact with long-term friends. I miss making music with the band that I've known since I was 14. I miss hanging out with them. Now, I have to seek out new people. A part of me doesn't want to engage in small talk and agenda-based discussions, but another part of me sees that I need to reach out.

We need solitude in order to hear ourselves clearly. Silence bears fruits only among those in good company.

*In this season of your life, where do you need to be on the spectrum of Solitude and Community? (Mark an '<', '>' or 'x' on the line below).*

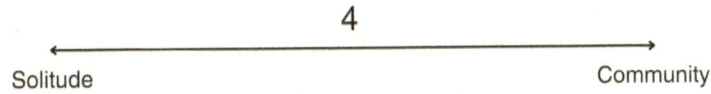

Solitude                                              Community

## COUNSEL

### A. Solitude

If you find yourself moving towards the side of needing to be by yourself, here are some suggestions:

### 1. Walk

Moving around your neighbourhood or in nature fosters a certain inner rhythm for thoughts to percolate. This is viscerally different from sitting down and thinking. When you are walking, you can be mindful of the present, or you can be contemplative. You don't have to be "emptying your mind" or self-reflecting. Walking gives rise to our intentions.

You could substitute walking for yoga, but I wouldn't necessarily put running, cycling, or even going to the gym in the same category. The reason is that our minds get pulled into the physical demands of the workout. Some might still be able to maintain a meditative state with rigorous routines, but generally speaking, slowing down might be more helpful for embracing solitude. (See Paradox 13. Stillness/Movement).

Practise walking with no destination in mind.

## 2. "No inputs from other minds"

If your intention is to rejuvenate, a good rule is to have "no inputs from other minds." This means no reading, no audiobook, no podcast, no phone calls. Reading the news or social media feeds is not true solitude.

When you try this rule, you might at first feel a bit "off," like you've missed your morning coffee. Hang in there. You've become used to the pleasures of distraction. You might need a "dopamine reset."[iv]

If you have been on a silent retreat before, you'll be familiar with the initial agony. But by the end of the retreat, you feel as if the palate of your senses has been cleansed; you feel the world around you a little more.

Solitude creates the spaciousness and clearing required to hear ourselves. Don't dilute it with distractions. There are other times to be stimulated and invigorated by the inputs of others. (See also Paradox 14. Inputs/Outputs).

Practise periods of no inputs.

## 3. Routine

Bake #1 and #2 into your weekly rhythm. Set reminders if you have to.

The experience of solitude is at odds with the way our society and technology have been developing, thus affecting the way we have been living. Especially when you are making significant transitions in your life, you need to protect solitude, so that the small voice inside you gets a chance to be heard.

Practise befriending your inner life by setting a rhythm to your days.

## B. Community

If you find yourself moving towards the side of needing to be more in community with others, here are some suggestions:

### 1. Find Your Tribe

Join a community choir, volunteer at a local charity, sign up for a Meetup group,[1] join people with common interests in your area. Use the internet or your local community magazine to find people who share your values and passions.

Do something you have never done before. There is always a time to do something for the first time. When you try out these new things, go without expectations. Simply allow yourself to experience new things.

Practise being with new people of common interests.

### 2. Be a Host

Bring people together. Invite friends for monthly dinners. Suggest a rotation for hosting. Bring a dish,[2] or host a fortnightly cheese-tasting. Arrange lunch with a colleague. Make up any excuse to come together just for the sake of it.

The thing about these suggestions is that you have to initiate. Make the act of meeting other people a part of your weekly or monthly routine. If you have a circle of friends, make it a point to reach out on a consistent basis. "But why should I be the one who's always reaching out?" Have that difficult conversation. Ask your friend, "Do you feel like it's a drag that I keep reaching out?" Maybe they feel that whenever you reach out, you end up talking all about yourself, or that they are just super busy with a work

---

1. Yes, meetup.com still exists. Check your local meetup groups.
2. In Australia, we say, "Bring a plate."

project. Or, they might say, "Actually, I'm really grateful you are checking in." They just hadn't gotten round to expressing their gratitude.

Reach out. The lucky person is that one who stays open to experience, minus expectation. Someone is lucky to have you as a friend.

Practise being a host; bring people together.

### 3. Be a Witness

When we encounter the word "witness," we might think of it in legal terms, such as being an "eyewitness" or "expert witness." Witnesses are typically cross-examined by attorneys to elicit information, clarify details, or challenge the credibility of the testimony.

But to be a witness to others when they are Crossing Between Worlds is to accompany the individual in their solitude. To be in the same world, at the same time, through this liminal space of bridge-crossing, is to share a given space and time together. It is to say, *I share your reality*, as you move from an old world to a new world.

Being a witness does not require specific actions. Rather, it requires a specific disposition. It requires a posture of patience, hope, and willingness to suspend your own agenda and be with another through times of uncertainty and tribulation. To be a witness is to be a midwife of hope for a friend.

Not only can you be a witness to others, you must also allow others to be a witness to you when you are moving and being moved towards a new life. A family friend was diagnosed with cancer and she kept mum about it. She was in her mid-forties. She didn't want to make a fuss about her condition, thinking it would be a burden and imposition to others. Thomas Merton said, "Suffering is wasted if we suffer entirely alone."[v] We yearn to let others into our lives when we're suffering, to be known and accompanied. To open our hearts to others in times of suffering is to give the gift of closeness. Allowing a friend or family member into our deepest caves of darkness is to say, *I trust you*, and *Can you be with me through these times?* This raw vulnerability may be the thing that you are avoiding. But suffering is wasted if you don't give others a chance to be there for you.

Practise being a witness, and allow others to be a witness to you.

## BROADEN YOUR NATURE

If you are high in Extraversion and Neuroticism, you may find the suggestions on Solitude confronting. You are essentially reducing stimulation from the external environment and, consequently, are made to face your inner world. This can be more difficult if you are on a diet of a constant stream of inputs.

People who are introverted don't necessarily find it difficult to be in community; they just probably need less external stimulation, and by nature, appreciate alone time and time to recharge after social interactions. Pay attention to what this season of your life asks of you.

---

*Related Paradoxes: 3. Introspection/Outrospection, 7. Approach/Retreat, 10. Grief/Love, 13. Stillness/Movement, 14. Inputs/Outputs.*

# PARADOX 5. YES/NO

**CONTRADICTION**

What is a yes when you can't say no?
Do I need to learn to embrace more "Yeses" to opportunities, or to assert more "Nos" to protect my boundaries?

**CLARITY**

**A. Yes**

"Those who say 'yes' are rewarded by the adventures they have. Those who say 'no' are rewarded by the safety they attain."

— *Keith Johnstone*

This might sound strange to some but deeply conflicting to others. This benign question can be deceptive:

## What do I really want?

Desire is the seed of knowing, deeply rooted in our psyche. Especially when you are at significant transitions, such periods hint at not only what you like, but also who you are going to become (see #2. Who Do You Want to Become? In Paradox 2. Future). For instance, a person who decides to leave a high-paying job in his 40s—because he can no longer work in a place that violates his values about the environment and how to treat people —now has to recalibrate in a new direction. If he stayed at his previous job, even though it paid well, the ongoing moral injury would likely inflict psychological symptoms like depression, anxiety, insomnia, and feelings of overwhelm and alienation.

At first blush, the question "What do I really want?" sounds highly self-indulgent. But affording ourselves the chance to carefully reflect on it can lead to deep reckoning. And what we have to reckon with is the idiosyncratic particularities of what makes us come alive.

Your biggest need is to figure out what you really want.

And no one can tell you what to want (see #2. Your Desire— or Is It Mimetic Desire?, in Paradox 8. Autonomy).

One of the best times to consider the question of your desire is when you are Crossing Between Worlds. To find clues, it may look like you need to take steps forward, but oftentimes, you are actually returning to the seeds of your childhood. Those seeds have always been there.

Let these words from the late poet Mary Oliver resonate:

> *You do not have to be good.*
> *You do not have to walk on your knees*
> *for a hundred miles through the desert repenting.*
> *You only have to let the soft animal of your body*
> *love what it loves.*[i]

## B. No

> "On matters of style, swim with the current...on matters of principle, stand like a rock."
>
> — *Thomas Jefferson*

When you are first starting out in your career, you have to learn to say yes to most things. But as your career progresses, you have to learn the fine art of saying no. If you can't say no to things that are not a "yes" for you, you run the risk of burnout and resentment. The potency of your Yes depends on your willingness to say No.

When we learn to say No, we can say Yes to the things that count.

Of course there isn't a blanket rule that you need to say either Yes or No all the time. Perhaps in some situations, you need to say Yes more, and in other contexts, you need to flex your No muscles more. That said, when making key transitions in your life, a quieter part of you knows whether it wants a Yes or a No. This part of you wants you to take heed.

---

Our Yeses will mean something when we can exercise our Nos, and our Nos will give us the freedom for our Yeses.

*In this season of your life, where do you need to be on the spectrum of Yes and No? (Mark an '<', '>' or 'x' on the line below).*

5

Yes ←——————————————————→ No

## COUNSEL

### A. Yes

If you find yourself moving towards the side of needing to say Yes to opportunities more often than not, consider the following suggestions:

### 1. Ask "What do I really want?"

Take 30-45 minutes to journal or mindmap. At the top of the page, write down the following prompt: "What do I really want?"

Break the page into three sections.
i. Personal
ii. Relationships
iii. Work

Be honest with yourself. Listen to your yearnings and let your answers freely exist on the page.

After you are done, ask yourself the following questions:
- If a friend wrote this, how would I describe that person?
- What does what I want in my personal, relationship, and work life say about who I
am and what I really care about?

Practise listening to what you really want.

### 2. Say "Yes! And…"

Remember that Jim Carey movie, *Yes Man*, where the protagonist attends a seminar that makes him say yes to *everything* that comes his way, no questions asked?

This tip is not quite so extreme, but it is about adopting a posture of willingness to embrace everything that comes your way.

A friend asks if you'd like to join them for lunch. You reply, "Yes!"

A colleague asks if you can help them with a project. You enthusiastically say, "Most certainly!"

Your spouse suggests getting a babysitter so that you can both go on a date night. You exclaim, "What a brilliant idea!"

This is not about becoming a spineless "Yes man" but more about what improv actors call "Yes, and...." This strategy of "Yes, and..." is a guiding principle that improvisers are taught to use by accepting what another improviser brings to the scene (See Paradox 15. Surrender).

I attended a small group improv class some years ago. The facilitator explained this "Yes, and" rule-of-thumb. I was sceptical. Already in my mind I was "Yes, but-ing" the idea. However, as each of us presented a scenario (e.g., "I am walking down the street eating my ice cream cone..." and the other replied, "Yes, and I am really enjoying the ice cream when a pelican swoops down and pecks my head"), the story became hysterically funny ("Yes, and so I build this ladder made of stacked up chairs to climb up the tree to find that bird and ask whether it actually wants my ice cream, not my head."). I was taken aback by the strange cohesion the "Yes, and" approach was creating, simply by embracing everything that came our way.

The real challenge is refraining from thinking of something smart to say. The key is to be all-embracing, and simply open the windows to experience.

Practise embracing all that is in front of you by saying, "Yes! And..."

## 3. Act Before You Think

Here are some common misconceptions. We think we need to

- Feel confident in order to do something with competence,
- Feel loveable in order to love,
- Feel good before we can do any good,
- Know before we act, and
- Find our passion before we become good at something.

The examples given above may seem reasonable, but in reality, things often unfold in the opposite way. We need to

- Become competent at something in order to build confidence,
- Give love in order to feel love,
- Do some good before we feel good,
- Act in order to know, and
- Follow our fascination before finding our passion.

We should think not only on our feet, but also *with* our feet.

There is wisdom in our lower limbs. We are not designed to be sedentary creatures. We are designed to grow, and growing takes place when we move, both in our inner lives and in our mortal flesh.

When my daughter was three years old, she thought with her feet by trying things, even if she might fall and get a stern warning or two for pushing boundaries.

Composers, movie directors, performers, writers, and storytellers know the importance of creating dynamic movement in order for a scene to come alive. They know how to move us.

We are designed to move and be moved.

In the spirit of Yes, give things a go first. Reflect on them after the fact. Not the other way round.

Practise thinking with your feet first, followed by your head.

## B. No

If you find yourself moving towards the side of needing to learn to say No more often than not, consider the following suggestions:

### 1. Be "Divided No More"

When you go against what you stand for, you violate an integral part of yourself. This type of moral wounding eats at you. Even when you think you have sufficiently distracted yourself and gotten those negative thoughts out of your mind, the inner division festers.

Quaker author Parker Palmer notes in his book, *A Hidden Wholeness:*

> Dividedness is a personal pathology...The divided life, at bottom, is not a failure of ethics. It is a failure of human wholeness.

Wholeness, by my estimation, is not some fluffy New Age concept. To go against what is a "No" for you on the inside, by saying "Yes" on the outside, creates a divided life. This division not only affects individuals personally, but it also impacts others. When your Yeses and Nos are not aligned with your inner and outer life, people around you are not getting a chance to really know you. What they experience of you is only a veneer.

One of my clients, Max, a handsome male in his late 20s, was dating a girl for more than five years. There were threats of them breaking up a couple of times. His partner cheated on him. She begged for his forgiveness. He forgave her. And then she cheated on him again. She confessed to him. She was painfully remorseful. She loved him and was racked with guilt and shame. He forgave her again. I asked him what made him forgive her, twice.

"It's the right thing to do, isn't it? I should just man up and not be so insecure about these things."

"Ok... it's the 'right' thing to do... but on the inside, does it feel *right* to you?"

He shrugged. "Eh..."

His apathy, low mood, and feelings of guilt continued. His well-being scores remained roughly the same as when I started working with him. I was increasingly worried about him and his lack of progress. I knew about his history, that there'd been a pattern of subjugating his own needs since he was a child. Even though his parents were together, they led separate lives. His father lost himself in alcohol on most nights, and his mother was too busy trying to keep the family afloat. Meanwhile, with four other siblings in tow, Max, the eldest, quickly learned to be a parent in the household, picking up the pieces for everyone else.

Some weeks after our conversation about his girlfriend, I met up with Max. As part of my routine clinical practice, I had him fill out an ultra-brief measure of his global well-being. To my surprise, his scores had improved. Naturally, I was curious. He spent the next 15 minutes catching me up, and then he said, "... and I decided that this relationship couldn't continue. I broke up with my girlfriend."

Most of the time, when a relationship breaks down, one would expect a dip in a person's well-being. Max, however, had a different experience. He said, "For the first time, I feel like the choice that I'm making is mine."

Muscles atrophy when we don't use them. Our "No" faculties atrophy when we don't use them. Even though Max had a late genesis of tending to his own needs, learning to flex between what was a Yes and what was a No gave him strength. More importantly, he could now begin to lead an undivided life. He can learn to truly forgive when he is now congruent with himself.

Clearly, things often aren't as simple as a Yes or a No. Here's a good principle from Brazilian author Paulo Coelho: "**When you say yes to others, make sure you are not saying no to yourself.**"

Practise saying No on the outside when it is a No on the inside.

## 2. Increase Autonomy by Saying No

Saying no is hard.

It's hard because it feels like we are letting others down.

Many of us would rather suffer on the inside than disappoint others.

In the past, I kept taking on project after project, even though I was already 110% over the brim. Why did I do that? The explanation in my head went like this: "I think I can work on this for a few evenings after I put the kids to bed…and maybe wake up at 6 a.m. to finish it up…Yeah, it's doable." Despite not being employed in the halls of academia, which meant that I had no incentives to publish peer reviewed articles, I would take on research studies, sign up for "extracurricular activities" outside of my role as a clinician in the hospital, and often say "yes" to reviewing studies as a peer-reviewer, even though I really didn't have the bandwidth for them.

Apart from my wife, no one else knew I was suffering because of these Yeses.

Here are some more examples of the narratives I used to convince myself: "This would be a good opportunity for me to get more exposed to this particular clinical research," "This would help me build a name for myself," "This would be good for learning more about how organisations operate," and the kicker, "What if I miss this chance and it's not going to come by again?"

Even though my rationale was meant to be self-beneficial, this led me to burnout. The only way I could turn things around was to base my decisions not on the potential of benefit, but on *autonomy*.

Given the lessons learned, as I operate from a place of autonomy, my default answer to new projects is a No, even if the benefits seem enticing.

The shift from "benefit" to autonomy means that I now anchor myself on things that can increase my sense of agency and control of my life (See Paradox 8. Autonomy). This means that I have to not just go with what might be useful, beneficial, or even helpful, but also be governed by a different principle, one that is about enacting true choices, much like how my client Max exercised a choice that was truly his.

Practise increasing autonomy, and not just seeking benefits.

### 3. Make a Big Decision to Avoid Small Decisions

Moving our thinking from "benefit" to a real consideration of autonomy isn't so straightforward. In order to make the difficult things easier, adopt the following principle:

**Make a big decision so as to avoid small decisions.**

If someone invites you to a gathering that you aren't actually 100% keen to attend, *and* you already have 19 other big commitments and deadlines tied down for the next eight weeks, say a gracious No.

If someone at work gives you a "perfect" project opportunity that might even lead to a promotion in the near future, but you actually only have 5% interest in the project and the potential role, bravely give a kind No.

Instead of saying a hesitant Yes and then regretting it later on, consider some variant of the following response: "Thanks for thinking of me. At the moment, I'll have to turn down the invite. But if things change in the next few weeks, I'll definitely let you know."

At the outset, instead of being confronted with in-the-moment small decisions or even the pressure to say Yes, make a pre-decision to say No.

Your Yeses depend on your Nos. The ability to make "a big decision" upfront by saying No requires you to know what you really want and what is important to you (See #1. What do I really want?, in Paradox 5. Yes).

If you are often put on the spot and have difficulties defaulting to a No, buy some time. Say to the other person, "Let me get back to you," so that you think it through clearly.

Practise front-loading your efforts to commit to a decision before the event arises.

## BROADEN YOUR NATURE

Highly conflict-avoidant and people-pleasing individuals are likely to struggle with the question "What do I really want?" Stick with it, especially if this is a period in your life where you find yourself needing course correction.

If you are high in Agreeableness, you have to be careful not to say yes to things that are a no. If you continue to do so, resentment will build. That's a huge price to pay if you continue to be conflict avoidant. Facing potential conflict now pays off later in the long run. Take a moment to distinguish between what is a Yes or a No for you.

---

*Related Paradoxes:* 8. Autonomy/Belonging, *15. Control/Surrender.*

# PART III: WELL-BELONGING

"The full achievement of what is unique in each of us lies not in our individuality but in our personality, and we can find that personality only in union with others."

— *Pierre Teilhard de Chardin*[i]

In this second section, we enter into the web of relationships and discover the transformative power of intimate connections. Our well-being is interwoven with our well-belonging. We will look at the tension of opposites between our need to connect and care for others and the need to increase autonomy and receive care from others.

# PARADOX 6. ACCEPTANCE/CHANGE

## CONTRADICTION

The first seeds of change grow out of full acceptance. Brute force to change can cause harm. Yet a resistance to change denies our instinct for growth.

Do I need to learn acceptance or make active changes?

## CLARITY

### A. Acceptance

*I. Others-Acceptance*

One of the hardest things to do is radically accept someone as they are, especially the people closest to you.

It's as if you have to fight against some kind of impulse. Somewhere deep in your bones you reject the person's actions, even though deep down you love them.

The reason it is difficult to fully accept someone as they are—even though you know intellectually it makes sense—is that it opens a floodgate of heated and conflicted emotions within. These feelings, often absent from the experiences of daily living, rush out of the hidden depths and onto the surface of everything like a tsunami.

I like to believe that I carry myself fairly consistently in most parts of my professional and personal life. However, I am of a different spirit when I am with my father.

As a child, I found myself shutting down whenever my parents argued. I was prone to turning inward, and I was somewhat of a "crybaby." I teared up easily. I suspect this left my dad feeling helpless, which turned into agitation. He didn't know how to handle me. Like a typical Asian father, he was stoic and stern. I didn't have the best relationship with him. During my youth, we fought on several occasions.

Now, as a 45-year-old man, more than 20 years later, I can still feel the tension of my childhood in my bones. Even though I do not hold any resentment towards him, I still feel a disconnect with my father. When the COVID-19 lockdown ended, my parents came over to visit and stayed with us in Australia for a few months. I was talking to a friend of mine about my frustration with my own knee-jerk reactions towards my father. He was just being himself. Given her spiritual practice at Thích Nhất Hạnh's Plum Village, my friend said to me, "Thay said, 'Love is understanding...' and our intolerance—" I interrupted her right there. The word *intolerance* had hit a nerve. I was surprised by my reaction to this. I was familiar with the saying "Seek first to understand, then to be understood," often attributed to Stephen Covey and the Prayer of St. Francis of Assisi. But the realisation that I had been intolerant caused a feeling of embarrassment to wash over me.

Thích Nhất Hạnh, affectionately known as Thầy (meaning "teacher" in Vietnamese) by his students, said,

> Understanding is love's other name. If you don't understand, you can't love...To know how to love someone, we have to understand them. To understand, we need to listen.

As I looked back, I realised that, while I have moved into a profession that uses deep listening as one of its instruments for healing, I actually stopped listening to my father a long time ago. Whenever he raises an opinion, I react reflexively and find myself snapping or shutting down. My wife sees this. She gives me a look. I give her back the *"What?"* look. I have become intolerant of my father.

I love my father. I just have a hard time accepting him for who he is. I've had to admit to myself that learning to accept my dad as he is was too big a leap for me. The pathway to acceptance seems to be more possible when I seek to understand, as Nhất Hạnh advises. And in order for me to understand, I have to open my ears to my ageing father, who is past eighty at the time of this writing. To open my ears exposes me in a way I find unsettling and uncomfortable, which is a strange paradox, given that I am comfortable with intense emotions in the therapy room. The time has come to leave the old world of my noise-cancelling ears towards my father and move towards one where I'm ready to listen and engage.

Here is what writer Wes Angelozzi says,

> Go and love someone exactly as they are. And then watch how quickly they transform into the greatest, truest version of themselves. When one feels seen and appreciated in their own essence, one is instantly empowered.

## *II. Self-Acceptance*

As if learning to accept someone you love as they are isn't hard enough, the identical twin of self-acceptance also tops the difficulty charts.

Self-acceptance is simple to grasp and hard to follow. Like most fundamental facets of our lives, we rarely pause to think about what it truly means.

Self-acceptance is not self-esteem, which is dependent on a subjective evaluation of one's own worth or value, often tied to external factors.

Self-acceptance means to accept what's natural to you. As mentioned in Part I, the Latin word for nature, *natura*, means both birth and character. (See Introduction, What Is Our Nature?)

And what's natural is, by nature, imperfect.

Self-acceptance softly defies external expectations and societal standards. To learn to accept oneself—and all of one's original goodness—is an act of defiance. It subverts the normative view that we must be more than we are.

It also requires an understanding that our imperfections are sources of beauty and grace. We do not hide away things that are of beauty, and the world could use a little more gracefulness.

The sing-songwriter and poet Leonard Cohen wrote in his song "Anthem,"

> *Ring the bells that can ring*
> *Forget your perfect offering.*
> *There is a crack, a crack in everything,*
> *That's how the light gets in.*

Acceptance, as the humanist theorists would argue, is the first seed of change. I once heard Carl Rogers say, "If I fully accept what I have, what I have is enough."[i]

That's how the light gets in.

## B. Change

We have a conflicted relationship with change. We yearn for things to be different, yet we cling to the familiar.

"Change is scary," said the anthropologist Gregory Bateson. "Not changing is even scarier."

Perhaps scarier than not changing is to change in a way that is not aligned with who you are, and who you'd like to become. When you are trying to make changes in your life, you first must be clear on the direction you want to head. Making changes in the wrong direction is worse than making no changes at all.

At certain periods of our lives, we get to choose, we get to *move* towards our intended goals. At other times, life does not ask for our permission for change. We are *being moved*—or rather, thrusted towards a place we would never imagine. Don lost his daughter Sylvia through a long battle with cancer. She was in her mid-twenties. One can only imagine the devastating impact of losing one's child. Don described her birth as an event that made him reevaluate his priorities. Though he separated from Sylvia's mother, his relationship with his daughter during her adolescence was both beautiful and tumultuous, since they were close but also frequently clashed. Her death brought him hell on earth, causing him to question the very purpose of his existence.

Years later, Don found his footing through a reexamination of what he was going to do with the second half of his life, amidst waves of unrelenting grief. "I kept fighting it," Don said. "But now I'm clear. **Life is trying to change me.** Life is trying to change all of us."

"When thinking changes your mind, that's philosophy," says the editor John Brockman of the book *What Have You Changed Your Mind About?* "When God changes your mind, that's faith. When facts change your mind, that's science."

I would add that when you change your own mind, that's an opinion. When someone changes your mind, that's love.

When we open ourselves to love, we become vulnerable. When we are vulnerable, we are woundable. But our hearts are not meant to be shielded from the world. Our hearts are meant to be broken, over and over again. Not shattered, but opened to the greater connection to the self and the world around us. Not hardened, but softened enough to absorb further love. Don's wounds from the loss of his only child will never be completely healed, but his love has only expanded through the course of his own journey and healing. Don is changed, not by choice, but by his willingness to allow life to ultimately change him.

Change is not always about growth, but growth needs something to change. And sometimes, change begins with an "insufferable frustration."[ii] We can no longer bear the pain of the status quo.

In a sense, change is loss. When we make a change for the better, we let go of old habits, and we let go of an old world, an old way of being. Franciscan Richard Rohr says, "Change is when something new begins. But transformation is when something old falls away."[iii]

In this context, when we say someone has "changed," what we really mean is someone has been transformed.

To experience deep change is to allow ourselves to be altered, to be transformed. Such transformation occurs when our identity expands. As you cross into another world, maybe you are now a spouse, a grandparent, a widower, a small business owner, a recovering addict, a mentor, etc. A new you grows out of you.

---

When we learn to fully accept, the door of possibilities opens up. When we learn to embrace change, we allow life to transform us.

*In this season of your life, where do you need to be on the spectrum of Acceptance and Change? (Mark an '<', '>' or 'x' on the line below).*

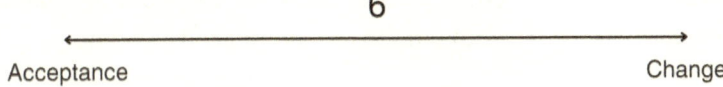

## COUNSEL

### A. Acceptance

If you find yourself moving towards the side of needing to accept others and yourself, see the following suggestions:

### I. Others-Acceptance

#### 1. Strength vs. Warmth

There are moments in your life when you need to stand firm, and others where you need to exude warmth.

We need both physical and psychological strength in order to get things done. We are not passive actors in a deterministic reality, and we need the gumption to shape the world around us.

Warmth, on the other hand, relates to the feeling of belonging, care, and affection. When we are learning to be accepting of others, we need to be open and soften our hearts, so that we can connect.

While strength and warmth can be complementary and not mutually exclusive, John Neffiner and Matthew Kohut, authors of the book *Compelling People*, point out that there is a "hydraulic effect" between strength and warmth. "When one goes up, the other usually goes down." They add, "Nearly everything you do to increase your strength diminishes your warmth, and vice versa."

In most social situations, those who project themselves with high strength can often be seen as assholes. On the other hand, those who dial up warmth tend to be experienced as friendly.

When we are learning to be accepting of others, the first thing we should do is dial up Warmth, and dial down Strength. Theologian John Dunne described empathy as an act of "passing over," where we leave ourselves and enter into the thoughts, feelings, and imaginations of the other.

Practise intentionally dialling up warmth, while dialling down strength, so that you can "pass over" to the other person you are trying to be accepting of (See Paradox 3. Outrospection).

**2. Allow**

To allow is to let the other person be. To let what's most natural to them express itself.

To allow is to put aside your best intentions, and let your ego die a little, without trying to control, convert, or change the existence of words and actions that come out of the other.

To disallow, on the other hand, is to reject.

To disallow is to say, "No." The "no" is often experienced as a dismissal of the person.

Clearly, there are situations when we have to say no, like when someone is abusive and violates our dignity (See Paradox 5.

No). But when we are trying to receive and bring the other closer to us, to connect and foster deeper bonds, we need to learn to give allowances.

Consider this perspective by Carl Rogers:

> People are just as wonderful as sunsets if I can let them be. In fact, perhaps the reason we can truly appreciate a sunset is that we cannot control it... I watch it with awe as it unfolds.
>
> I like myself best when I can appreciate my staff members, my son, my daughter, my grandchildren, in this same way.[iv]

How do we learn to let others be, to "allow"? Allowing is a posture to adopt when you are relating with others. Like learning a yoga pose, you begin by trying to get your body to follow your mind. And then, as you slowly figure out where your hands and feet need to be, you breathe out a sigh. This physiological sigh is one of letting go (See Paradox 15. Surrender).

There's no need to control, convert, or change the other. To allow someone to be who they are is one of the truest gifts we can give.

Practise the art of allowing others to fully express their nature.

### 3. Listening to Be Changed

Try listening to a loved one as if for the first time. It's hard, isn't it? The actor Alan Alda describes, in his book *If I Understood You, Would I Have This Look on My Face?*, the real challenge is in being responsive to others. As he recounts, the director Mike Nichols repeatedly told Alda and his co-actress in the Broadway musical *The Apple Tree* to relate better. Alda says, "Finally, he couldn't stand it anymore. 'You kids think relating is the icing on the cake,' he said. 'It isn't. It's the cake.'

What is "the cake?" Alda goes on to describe how it took him years to understand this seemingly straightforward idea of relating:

> It's being so aware of the other person that, even if you have your back to them, you're observing them. It's letting everything about them affect you; not just their words, but also their tone of voice, their body language, even subtle things like where they're standing in the room or how they occupy a chair. Relating is letting all that seep into you and have an effect on how you respond to the other person.

Renowned improv teacher Keith Johnstone says something similar. "Instead of telling actors that they must be good listeners (which is confusing), we should say, '**Be altered** [emphasis mine] by what's said.'"[v]

Alda and Johnstone's principles aren't just about acting. They're about how we allow our listening to change and affect us. Most of the time, when we are negatively affected by what a loved one says to us, the problem is not what they said at that moment, but more so the *memory of their* words, facial expression, and body language that conjures up our past. To have the faculties of a long-term memory is not a bad thing—that's how we learn. What we need to do is suspend the projections of the past and listen carefully to the words unfolding right in front of us.

To listen without prejudice does not mean to whitewash a mean-spirited person who is attacking you with their words. Rather, it is a way to recalibrate the way we listen so that we can seek to truly understand the other.

Practise letting your listening change you.

## II. Self-Acceptance

### 1. Nature, Nurture, Need

The pathway to self-acceptance is to nurture our nature, informed by our needs.

And our needs often show up like our long-lost Uncle Bernard in specific seasons and chapters of our lives.

As mentioned in Part I, we might start understanding ourselves using the Big Five Personality construct as a starting point (See What is Your Nature). But that's just the first step. Remember: It's not just what's in your nature, but also who you are becoming that matters. It's both the 'seed' and the act of cultivating the growth of the seed in the right manner. It will need a certain amount of water and light, and the right type of soil.

So what can you do?

*i. Identify Your Nature:* List your traits using the Big Five Personality construct as a starting point (See the Appendix A). Speak with people who know you; ask whether they see you the same way in the Big Five. Note down any significant or different points of view.

*ii. Reflect:* What needs nurturing? Maybe you are high in Openness to Experience and low in Conscientiousness. Currently, in this season of your life, you notice that being too disorganised and not doing anything about it has cost you greatly in both your professional and personal roles (e.g., not keeping track of prior commitments, feeling overwhelmed). Your traits are not set in stone. You have to place them in fertile ground to prune and grow them.

*iii. Cultivate:* In this process of being and becoming, you are *broadening* your nature,[1] becoming more of what is asked out of

---

1. This is why each of the 15 Paradoxes ends with "Broadening Your Nature."

you in this specific time in your life. This takes time, so be patient and consistent with it.

One might say this sounds more like *changing* oneself than "self-acceptance." I disagree. We gain self-acceptance when we engage in a full expression of who we are. We cultivate what is within us.

This is also not about trying to be someone else. Trying to be other than what is in your nature is to deny and force something else upon yourself. Engaging in comparison will breed self-denial of your true nature. Comparison is like porn: you can't help but look. And if you look long enough, you might mistake it for reality.

There is a saying: "Compare and despair." According to the teachings on the causes of suffering (dukkha) found in the Four Noble Truths in Buddhist literature, **comparison is a source of suffering.**[vi]

Spend less time comparing yourself with others, and spend a little more time cultivating your nature. Plus, if you want to understand others, you must have a good enough understanding of how you perceive others through the clarity that you have of yourself.

Practise nurturing your nature, informed by your needs.

## 2. Fierce Kindness

Some people switch off when they hear the words "Be kind." I suspect this is because we associate being kind to others with being a "softie."

Kindness is not a weakness. Kindness requires tenacity, a form of inner-resistance to reactivity.

To inhabit a type of fierce kindness[vii] is to take pause, stand firm, and allow ourselves to go through what the Sufi poet Rumi calls "The Three Gates of Speech."

*Before you speak, let your words pass through three*
   *gates*
*At the first gate, ask yourself, "Is it true?"*
*At the second gate ask, "Is it necessary?"*
*At the third gate ask, "Is it kind?"*

We can learn to speak to ourselves by passing through these three gates. Often, we pass through the first two gates of truth and necessity, but the third gate of kindness reminds us to not let the self-critical side get the better of us.

If negative comments can't pass through these three gates, don't let it get to you. Other people have a say but not a vote. Using these gates as filters, you get to choose what you metabolise in your thought process.

Practise fierce kindness by passing through Rumi's Three Gates: *"Is it true? Is it necessary? Is it kind?"*

### 3. To be Critical Without Criticising

Our self-talk is quite revealing. Listen to your own reactions when something goes wrong. "What an idiot," or "Stupid fool! What were you thinking?" you might exclaim to yourself—or something more profane than that.

Most people would nod in agreement when we say that we can be our worst enemies. I think that's true, only because we are able to hit right at the nerve centre.

We have to learn to be critical without being self-criticising. How? Be specific, not global. Be detailed in what exactly you did wrong rather than attacking your core identity.

When something goes wrong, start with "fierce kindness" as mentioned above, and then be highly specific. "Ok. I messed up. How did I forget to get that parking ticket that led to that fine? I was distracted with the podcast I was listening to… and I was running late for my 9 a.m. meeting. And then Mom called ... My mind was elsewhere and my feet were scurrying..."

Practise being highly specific with yourself. Resist being global; prevent self–*ad hominem* (i.e., self-attack).

## B. Change

If you find yourself moving towards the side of needing to make changes, see the following suggestions:

### 1. The Dailies, Strategies, Skills, Meals (DSSM) Framework

The Dailies, Strategies, Skills, Meals (DSSM) framework gets to the heart of any real changes you are trying to make. The aim of DSSM is to help make change implementable and sustainable. In turn, when we are able to change, we enable ourselves to relate better to people we care about.

Let's go over each of the sections to understand what they are and how they relate to each other:

| Name The Season You Are In: <u>Healing from Hurts (A recent relationship breakup)</u> | | | |
|---|---|---|---|
| **Dailies** | **Strategies** | **Skills** | **Meals** |
| - Morning routine: wake up at 6:30am. Quiet time for 15 mins.<br><br>- Ensure lunch breaks.<br><br>- Allow 30 mins to wind down instead of crashing into bedtime | - Prevent total depletion from work (see <u>#3. Give 80%, not 100%, in Paradox 12. Stress</u>).<br><br>- Listen to my body. Allow rest (see <u>Paradox 1. Self-Care</u>).<br><br>- Allow time to be alone daily but connect with a friend weekly. | - Learn how to say No when it is not a Yes (see <u>Paradox 5. Yes/No</u>).<br><br>- Learn to be attentive to my needs and not override them.<br><br>- Improve my ability to focus on the task at hand. | - Curate what types of content I actually consume, and stop mindlessly scrolling on the phone.<br><br>- Have proper meals during lunch. |

*An Example of the DSSM Framework (See also Appendix C)*

### Dailies

Dailies refers to the daily activities you engage in. From the moment you wake up, how you manage your work schedule, exercise, when you take breaks, etc. We can think about "Dailies" as habit formation.

How you design your daily life has a profound impact. Change your days, you change your life.

### Strategies

Strategies refer to a set of plans and organised course of action or approach to help you achieve specific goals. What are some things we can tweak? What are some changes we can make to our environment, the tools we use, etc. A Strategy can be short term or long term, as well as adaptive to the circumstances. We can also think about "Strategy" as a set of road signs to help us navigate along the way.

Unlike Dailies, Strategies act as guides. Dailies are the actions you execute upon, while strategies serve as a roadmap to what you do on a daily basis. (You may have noticed that throughout this book, Strategies are provided in each of the 15 Paradoxes under the *Counsel* section).

Some Strategies might evolve to become guiding principles in your life. While Strategies apply to specific contexts, principles are more generalisable across situations. For example, "Make a big decision so as to avoid small decisions" is a principle that I apply not only to work, but also to other areas of life (See 3. Make a Big Decision to Avoid Small Decisions, in Paradox 5. No). For example, instead of debating when I should release my newsletter, I commit to releasing it every Friday.[viii] Instead of deciding when it's the time to go for family adventures, we commit to little fun explorations around the country once a month. Instead of hemming and hawing when my wife and I should spend alone time together, we reserve Friday for our weekly lunch date (after I send out the newsletter).

### Skills

Skills refer to a learned ability.

Broadly speaking, skills consists of five domains:

*i. Technical skills* (e.g., how to use a particular software application; how to fix a leaky tap; how to repair a car);

*ii. Relational skills*[2] (e.g., how to engage in small-talk; how to manage a team at work; how to deal with conflict resolution),

*iii. Practical skills* (e.g., financial literacy; cooking; time management);

*iv. "Inner-game" skills* (e.g., how to think clearly; learning how to learn well; emotional regulation), and

*v. Fun skills* (e.g., playing the piano; picking up a new sport; dancing).

If you are making a career switch from an accountant to a baker, you might need to improve specific technical skills in baking. If you are recently divorced, and for the first time in your adult life you find yourself needing to expand your social circle, you might need to improve your relational skills. If you are leaving full-time employment and are starting a new business for the first time, you might need a crash-course in business-management. If you want to return to school to earn a degree, you might need to improve an inner-game skill like your ability to learn well. Finally, if you are beginning to see how distant any form of leisurely activity is from your life, you might be inclined to work on a "fun" skill by picking up the ukulele.

Once you start adopting an attitude that skills are things that are "learnable," and not innate traits (i.e., "you either have the talent or you don't"), in that instant of a mindshift, the road ahead becomes wide-open to you. However, you can improve on anything—but not everything. The real challenge is to identify

---

2. I dislike the term "hard" vs "soft" skills. While this makes sense in a computing analogy—i.e., hardware vs. software—it falls apart when we start to think of social skills as "soft" skills. It's actually a difficult/hard skill to improve at.

the top areas you need to focus on that have actual leverage on improving your life given the current season that you are in.

**What are the top three skills that you need to focus on that have leverage as you are Crossing Between Worlds?**

Whereas Strategies are often a one-time design, a Skill is an area you work on for a period of time. The process of skill development should manifest itself in your daily activities, guided by the strategies you apply.

*Meals*

Meals refer to nourishment.

If we do not take care of what we eat, we are at risk of failing in our attempts to make changes. Running on empty is a sure-fire path to burnout, simply because we are not nourishing our bodies with the nutrients required for them to do what we intend to do.

Meals are about what we eat and when we eat. Whenever I ask people in my clinical practice about their meals, I discovered that they often tend to "override" the signals of their body. They skip meals or, conversely, indulge in over-eating in the evenings. More so in Australia than in Singapore, alcohol consumption is also a topic that I have to ask about routinely. People tend to use alcohol as a social lubricant and fail to appreciate that it is chemically a depressant. That is why it makes you feel good, and then it makes you feel lousy.[ix]

Broadly speaking, "Meals" also refer to what we **input** in terms of what we read, watch, and listen to. Garbage in, garbage out. We can become consumed by the nonsense that we consume. At every turn, we are lured into the gluttony of everything out there on the web, in the palm of our hands. We hold it much more than we hold the hands of our loved ones.

**You are what you feed.** If we take care of the inputs that enter our bodies and minds, we stand a fighting chance to make the changes we want to make (see Paradox 14. Input). If we fail to appreciate the embodied nature of our being, we make the hard things harder to do. When we are making changes, it is not mind over body. The mind is there to take care of the body and itself. Feed them well.[x]

Practise using the DSSM as a framework for change.

## 2. Subtractive Changes

When we think about making changes, we often default to add-ons. The "more" mentality leads us to thinking that if I want to get to X, I need to get Y. Our tendency to overlook the counter-intuitive "less" mentality leads us to overburden our minds and schedules.[xi]

If you want to make changes, think about not just the pluses, but also the minuses.

What do I need to do less of? What do I need to reduce in my schedule in order to do what I really care about? What do I need to let go of?

If you have been wanting to get back to painting, make time by subtracting Netflix in the evenings. If you have been wanting to be more productive with writing in the mornings, stop reading the news the first thing after you wake up.

Practise subtraction before addition.

## 3. Change the Space

Change must come from *within*, but change can also come from the spaces *between* us and the world *around* us.

Winston Churchill said, "We shape our buildings, and afterwards our buildings shape us." Our everyday spaces structure and shape our behaviour and well-being. "Space is like a secret script directing our actions," says the environmental psychologist, Lily Bernheimer. "But like the actors in a play, we maintain the illusion that our actions are unscripted." She adds, "We know intuitively that space is essential to who we are... But oddly, we don't acknowledge how much it moulds us."

Do colours in our surroundings matter? Experiments showed that violent drunks were dramatically subdued when placed in a pink holding cell.[xii] Does the placement of your chair in an office space make a difference? Research indicates that we actually concentrate better, with increased cognitive performance, when sitting with our backs to the wall—or what are called ninja-proof seats. Why did soldiers who were using heroin have an astonishingly low rate of relapsing once they returned home to America? The standard relapse rates are generally around 87%, but only 12% of Vietnam veterans experienced any episode or re-addiction upon returning home. It wasn't the lack of access. In part, it was that their time in Vietnam was a sharp disconnect from normal lives in the U.S. Bernheimer noted, "It was a different world, and they were different people there."[xiii]

Shifting spaces has a way of changing our state of mind. (I just reached a plateau writing at home, for example, and now I've moved to a local library and the gears are turning again.)

Spaces and places matter more acutely when you are at pivotal moments of transition in your life. Find a special place to go to on a routine basis. Go to a specific beach to honour someone who has passed away. Sit in a place of worship as you contemplate the next steps of your life. Go to a cafe to write if you are trying to complete an essay. Visit a museum to be in the company of the greats.

Practise being an architect of your environment to support change.

## BROADEN YOUR NATURE

Introverted people are likely to struggle with asserting strength, and Agreeable people have more ability to put on the brakes and be less assertive when necessary. Said another way, if you are more Introverted, you are likely to feel like it is more of a stretch to assert strength, compared with more Extroverted individuals. If you are more Agreeable, you are likely to have the ability to put on the brakes and stand down on unimportant issues, compared with less Agreeable individuals.[xiv] In both aspects, you need to know when to assert Strength and when to pick your battles and invoke more Warmth to relate to others (see #1. Strength and Warmth, in Paradox 6. Acceptance).

If you are low in Conscientiousness, you are likely to struggle with organisation. Use the Dailies, Strategies, Skills, Meals (DSSM) framework to your advantage. Even though it might be challenging at first, print out the DSSM worksheet and pin it to your wall (See the downloadable version in **A Gift for You**). Make sure it stays visible to you whenever you start your day.

---

*See Related Paradoxes: 2. Present/Future, 5. Yes/No, 10. Grief/Love, 12. Recovery/ Stress, 14. Input/Output, 15. Control/Surrender.*

# PARADOX 7. APPROACH/RETREAT

## CONTRADICTION

*When should I pull away and retreat from the world? But I'm told that's not good for my mental health...*
*Do I need to learn to approach what I fear, or do I need to rejuvenate by retreating?*

## CLARITY

**A. Approach**

I mentioned in an earlier part of this book (Paradox 1. Self-Forgetting) that I was once stuck at the beginning of a zipline for what seemed like an eternity because I was too afraid to make the leap.

About a year after that incident, on a different obstacle course in the scout camp, the confidence jump, I was faced with the same sadistic instructor, Jason. My fear of heights has not abated.

But after three days of pent-up anxiety, I made an angsty

teenage promise to myself: *I will prove to this particular nut-job instructor that I am not what he thought me to be.*

I'm standing at the ledge, two storeys high. I look down. Yikes. This is even harder than I thought it would be. I see the blue gym mat I'm supposed to land on. Before Jason can mutter to his other instructor, "This is Daryl. He's a chicken—," I make the leap. In mid-air, I feel a wave of exhilaration run through my body. *This is happening.* I land on the blue gym mat—I feel another strange sensation. The next thing I know, my white St. Gabriel's sports tee-shirt is coloured in blood. Where did this come from? I hear whispers around me saying that I was supposed to land on my behind on the mat. I must have thought I was Spider-Man and landed on my feet. My knees hit my chin, my upper teeth bit into my lower lips, and the floodgates opened. I can't recall who, but someone rushed me to hospital.

I spent the next two weeks as a stitched-up puffer fish.

Injury and hideous appearance aside, I serendipitously discovered that it is actually possible to approach what I fear. (See the Counsel section of this paradox)

Approaching one's fear is inherently confronting. But since then, my height phobia has diminished significantly. Admittedly, my intentions at that time were ego-driven: to shut the foul-mouth instructor up. I didn't like him. He swore too much.

Patricia Madson, actor and author of *Improv Wisdom*, says, "Turtles are a good model, since they make progress only when they stick their necks out."[i] I think she's right. There are seasons in your life when we need to stick our necks out, go beyond the default and what's expected of us, or for that matter, what we expect of ourselves. In such instances, the useful approach is to move to the edges.

When we are Crossing Between Worlds, we find ourselves in these Edge States (See Liminality). This is a good time to ask ourselves, *What do I really want? Where do I really want to go?*

*Why?* (See #2. Psychological Movement, in Paradox 13. Movement).

## B. Retreat

> "Hiding is a way of staying alive. Hiding is a way of holding ourselves until we are ready to come into the light."
>
> — *David Whyte, Consolations.*

To retreat is not an admittance of defeat. To retreat is especially necessary if the season of your life is one of "wintering."

Wintering seasons may not be cherished, nor welcomed, because they often happen at critical junctures, such as periods of loss, health failures, or significant changes in life circumstances. Rarely do we choose periods of wintering.

Writer Katherine May provides a beautiful assessment about wintering:

> Wintering brings about some of the most profound and insightful moments of our human experience, and wisdom resides in those who have wintered. In our relentlessly busy contemporary world, we are forever trying to defer the onset of winter. We don't ever dare to feel its full bite, and we don't dare to show the way that it ravages us. A sharp wintering, sometimes, would do us good. We must stop believing that these times in our life are somehow silly, a failure of nerve, a lack of willpower. We must stop trying to ignore them or dispose of them. They are real, and they are asking something of us. We must learn to invite the winter in.[ii]

Some seasons call for us to stick our necks out. At other times, we need to incubate in our shells.

Wintering compels us to retreat and to hide. Katherine May adds, "Winter is not the death of the life cycle, but its crucible."

In such times, we need to honour the need to hide away. We need spaces and places in which to enter this metaphorical "turtle shell."

To learn to retreat is to be season-minded. It is the right action, as nature will have her way. Here's May once again:

> Plants and animals don't fight the winter; they don't pretend it's not happening and attempt to carry on living the same lives that they lived in the summer. They prepare. They adapt.

When the world has gone hyper-busy and lost its bearings to the frenzy of hustle culture, we may need to retreat, to recompose, and reimagine where our life needs to go––and stop being so stubborn.

---

There are times where we are called to approach what we fear in order to foster connection with the world outside, and there are seasons where we need to retreat in order to encounter the world inside.

*In this season of your life, where do you need to be on the spectrum of Approach and Retreat? (Mark an '<', '>' or 'x' on the line below).*

7

⇐──────────────────────────────⇒
Approach                                                      Retreat

## COUNSEL

### A. Approach

If you find yourself more on the side of needing to approach what you would normally avoid, here are a few ideas to tip you in the right direction:

#### 1. Approach the Internal Fear

I didn't see it that way at that time, but years after the confidence jump incident that I described earlier in this Paradox, it dawned on me that the deeper lesson for me was not about approaching my fears or proving others wrong. In approaching what I feared, I realised that **what I needed to approach was actually internal, not external.**

We think we are avoiding the object of our fears. But the thing that we fear is *not* the source of our fear. It is a trigger to the fears inside.

In the case of height phobia, the trigger was the feeling that I got when I was looking down from an elevated position. It made my stomach queasy and made my legs shake like Elvis. In turn, these physical sensations triggered a flood of catastrophic images in my head. It was these vivid movies in my head that got to me. I saw myself at my own funeral, my loved ones mourning in the aftermath of my blunder. This all sounds crazy, but at the time, it was an intense internal experience. Unless I was asked, I don't think I would have been able to articulate this as a teen. The reason that cinema reel in my head bothered me so much was because I didn't want to cause pain to people in my life. Even saying this now sounds absurd to the present me, but that was an "emotional truth" for me at that period of my life.

Maybe you have fears. Learning to speak up at a meeting,

giving a public talk, quitting a life-diminishing job, or leaving an abusive relationship. First, be clear that these are the external stimuli of an internal fear.

Second, take a moment and ask yourself: What is the story inside? What inner fear does this trigger?

Maybe the thought of speaking up triggers a gut-level reaction of being judged and disliked by others. Maybe the act of quitting a job or leaving a relationship triggers a voice inside you that says that you are a quitter, just like you have been since childhood, even though your job eats at you, or even though your relationship has become abusive (See #3. Grit and Quit Quadrant, in Paradox 1. Self-Care).

Finally, when we approach our inner fears, we need to let the following question ferment: **What do I have to learn?**

Maybe your personal learning is to experiment and trust that you have something to offer when you speak up. Someone else's deep learning might be to attend to their emotional needs, not brush them away. For another person, it might be the realisation that you can be loved for who you are, and not be living under the perpetual cloud of fear.

Practise approaching your inner fear. Do not mistake the trigger for the fear inside.

## 2. Test and Reevaluate

Once we have a gasp of the internal fear that is triggered by an external stimulus, it's time to be playful.

I don't mean this to sound like some cognitive-behavioural therapy (CBT) trope. But what if we actually allowed ourselves to test and reevaluate fundamental beliefs that bind us?

Our minds are a prediction organism, creating mental models inside of what the world is like on the outside. Some of these predictions need to be tested—and then updated.

Looking back, at that point in my life, I overidentified with my "fear of heights" as part of who I was, that "this is me."

Before the confidence-jump incident, I had never thought to challenge myself and test my assumptions. My knee-jerk reaction was to jump forward to a catastrophic endpoint where I am crippled and my poor mother will have to take care of me for the rest of my life. Or where I've died from a fall from great heights. I could see the vivid images of the ambulance and sirens swirling, my dwindling demise that would lead to my pitiful funeral.

Don't get me wrong, I still have no plans to sign up for a bungee jump in New Zealand. The point is that I've learned to develop a certain friendship with the fearful feelings inside, stored in my body, and the cinematic vivifications of my mind. I'm now at least willing to test my assumptions and be wrong.

Be your own scientist. Design mini-experiments. Write down your beliefs (e.g., "I will be shot down if I speak up at the meeting"), give it a go (e.g., offer up one idea of your own), and then keep your eyes and ears peeled. Watch and listen to the reaction of others.

Now, update your prior beliefs. This final step is often taken for granted. This is the moment where the rubber meets the road, in terms of emotional learning. Journal and reflect on this. Even if you indeed get a negative reaction from others, the important thing you can learn from it is that you are still fine, standing on your own two feet.

Practise challenging and testing your assumptions, and update your beliefs.

## 3. When in Doubt, Ask Yourself, "What is the Courageous Decision to Make?"

Sometimes we are so torn apart by the competing voices in our head. At such instances, a good question to contemplate is "What is the courageous decision to make?"[iii]

In *The Screwtape Letters,* a book dedicated to his close friend, J.R.R. Tolkien, C.S. Lewis wrote a masterpiece of satire based on the wise old devil advising his nephew Wormwood on how he should overthrow the world. Screwtape counsels, "To make a deep wound in his charity, you should therefore defeat his courage." Screwtape elaborates, "Courage is not simply *one* of the virtues, but the form of every virtue at the testing point...at the point of highest reality."[iv]

Intriguingly, Screwtape says to his nephew, "The emotion of fear is, in itself, no sin." But, he stresses, "the *act* of cowardice is all that matters."

This is not a lecture about angels and demons. From Latin, courage is *cor,* or "heart." We need to "take heart." Because there are so many unknowns when we are making a leap in our lives, courage is a prerequisite. On this bridge-crossing journey, let's ask ourselves, "What is the courageous decision to make?"

Practise the virtue of virtues: Courage.

## B. Retreat

If you find yourself more on the side of needing to pull away, consider the following:

### 1. Set Up Periodic Times to Retreat

As a practising psychologist for the last 20 years, I've seen many individuals who have a pervasive inability to rest.

It takes courage to approach what we fear, and it takes courage to retreat.

We're enticed to live as busy bees. After all, we are being productive, aren't we? The push for hyper-productivity can distract us when the season of our time is to retreat. We don't know how to rest. (See Paradox 1. Self-Care).

Rest is not an indulgence for certain seasons of our lives. We need it daily. That's why our body sleeps—if we don't fight it. We need moments of respite in our waking hours, too. If we are trying to be less distracted and more focused in our work, we need to learn to allow our minds to idle, wander, and meander. Cognitive scientists argue that in order for us to be effective in focused mode, we need to juxtapose periods of being in the default mode network (DMN).[1] The DMN is a network of brain regions that activates during rest and self-referential thought, such as daydreaming or introspection. It typically deactivates during focused, goal-oriented tasks (See Paradox 12. Recovery/Stress).

Most people do not have the luxury of pulling away from work commitments on a whim and running to the mountains. But we can bake this sort of rest into the cycles of our routine. Plan ahead. Block off periods in your calendar. Think not only in yearly terms, but quarterly, monthly, and even weekly and daily periods. Perhaps on your usual walking exercise, once a week, you walk without a podcast playing in your earbuds. Perhaps you could institutionalise lunchtime on a daily basis, so as to protect that hour from outside inputs (See #1 The Dailies, Strategies, Skills, Meals (DSSM) Framework, in Paradox 6. Change).

Practise subverting the norm of working like a factory, and allow yourself to retreat and rest.

## 2. Find a Place to Go

After you've committed times for retreat in your schedule, pick key places that you can go. A nearby park, a trailwalk, a place of worship, or the riverbank. (See #3. Change the Space, in Paradox 6. Change).

We must find places that we can call sacred, or "set apart" from ordinary places. Secular spaces can become sacred if the

---

1. Or what I like to call, "Do Mostly Nothing." (DMN).

conditions are fitting. Oftentimes, these sacred places provide a sense of safety and comfort. They do not demand anything of you. You feel your body respond with a sigh of relief at being there.

Allow your feet to take you to these places regularly.

Practise routinely going to places you deem sacred and special.

## 3. Explain Your Needs to Your Loved Ones

This is strangely, one of the biggest challenges I face when I need some time alone. I feel guilty telling my wife and kids that I need to "retreat."

While I do have my daily, weekly, and monthly periods to pull away, I still find it a struggle to say that I need to retreat for a few days on an annual basis.

I've worked on this for four or five years now, and yet every excuse I can think of still creeps up. I know where I want to go (a Benedictine Monastery in New Norcia), and when I want to go (January). But I've yet to do it.[2]

Several months ago, in one of our spousal tiffs about parenting and the dishes, I was burnt out from the demands of juggling work and family life. I blurted out that I just needed some time to recharge. My wife replied, "Why didn't you say anything about this?"

"I... I... it's just hard," I said.

"Why is it hard," she asked.

"I don't know."

"What do you need?"

"I think I just need two or three days away, like I could drive down to New Norcia or something," I replied.

---

2. At the time of this writing, I've emailed the New Norcia Guesthouse to book a retreat.

"Then go do it." I think she was still mad at me, but she was making more sense than I was at that point in time.

It probably doesn't require a quarrel to unearth what you need. Pay attention to your needs for retreat. I don't see retreat as escapism. It's for replenishment and recalibration. I have reconciled that, given my temperament, I need a lot more solitude and time for contemplation than most. If I denied my nature, I wouldn't be able to attend to the seasonal changes in my life.

Practise explaining your needs for retreat to your loved ones. I bet they will understand.

**Broadening Your Nature**

If you are high in Extraversion and you are in a period of your life that calls for Retreat, this might feel foreign to you. Allow some spaciousness to stretch towards where you normally wouldn't go —inward. If you are low in Extraversion, chances are you need more periods of retreat.

If you are high in Neuroticism, you might already be prone to withdraw from others when you are overwhelmed. Depending on where you are, you still might need space to recompose yourself. Make a distinction between withdrawing due to your default reaction and responding to the needs of the times.

---

*See Related Paradoxes: 1. Self-Care/Self-Forgetting, 2. Present/Future, 4. Solitude/Community, 6. Acceptance/Change, 11. Recovery/Stress, 13. Stillness/Movement.*

# PARADOX 8. AUTONOMY/BELONGING

## CONTRADICTION

I should be a fiercely independent person and not depend on others. Should that always be the case?

Do I need to learn to be more autonomous, or learn to rely on others when I need help?

## CLARITY

### A. Autonomy

*Converting Autonomy to Agency*

To be independent in our choices and actions is to exercise what it means to be a self-governing, autonomous person. When we learn to exercise our will, we not only steer the boat in the direction we want to go, but we find out what we are truly capable of.

This attitude is not as simple as positive thinking. It's not just believing that something good will happen to you. It is engaging and exercising your autonomy with a sense of agency that you can bring something good into this world.

*Slippage of Autonomy*

That said, not all of our choices are truly "independent." When I am contemplating buying a book, I inadvertently find myself reading the recommendations, even though I know they are all going to be filled with praise and not criticism. The thing is, it's not what's being said, but *who* said it that I care about. I recently bought a book on fitness based on the fact that a well-known scientist wrote the advance-praise for it. I'm still going to exercise my judgement about the book; the proof of the pudding is how applicable the exercises are to my situation—and that I feel compelled to actually do them (what good would a book on exercise be when I don't use them?).

Most of us wouldn't simply give up our autonomy. Rather, what really happens is that we let it slip from our hands.

How does this happen? How do we lose the grip of our autonomy? There are two possibilities:

1. Choice: When we fail to exercise our choices.

2. Mastery: When we have yet to master the skills that are required.

*Choice*

The truth is that we are, at times, at the mercy of circumstance. We don't get to choose our parents, the family we are born into, our country of birth, our genetic makeup, etc. And if we are not careful and fixate on inherited aspects that constrain us, resentment can fester.

Once I heard a young person say, in a fit of frustration to his father, "I didn't ask to be born!" That's true. There wasn't a consent form for that with the OBGYN. But what would lead someone to exclaim such a thing? There is a lot implied in that single sentence.

Each of us has not only the *right*, but the *responsibility* to exercise our will. This takes shape in the way we make our choices (See Paradox 15. Control).

Joseph, a client of mine in his mid-thirties, was so upset about the advice he was given by his dietitian. He'd suffered a lower back injury during a workplace incident and was in constant pain. As the months went by, he found himself more and more confined at home, and he soon became overweight. "The dietitian gave me some generic pamphlet on meal planning and said that I should do regular exercise, like jogging." He added, "I was infuriated. I told her that if I could run, I would be sprinting laps every single morning." At least his dietitian was responsive and took note of his circumstances. Time was running out in the session, so she proceeded to schedule a follow-up appointment for him; the earliest available slot was in three month's time. Joseph said, "So now I just have to wait another twelve weeks before I can sort my life out?"

I could see he was upset. I said, "Mate, are you saying that you are gonna put this *on* her?"

"But she's not doing her job!" Joseph said.

"Yeah, but this is *your* life.... What if you did what you can about your diet in the meantime?"

Most of us are taught to rely on experts. But I don't believe we should outsource the responsibility of taking charge of our well-being to others, especially with the resources we have available today in the palm of our hands. We do not lack information.

Joseph unintentionally assumed a passive approach towards his own health rather than taking an active role in shaping his future. I suggested that he take matters into his own hands and learn as much as he could by himself. With the likes of modern-day health and science experts such as Mark Hyman and Andrew Huberman, we do not suffer from a shortage of relevant advice. Joseph asked for recommendations, so I gave him some podcasts, video links, and reading resources, but I wasn't sure he was going to rise to the occasion given the pain he was already enduring.

Besides, information does not equate to transformation—but it's a start!

I met with Joseph some weeks later. He proceeded to tell me that he had kicked off a ketogenic diet regime, started meal-planning, and was beginning to see results. He did his homework. He created his own pseudo–lesson plan on diet and exercise, given his limited mobility. To be sure, he consulted his GP during one of his routine follow-ups. He was given the green light.

In short, he took charge.

---

"Just remember," Edith's mom said to her when she was sixteen, "no one can take away from you what you've put in your mind." These words were uttered to her as they were deported to Auschwitz.

In her autobiography, published more than 70 years later in 2017, when Eidth Eger turned ninety, she makes a distinction between victimisation and victimhood. "Suffering is universal. But victimhood is optional." She adds,

> We are all likely to be victimised in some way in the course of our lives. At some point, we will suffer some kind of affliction or calamity or abuse, caused by circumstances or people or institutions over which we have little or no control. This is life. And this is victimisation. It comes from the outside... In contrast, victimhood comes from the inside. We become victims not because of what happens to us, but when we choose to hold onto our victimisation.

All of us can easily slip into victimhood, especially when resentment builds, and especially when the gravity is as profound as the Auschwitz concentration camp, the loss of her parents, and the horrors of the death march that killed most of her companions. But Eger is quick to point out, "there is no hierarchy of suffering." As a practising psychologist during her adulthood in the United States, Eger was speaking about the various sufferings that she attended to in her clinical practice. "There is nothing that makes my pain worse or better than yours, no graph on which we can plot the relative importance of one sorrow versus another."

Edith Eger's refusal to be defined as a victim, as well as her desire to help others overcome traumas and discover themselves, was what kept her alive. Hence, the title of her book, *The Choice*.

### Mastery

While we need to exercise our choices, we also need to discern what aspects of our lives require mastery learning.

Mastery learning is an individualised process of step-by-step advancement. Only after achieving proficiency does the learner proceed to the next step, at their own pace. In the process, we increase our capabilities in those specific domains, which in turn leads to a greater sense of self-determination and autonomy.

Frederick described himself as having a conflict-avoidant personality. Listening to this 40-year-old man speak in-depth about the people in his life, it is obvious that he was a very caring —and even sensitive—individual. His two kids loved him to bits, and he has been a very present parent, rarely missing any school or sporting events. His wife, Evangeline, however, was at her wits' end. She said that trying to figure out what Frederick wants was like trying to dig up a boulder buried six feet under ground.

Whenever there was a quarrel or disagreement, he would shut down, she said. "He becomes almost mute. I feel bad about getting angry at him, because he's not really being mean or anything. But he just gives in. He's so passive!"

Meanwhile, in the corner of my eye, I saw Frederick, seated at the end of the couch, nodding his head in gentle agreement to his wife's commentary.

I later learned that, growing up as the second eldest of four siblings with an alcoholic father, he'd watched his brother get beaten up by his dad for wanting to rebel against his wishes. He learned not only to "back off," but he also did whatever he could to keep his younger siblings away from the tyranny of their explosive father, especially in the evenings. Meanwhile, his mother was very appreciative of the help he gave and often praised him for being a "mature and caring" person.

Frederick was visibly emotional when narrating this story. This information was not new to Evangeline, but it struck her that she didn't know the extent to which it had actually affected him, since they had previously talked about the past only briefly and factually.

Over the years, Frederick had grown to be a highly compassionate person. But, meanwhile, a part of him had been relegated to the back seat, which was showing up as an issue in his relationship with his wife. What had gotten Frederick this far in life was not going to get him where he needed to go.

Framing the road ahead as a "skill" to be developed resonated with Frederick, because he had previously found it too abstract to do anything about it on his own.

The "skill" that he needed to work on was mastering his "Preferences." He and wife exclaimed when I said this. "That's it!" said Evangeline. Frederick chimed in, "But I never say, or even really know, what I want."

I said, "It's like learning to sing in a choir. Without practice, instead of singing in harmony, we end up singing in unison, i.e., in the same key. In order to sing in harmony, we must learn two things: First, we have to learn to listen attentively to others. Second, we have to learn to listen to ourselves. When we don't hear ourselves, we are prone to following in the exact register as the other."

"Ok," Frederick responded hesitantly, while I worried whether the analogy made sense. "I think my first step is to take some time to figure out what I want... and that it's ok to voice what I want."

That's the road of mastery. We take one step at a time, in a specific direction, levelling up each step of the way before proceeding further. Frederick's road consisted of taking moments to check in with himself about what he really wants and prefers, even if there were conflictual feelings within, and then vocalising them. As he was Crossing Between Worlds, Frederick learned to sing not in unison with others, but in harmony with them.

---

Our voice gets muted amidst the opinions and desires of others. Autonomy is our right, but we have to take responsibility for it. Autonomy requires an assertion of the will. Autonomy is the practice of our Yeses and Nos (see Paradox 5. Yes/No). Mastery means acquiring the necessary skills to get a handle on life.

If we don't exercise our choices, we lose touch with who we are and what we truly want. Not exercising our autonomy regularly can result in a loss of our sense of self.

Autonomy grows from agency, and agency comes from how we exercise our choices and develop mastery. This is required of us when we make the transition into a new phase of our life.

## B. Belonging

> "Your task is not to seek for love, but merely to seek and find all the barriers within yourself that you have built against it."
>
> — *Rumi, Sufi poet.*

We are a being and a belonging.

When we are born, we belong to someone by default, and as we grow, we seek to belong to others.

When we are in a relationship with someone, we open the doorways of our hearts to the other. These door-openings of our hearts are a true gift, and they inspire others to do likewise. Others feel moved by us, and may want to reciprocate that by opening the doorways to their hearts. This creates a virtuous loop that invites us all into the house of belonging.

I sometimes hear people proclaim, "No one can make you 'feel' a certain way…" I don't think that's true. Quite the contrary, though we can't control others, we can influence and affect how others feel. You feel good about yourself when you are with someone who is a deep listener, cares about your well-being, and is curious to learn more about you. You'd feel quite another way when you are in the company of a self-absorbed show-off.

So we let only people we trust into this house of belonging. As we do so, we are invited to reimagine what the Self is. We think that the Self is "me," the individual. The Self is not just you. It is **who you are and who you love.** We exist in a web of relationships.

Seen in this light, mental health is not just an individual "mental" activity. Mental health is, to a large extent, *relational* health. For better or worse, we have an effect on each other.

We are part of this house of belonging. And as we find solace in our kith and kin, we invite others in as well. This self-expansion project is one we are called to move towards. To grow friendships, fall in love, take care of ties within the family.

To belong is the relationship of melody and harmony. The melody of a song doesn't exist in a vacuum, but within the embedded context of a harmony. The Self, the human being, exists only in the context of the people we belong to. As the poet David Whyte writes,

> *There is no house*
> *Like the house of belonging.*[i]

These four walls are not a prison, but a home. Our task is to build this home—and remove barriers within ourselves to love freely.

---

In order to individuate, we must learn to belong. In order to be together, we need to learn to be autonomous.

*In this season of your life, where do you need to be on the spectrum of Autonomy and Belonging? (Mark an '<', '>' or 'x' on the line below).*

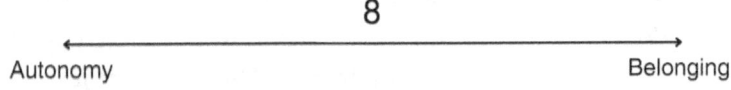

Autonomy            Belonging

## COUNSEL

### A. Autonomy

If you find yourself more on the side of needing to be more autonomous, consider the following:

### 1. Exercising Choice

The late psychiatrist William Glasser had a theory that has implications for how we lead our life. He called it Choice Theory.[ii]

Choice Theory is based on a simple premise: every person has the power to control themselves and limited power to control others. When we apply Choice Theory, we take full responsibility for our own actions, and at the same time, refrain from attempting to direct other people's choices and decisions. In turn, Choice Theory advocates for supporting other people's choices.

Sounds straightforward, doesn't it? In theory, yes. In practice, it can be a challenge. Not only do you need to relinquish the need to control others, however good your intention, you also need to assert your will and take action.

The opposite of exercising our choice is to *outsource* our choice-making. Married couples can attest to this. A husband goes along with what the "Boss" (i.e., wife) wants, only for the wife to gripe about always deciding what's for dinner.

To exercise our choice is to open up our desires to others. This is not to say that we must always *insist* on what we want. Rather, when we lay out our preferences, we invite the other person to do the same. A real connection is more likely to happen when both parties are willing to be vulnerable about their desires and hear the desires of the other (*See #1. "What do I really want?," in Paradox 5. Yes*).

Practise tuning in to your preferences, wishes, and desires.

## 2. Your Desire—or Is It Mimetic Desire?

How many of our choices are informed by what we intrinsically want, versus us wanting what others want?

In HBO's *The White Lotus*, a television series about the exploits of various guests and employees of the fictional White Lotus resort, one of the characters, Ethan, accuses another, Cameron, of the following: "You have a case of something called mimetic desire."

Ethan explains what we previously mentioned in "What Not to Do When Crossing Between Worlds" about René Girard's concept of mimetic desire, "If someone with higher status than you wants something, it's likely that you want it too."

At bottom, desires are important. They are what make us

human. Enduring desires tell us what we yearn for and who we are.

But first, we must separate our authentic enduring desires from our mimetic desires.

When we fail to make that distinction, we lose our autonomy.

Luke Burgis, author of the book, *Wanting,* recommends making a list of people who have an influence on your desires. Think of people you know, and think of people in the wider world. In my clinical practice, especially with young adults, I often ask, "Who do you follow? And why? What draws you in?"

It's intriguing that we borrow the old cult analogy of "influencers" and "followers" to describe YouTube video channels and music on streaming platforms. Who we "follow" gives us a glimpse into not only what we like, but also into our deep longings.

Mimetic desires derail us from meaningful desires. We end up chasing things we don't truly want. "Mimetic desire is a paradoxical game," says Burgis. "Winning is how you lose."[iii] In *The Courage to Be Disliked,* Ichiro Kishimi and Fumitake Koga provide an effective litmus test for the meaningfulness of our desires: Our desires are misleading if our intention is to make others like us. Kishimi and Koga add, "Conducting yourself in such a way as to not be disliked by anyone is an extremely unfree way of living."

Practise exercising choices that are informed by *your* desires, not mimetic desires. In turn, making autonomous choices can inspire others to listen to their own desires.

### 3. Figure Out the *What* Before the *How*

In school, you are *told* what to learn. In life, you have to *figure out* what to learn, what's worth learning at specific chapters in your life.

Each of us must figure out where our growth edge is. Many of the paradoxical ideas in this book provide clues to where we need to go. That said, you must still make a conscious choice about what exactly you need to work on.

As a start, you need to deconstruct the parts into doable steps. Recall the story of Frederick earlier in this Paradox. Before he became less conflict-avoidant, he had to learn to express what he wanted, then he had to learn to privilege his preferences and wishes. Then he needed to learn to take some "risks" in vocalising them. Later, he needed to learn that when others don't agree with what he wants, he needn't take it as a downright personal rejection, but rather just remember other people are allowed to agree or disagree with his ideas.

One way to begin this process is to **list, rank, and deconstruct**. First, list down all of the things you feel you need to work on. Second, rank them in order of priority based on what's most important to you. Third, start by breaking down the top priority into workable chunks.

For instance, maybe you have recently worked up the courage to end a relationship that has been abusive and life-diminishing. You find yourself in a liminal space of grief and solitude, as well as hope in the face of new possibilities. You list the following things you would like to get better at:

- Setting personal boundaries.
- Learning not to say yes when I mean no. (See Paradox 5. No)
- Being less isolated, i.e., learning to approach and be with others. (See Paradox 7. Approach).
- Learning to be less socially anxious.

Now that you've listed them, it might be a challenge to rank them in order of priority. For some, thinking in terms of importance would be enough. For others, it might help to think about the ranking process in terms of *leverage*. That is, what is the one thing that I can work on that would actually move the needle in the right direction? Sometimes this is referred to as the Pareto Principle, or the 80/20 rule. You want to work on the 20 percent of things that yield 80 percent of the results—not the other way round.

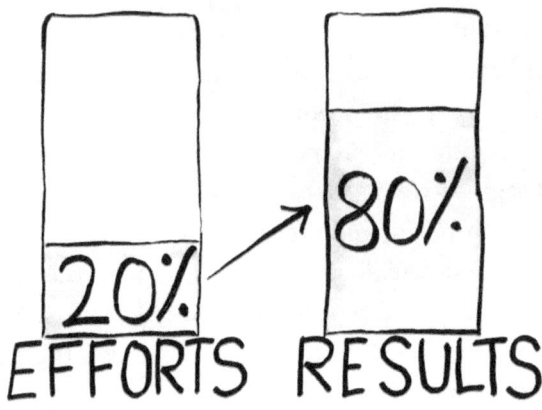

After some reflection on your list, you realised that to "learn to be less socially anxious" might be the thing that will create the most initial leverage for you. Now you can start to deconstruct this goal into its component parts. You can read as much as you can on this topic or see a therapist to help you with this part of your development.

Now that you've figured out *What* to work on, you can work on the *How*.

It turns out the goal of dealing with social anxiety has got two sub-areas that you can be working on. One, learning to focus on others rather than worrying about what others think of you, is an area to practise (See #2. Engage Like a Journalist, in Paradox 3. Outrospection). Second, when socialising, you can learn to take heed of your comfort level. Instead of forcing yourself to hang out with people you are actually not interested in hanging out with, you can pay attention to your comfort level as a barometer. This will also help you with your goals of "setting personal boundaries" and "learning not to say yes when I mean no."

Practise taking the time to figure out what you need to learn in order to create an impact in your life. Work through each stage at your own pace. And celebrate the wins—you are becoming more of who you really are.

## B. Belonging

If you find yourself on the side of needing to be more in relationships, consider the following:

### 1. Who Do You Belong to?

This is a reflection exercise. Take a moment to pause and contemplate the following:

> *i. Who are the people who have loved you into being?*
> Slow down for just a minute and picture them in front of you. What is it like to "feel" them in your consciousness right now?
> *ii. How have they shaped you?*
> Think about the influences these people have had on you. You are who you are now because of them.
> Next, take a moment to reflect the other way round.
> *iii. How has your relationship with these people shaped them?*
> Given that these people have had a profound impact on you, how do you think your reception of their love has had an impact on them?
> Finally,
> *iv. How can you pass this on?*
> How can you spread this spirit to others in your life? What elements do you wish to share with others that were first experienced with these people who shaped you?

## 2. Name the Barriers to Love

Recall the opening line from Rumi in this section, "Your task is not to seek for love, but merely to seek and find all the barriers within yourself that you have built against it."

As time goes by, the walls that we have built around ourselves no longer protect us from the world outside; they imprison us from our original intent.

Think of the people you care about. What barriers have been built or coagulated over time that prevented greater intimacy?

A father of a teenage son described to me his futile attempt in trying to discipline his son so that the son wouldn't go down the same wrong path the father had in his younger days. The father noted something revealing, "I think my son thinks I don't like him...and that's just not true." He fought back tears.

We often think that liking is a lower cousin to loving someone. Being liked is different from being loved. You can love someone you don't really like, perhaps out of duty, filial piety, or respect, but to feel like you are *liked* for who you are leads to a deep feeling of belonging to the other. "*You* like *me*." Being liked goes deeper, especially when it is by someone who cares for you, someone whose respect and acceptance you yearn for.

I never grew up watching Fred Rogers in Singapore, but after watching the 2019 documentary *Won't You Be My Neighbour*, I became acquainted with his body of work as a preschool television personality in the series *Mister Rogers' Neighborhood*, which aired from 1968 to 2001. One of the scenes that moved me was when he said to a child, rather intently, "You know, I like you." The child said, "Really?" He replied, "I do. It's you that I like."[iv]

Mister Rogers was not only the series' host, producer, puppeteer, and writer, but also the musician behind the show's songs. Here's one of the enduring tunes that he wrote:

*It's you I like.*
*It's you I like.*

*It's not the things you wear*
*It's not the way you do your hair*
*But it's you I like.*
*The way you are right now*
*The way down deep inside you*
*Not the things that hide you*
*Not your degrees*
*They're just beside you.*
*But it's you I like.*
*Every part of you*
*Your skin, your eyes, your feelings*
*Whether old or new.*
*I hope that you'll remember*
*Even when you're feeling blue*
*That it's you I like*
*It's you yourself*
*It's you —*
*It's you I like.*

Returning to the story of the father, I asked him, "What's getting in the way of your son feeling and knowing that you actually like him?" He said, "I think we just got so entrenched in the daily problems… and I think I just need to tell him that I love him."

"And specifically," I added. "That you *like* him. Tell him what you like about him as your son—in detail."

The father soon realised that he'd put up an emotional barricade with his son. He was afraid of being soft around him, fearing it would make him look vulnerable and weak. He said he felt "queasy" at first as he took my advice. He had never experienced that kind of emotional intimacy from an adult in his own growing-up years, so this was a foreign territory to him.

To be truly liked is not the same as receiving a "like" on Instagram. To be liked by someone who cares about you is to feel a sense of belonging.

But first, we have to name the barriers.

Practise identifying the walls that separate you from a deep connection with others.

### 3. Invitation to Play Together

Play is an antidote and an aphrodisiac.

It is not only an antidote to the drudgery of life, but also an antidote to our excessively utilitarian approach to living, i.e., "I do X to get to Y." What we do often becomes a means to an end, a way to get to our goal; we end up instrumentalising people and things.

Play researcher Stuart Brown defines the properties of play as,

- Apparently purposeless (done for its own sake)
- Voluntary
- Inherent attraction
- Freedom from time
- Diminished consciousness of self
- Improvisational potential
- Continuation of desire[v]

Take a moment and go through the list above again. Play's purposelessness is paradoxical. The qualities of play helps us step outside of chronological time and into what is called *Kairos* (i.e., timelessness; see #2. Who Do You Want to Become?, in Paradox 2. Future).

Play is a remedy for depression.

Stuart Brown goes so far as to say, "A lack of play should be treated like malnutrition; it's a health risk to your body and mind." I think that many of us are play-malnourished. We are play-hungry. It's not necessarily a bad thing to have goals, but many of our adult activities are dominated by achievements and goals, seven days a week.

As a "Play Sabbath," you can make room once a week from the daily grind. If you do so, the people around you will thank you, because a different "you" will learn to come to the fore.

Play is also an aphrodisiac. Couples therapist Esther Perel notes that

> In long-term relationships especially, cultivating novelty—whether through stories or experiences—is key for sustaining passion...Novelty breeds testosterone, it sparks your curiosity, encourages exploration, and shows that even this person who is so known to you is still somewhat unknown, with untold dreams, longings, silliness, and surprises. [vi]

Perel says, "What holds many of us back from trying new things with our partners is the inherent vulnerability of it."

It's no coincidence that we describe the act of "foreplay" as tantalising activities that lead to sexual intercourse. But maybe playfulness in and of itself is what's needed in our intimate relationships.

Play is an invitation to drop our guard and unburden ourselves from the weight of constant earnestness—even if just for a moment. Play invites us to take some risks.

When you are at an impasse, consider what it means to play together. Engaging in play is the freedom to love.

What does play look like? Do something fun with the people you love. Go bowling. Throw a frisbee. Convert your dining table to play a game of ping-pong. Get a new board game. Go sit on a swing together. Jump into the ocean together. Do something silly.

Albert Einstein said, "Play is the highest form of research." I think this is true because the form of research we get into when we are playful is a form of "me-search." And if we play together, we get into "we-search." All of us are searching for a place to be free, free to discover who we can be, and free to love each other.

"If we can play together," says toy designer Cass Holman, "We can live together."[vii]

Practise using the freedom to play and create levity. Have some fun with each other. Play is the gateway to being in love.

## BROADEN YOUR NATURE

If you are high in Agreeableness, you might find it challenging to assert your autonomy. Remember Edith Egar's distinction between victimisation and victimhood; the latter is optional. Don't let resentment fester; learn to exercise your will.

If you are high in Neuroticism, you might experience difficulties with closeness and connection. We all have a need to feel belonged. But sometimes, our tendency to withdraw and proneness to negative evaluation might make it harder to repair ruptures in our relationships. Be cognisant of this and pay attention, especially if this is the season that requires you to build bridges of connection with people you care about.

---

*See Related Paradoxes: 2. Present/Future, 3. Introspection/Outrospection, 5. Yes/No, 7. Approach/Retreat, 10. Grief/Love, 15. Control/Surrender.*

# PARADOX 9. CAREGIVING/RECEIVING CARE

## CONTRADICTION

*In giving, you receive. In receiving, we allow others to feel the inherent joy of being able to give.*

*Do I need to learn to give care or to receive care?*

## CLARITY

"Nobody is so poor that [they have] nothing to give, and nobody is so rich that [they have] has nothing to receive."

— *Karol Józef Wojtyła, Pope John Paul II.*

### A. Caregiving

Some things *do* need fixing. But caregiving is not fixing.

To fix is to cure. Our attempts to "cure" someone with our rational advice can sometimes cause grief, because it runs the risk of invalidating someone's true inner experiences. Attempts to "cure" when things don't need our "fixing" cause further separation between people.

Just think of a time when all you needed was to confide in someone. Our impulse to seek out a listening ear is desirable because we are trying to reach past the threshold within. On the flip-side, you as a caregiver need to suspend all urges to solve, over-rationalise, or "fix" the situation. You need to learn to leave your ideas behind and listen carefully to what needs tending to. For example, telling a person who is grieving the loss of another to "move on" is communicating to them that they should be out of the grieving process by now. When one is indeed in the season of grief, they can't deny the attention that it needs. As someone who cares for another who is grieving, we need to be willing to sit beside them in the valley of loss, not try to "fix" it.

Put another way, caregiving is the act of directing our undivided attention towards someone we care about. Simone Weil said, "Attention is the purest and rarest form of generosity."[i]

When our attention is divided, it is like drinking from a straw with holes in-between. Pure attention pipes through from one end to another. Leaks of attention are not just unsatisfying, but literally frustrating.

*Condescension*

Caregiving also runs the unintended risk of creating a power imbalance. One can take a one-up position in trying to help someone. The person receiving your help might feel belittled. Some sensitivity to the possibility of this happening is useful.

As a psychologist, I am mindful about the impact of my words. I do not want to come across as chastising or coddling. This is because it takes an act of risk and trust to share something painful and perhaps "shameful." If I am not paying careful attention to this interior dynamic, I may cause further shame, as the person might retreat deeper into their inner cave.

*Sick Organisations*

To engage in caregiving, you have to take care of the source of that wellspring from which life flows. Unfortunately, those whose jobs are to provide care are often not cared for with dignity themselves.

One of the greatest risks for burnout in the workplace is for people to work in "sick" organisations.

How do you tell if an organisation is sick?

A sick organisation treats the people who deliver its service solely as a means to an end. It fails to notice that those who give care also need to be part of a community of care. It dispenses "well-being" catchphrases and is surrounded by the rah-rah cheerleading of "self-care" without addressing the need for communal care.

Ultimately, the greatest violation is the violation of the dignity of the human spirit.

An organisation that is sick is not able to heal those whom it seeks to heal. Rather, it perpetuates the underlying disease.

An organisation that is designed to help others needs to make sure that people who are in the caring profession are cared for themselves.

The moment we push for more, as if we are productive bots in a sausage "caring" factory, we engage in a form of violence.

Thomas Merton addressed this exact issue more than 50 years ago:

> There is a pervasive form of modern violence to which the idealist...most easily succumbs: **activism and over-work** [emphasis mine]. The rush and pressure of modern life are a form, perhaps the most common form, of its innate violence.
>
> To allow oneself to be carried away by a multitude of conflicting concerns, to surrender to too many demands, to commit oneself to too many projects, to want to help everyone in everything is to succumb to violence.
>
> The frenzy of the activist neutralises his (or her) work... It

destroys the fruitfulness of his (or her)...work, because it kills the root of inner wisdom which makes work fruitful.[ii]

The dangers of working in a sick organisation also puts you at risk of moral injury. Moral injury occurs when the system pushes us to a point of violating our deeply held principles, beliefs, and values. Being pushed into doing more than we can wounds us in the long run.

We have to look out for each other within an organisation, a team, a family. We are each other's healthcare workers.

## B. Receiving Care

We would rather give care than to receive it.

To receive care means to *need* someone else, to depend on them to nourish and tend to us.

The only way for the gift of care to flow is for someone to give care and for another to *receive* care. The gift we can give others is to allow them the joy of giving us their unmixed attention.

Allowing someone to love you and attend to your needs, is a gracious act. To assert a wall of independence is to deny others from reaching, touching, and being part of your life.

This morning at the shops, I saw a photo frame with yet another trope that read, "Believe in yourself." But you can only believe in yourself if you are believed in by others. If we accept that we exist in a web of relationships, and the notion that "the Self is not just me," then we need to engage in this mutual dance of caregiving and care-receiving.

Learning to receive care requires us to expand our limited view of the self. Again, **the Self is not just me.** We are loved into being. We are tasked with helping each other become who we really are. Individual endeavours require others. We are not separate from others (See Paradox 8. Belonging).

When I was a child, I was hospitalised for an unknown

stomach issue that was causing acute pain. The medical professionals were concerned that I might be at risk of a burst appendix. My mom stayed with me through the admission. The next day, my sisters and father came to visit me. They walked into the ward, and there they stood around my bed, surrounding me. I was the centre of attention. For some reason, I felt overwhelmed, and I began to cry. Immediately, I began to feel embarrassed by my unwarranted reaction. I hated that I looked like a crybaby. Looking back, I now realise the floodgates were triggered by a mixture of feeling the care from everyone in the family all at once, plus a thick topping of guilt. Being the only son—perhaps especially in an Asian context—I was told about the type of privilege I would have—especially being the youngest in the family. For as long as I could remember, I resisted that idea. I didn't want to be treated "special" just because I was male and the youngest. But in that moment, though it seemed appropriate that everyone would show their care for me, I felt a block within. This prevented me from receiving any feelings of care for me, except for those coming from my mom.

Years later, in one of my first (proper) jobs as a youth facilitator, we used a video segment of John Foppe's life as part of our talk.iii One of the scenes is etched into my memory. Foppe, born without any upper-limbs, talked about how he had to learn to towel-dry himself after a bath, open a soda can with his toes, and learn to drive without arms. Clearly, despite his severe constraints, Foppe had become a fiercely independent person through what he described as "tough love" that he received from his parents. That said, once a week he would request his nephew come and pick him up to take him grocery shopping. He said that, while his inner-resilience and self-mastery had grown over the years, getting his nephew's help once a week was a reminder to him that we are all *inter*-dependent on each other—plus, he got to hang out with his nephew regularly.

Indeed, help might be something we'd rather do without. But

at bottom, this symbiotic relationship of giving and receiving care is the true nature of living in relationships.

---

In giving, you receive. In receiving, you allow others to experience the gift of giving.

Caregiving can be second nature to some. For others, receiving care can be a foreign position to be in. Meanwhile, others would benefit immensely from the gift of being allowed to offer care.

*In this season of your life, where do you need to be on the spectrum of Caregiving and Receiving Care? (Mark an '<', '>' or 'x' on the line below).*

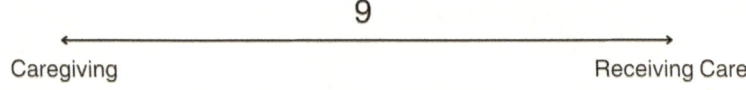

Caregiving                                                               Receiving Care

## COUNSEL

### A. Caregiving

If you find yourself more on the side of needing to be generous with caring for others, consider the following:

### 1. Get Closer

It's harder to connect when we are further in distance. Get closer. Move physically closer towards the other. Spend time being in that space, even if words fail to form in fluent fashion. Inhabit that space between you and the other. By learning to be present in that space, you can learn to open your eyes, ears, heart, and mind to what's really needed.

We can have all sorts of good ideas from a distance, which might not be helpful at all to the other person in reality. When we get closer, we make contact with reality and the real need of the other person. When we get closer, we suspend our good intentions and listen closely to the voice and need of the other in front of us.

Author and Quaker teacher Parker Palmer says,

> If we want to see a wild animal, we know that the last thing we should do is go crashing through the woods yelling for it to come out. But if we walk quietly into the woods, sit patiently at the base of a tree, breathe with the earth, and fade into our surroundings, the wild creature we seek might put in an appearance. We may see it only briefly and only out of the corner of an eye—but the sight is a gift we will always treasure as an end in itself.[iv]

I'm not saying that we should treat people we care about as wild animals. Rather, we need to figure out a way to be with them. We can't force someone to accept our good intentions. But we can move towards the person we care about.

Practise moving closer.

## 2. Go Slower

"Nature does not hurry, yet everything is accomplished."

— *Lao Tzu.*

Once we go closer, we can remind ourselves to slow down. Caregiving requires us to subvert the urge to go faster. Caregiving requires us to be unhurried.

When we slow down, we are more able to let go of our urge to "fix," thus creating a space for the relationship to exist.

Recall: Caregiving is not fixing.

Perhaps the young and the old suffer the most from our frenzied addiction to acceleration. Early in my career in Singapore, I met a father who was fixated on fixing his twelve-year-old son's ADHD. His son was not able to sit down and do his work; he was hyperactive and bouncing off the wall. The boy had already been diagnosed by a private psychiatrist and was put on a psychostimulant, Ritalin. Still, his symptoms were not 100% attenuated.

I sympathised with the father's plight. I could see that he was really trying to help his son. Given that I was a rookie, I consulted with my clinical supervisor and read everything I could get my hands on about ADHD. In gist, much advice was about intervening with behavioural strategies to improve emotional regulation and attentional focus. The father was always in a hurry. He was a busy man running his company. I asked how he managed his schedule between work and family life. He essentially replied, *I manage things very well, thank you very much.* Nonetheless, he added that it was his wife who brought their son to most extra-curricular activities throughout the week. I hadn't planned to do this, but I took a piece of A4 paper, drew a seven-column table, and asked his son to fill in his weekly schedule for me. After he was done, I looked at it. I couldn't help myself. I uttered, "Looks like you are busier than a CEO." His schedule was jam-packed with tuition classes, martial arts training, and more tuition classes on the weekend as he was going to take the Primary School Leaving Exams (PLSE) at Primary Six, which determines which prestigious secondary school you get into—or not. The only period that was free was Sunday morning from 7am to 10am, before the family went to Church.

The boy started to cry.

"What's going on?" His father asked.

"I'm just so tired," the boy replied.

Once the abstract became concrete through the clarity of his schedule it only made sense that the proper intervention was one of subtraction, not addition (see #2. Subtractive Changes, in Paradox 6. Change). We started to look at what extracurricular activities he could drop so that he could have periods of unscheduled play and rest, so that he could experience his childhood more by not being hurried from one structured activity to the next, seven days a week.

In an age where speed and productivity are prized above all else, it's easy to feel left behind. Quite simply, many struggle to catch up with this frenzy of efficiency. This is perhaps one of the reasons kids enjoy being with their grandparents. They are not in a mad rush.

> "How far you go in life depends on your being tender with the young, compassionate with the aged, sympathetic with the striving, and tolerant of the weak and strong. Because someday in your life you will have been all of these."
>
> — *George Washington Carver*

Practise manually shifting your gear one step slower.

### 3. Love People, Use Things.

Love people and use things. Don't love things and use people.[v]

If you are caring for others in an organisation setting, a team or family, one of the most important principles is to treat people not as a means to an end, but as an end in themselves.

When people feel used, we rob them of their dignity. In our relentless pursuit of corporate success, we run the risk of dehumanising people. "After several workshops with different groups," says conflict resolution specialist Donna Hicks, "it became clear that a major source of anger, resentment, and bad feelings among people who had to work together could be traced back to incidents in which individuals felt that their dignity had been violated...What exactly gets injured? Our dignity."[vi]

If we want to care for the people in our teams, there are three aspects that can serve as countermeasures to dissatisfaction. Look at the Development, Appreciation, and Contribution (DAC) diagram.

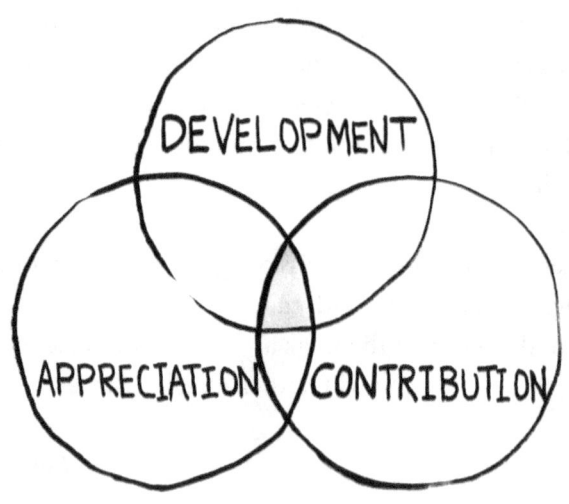

### Development

First, care for the people in your team by investing in their development. This not only consists of their professional role in the organisation, but also their personal development. A person has the potential to bring their full selves into what they do, and if we encourage, support, and cultivate their inner growth, we make them feel more like part of the team.

When someone is growing and developing, this becomes inoculative to burnout. When someone does not feel like they are developing, they feel stagnant.

*Appreciation*

Second, learn to articulate your appreciation for others. Don't make blanket statements; be ultra-specific. Pay close attention to what they are doing. Say exactly what you appreciate about them, what they did, and why it matters to you.

We feel valuable when we are valued.

When someone does not feel appreciated, they will feel less valued or even devalued.

*Contribution*

Last, we are caring for others when we allow people to contribute to an organisation in meaningful ways.

We can invite others to contribute by bringing their gifts and ideas, which might be either taken for granted or entirely missed on most occasions.

But do not conflate *contribution* with delegation.

Delegating work to someone is *your* agenda—and yes, we do have to delegate tasks to others from time to time. In fact, some of you might need to learn how to delegate more of your work. Contribution, on the other hand, is less about your agenda and more about what they can bring to the table.

My ex-colleague was a highly committed psychologist and always took on any project our boss assigned. She was hyperproductive and highly conscientious with her work. Even with all that busyness, she didn't feel like she was contributing. She felt like a cog in the wheel. She wasn't able to bring her gifts to match the needs of the organisation.

When someone does not feel they are contributing, they will feel less like part of the team.

Let's take a closer look at the finer details of the DAC venn diagram:

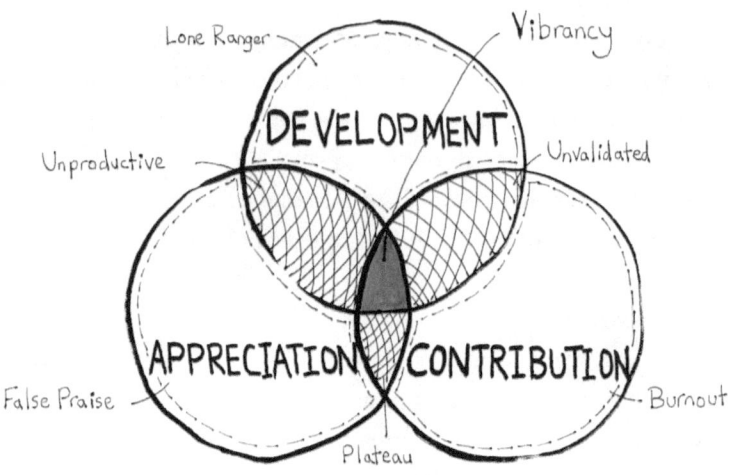

- *When there is Development and Appreciation, but no Contribution =* **Unproductive**
- *When there is Contribution and Development, but no Appreciation =* **Unvalidated**
- *When there is Appreciation and Contribution, but no Development =* **Plateau**
- *When there is Development, but no Appreciation and Contribution =* **Lone Ranger**
- *When there is Appreciation, but no Contribution and Development =* **False Praise**
- *When there is Contribution, but no Appreciation and Development =* **Burnout**
- *When there is Contribution, Appreciation and Development =* **Vibrancy**

As mentioned, I would argue that we can also think of families as a dynamic organisation. Our family is the first band of people that we are involved with. The DAC diagram can also be useful for taking care of a family. Kids need not only to develop, but also to feel appreciated by their caregivers—and like they are contributing members of the family in what they do and the home environment they create (e.g., keeping the house tidy).

Practise attending to the three factors of Contribution, Appreciation, and Development when you are caring for a team.

## B. Receiving Care

If you find yourself more on the side of needing to receive care, consider the following:

### 1. Request Closeness

Esther Perel once quipped about how we touch the touchscreens of our iPhones more than we touch the hands of our partner.

The problem is, we don't know how to ask for closeness.

Even though we might be making big changes and transitions in our lives, we don't want to impose upon or trouble others. Yet sometimes the other person doesn't have a clue about our emotional need for intimacy.

Learning to ask for time together, spending time doing some activity together, requires us to confront our *neediness*. We don't like that word. It connotes a kind of dependency and insecurity, an implication that we are not self-sufficient.

The truth is, we are need-full. We need each other. (See Introduction, Why Needs?). Revealing our needs—that we have needs in the first place—is scary. It takes a level of vulnerability to say to someone, "Hey, would you be free to come hang out next week? I just need some company…"

I find this a challenge. Maybe it's because, temperamentally, I'm more introverted. But every now and then, my wife says to me, "You know that I can't read your mind, right?" I have to consciously remind myself to explicate my thoughts and preferences to her, and not just assume that "she knows." Even as trivial as asking friends, I find it hard to say, "Hey bud, you wanna catch up?" Why is this so difficult? It's because I don't want to impose on others. Everyone's busy or going through their own shit. But frankly, every time I ask my mates to spend time together, the reply is often, "Yeah, sure. When are you free?"

Underneath it all, the real question we are asking each other is "Am I safe with you? Is it all right for me to reveal my wishes, my unspokens, my hidden truths, my guilt, my shame, my yearnings to you? Or are you going to try to fix me like a broken table? Will you reject me?"

Parker Palmer said, *"We need safe spaces for truth-telling."* We need relationships where we can be honest with each other about our needs.

Practise asking people to spend time with you.

## 2. Help

> "There are only four kinds of people in the world: those who have been caregivers, those who are currently caregivers, those who will be caregivers, and those who need caregiving."
>
> — *Rosalynn Carter*[vii]

As we age, we are confronted with the fact that we need others to help us. We may have been caregivers most of our lives, but if we let others in, we need to become receivers of care as well.

Maybe we should learn to receive care before we get old. Allowing others to tend to us provides an opportunity for them to experience the gift of caring.

When do I actually need help? When I feel like I need more perseverance. How many times has it crossed your mind to push on instead of asking for help, instead of letting someone else in? (See #2. Lighten the Suck-It-Up Muscles, in Paradox 1. Self-Care).

One of the inner barriers to letting others into our lives, especially to letting them lend us a hand, is self-rejection. This doesn't often surface in obvious ways. It often exists under the hood, hidden from the social exchanges, and maybe not even in your conscious awareness. Self-rejection can come in the form of feelings of unworthiness or arrogance. To feel unworthy means to feel like your needs are not worth attending to. To feel arrogant is to put yourself on a pedestal, that you are above it all, and you are better than others. Henri Nouwen noted, "Isn't arrogance, in the final analysis, just another way of dealing with the feelings of worthlessness?" He added, "Whether I am inflated or deflated, I lose touch with my truth and distort my vision of reality."[viii]

Ultimately, self-rejection rejects *everyone*. When we learn to see that the Self is not just me, we expand our sense of self when we let others in.

Practise asking for help. Trust is built more by asking than offering help.

### 3. Vocalising Appreciation

I often think about how things go in circles. Take for example, if one is experiencing a good conversation. It feels like a good back-and-forth game of table tennis. You ask a question, and the person responds. The other person then throws back a related question, and you respond, and maybe one of you goes a little deeper. Contrast this to a not-so-good conversation. You ask a question, and the other responds. You wait a second, and you find yourself needing to ask another question, and indeed the person does respond with a sentence or two. But there's no follow-up inquiry from the other person, no "And what about you?" You end up doing all the heavy lifting of the conversation.

Earlier, we addressed the importance of expressing appreciation of the other when we are caregiving. We also need to vocalise our gratitude when we are the receiver of care and attention.

*Expressing appreciation keeps the circle going.* Our relationships grow when there is a circulation of back-and-forth. Funny how it's much easier to vocalise our gratitude to a casual friend or an acquaintance than it is to people close to us. Sometimes, we take it for granted that "They know I appreciate them."

In his seminal book *The Gift*, Lewis Hyde characterises a genuine gift as something that is given *freely*, *received* by the other, *transformative*, *indebted*, and *circulative*. When we vocalise our sincere appreciation, we keep the circulation of friendship or kinship going. It is a gift to the other when they feel that their gift is well-received.

Practise articulating your appreciation. Be specific. Don't keep your gratitude inside. Share it.

## BROADEN YOUR NATURE

If you are high in Introversion and Neuroticism, you might have a tendency to withdraw from others. Listen to the signs of your times. If this particular season is calling you to give or to receive care, to do so, you have to come out of your shell and dip your toes into life.

If you are high in Agreeableness, you might find Caregiving easy because you are highly compassionate. On the other hand, you might find Receiving Care more challenging. Remember, learning to receive well is a chance for intimacy.

---

*Related Paradoxes: 1. Self-Care/Self-Forgetting, 4. Solitude/Community, 7. Autonomy/Belonging, 10. Grief/Love.*

# PARADOX 10. GRIEF/LOVE

*SPECIAL NOTE: We are now at the nerve-centre of this book. This Paradox is one of the most significant. You are probably no stranger to Grief and Love. The relationship between Grief and Love is the most fundamental element of Crossing Between Worlds. I urge you to give this Paradox some space and time, and allow yourself to revisit it at a later stage as well.*

## CONTRADICTION

*In the face of loss, we can feel lost. Can I protect myself from the pains of grief, or can I allow myself to experience the deep waves to change me? Can I learn to understand the call of love in my life? How do I learn to love well?*

*As I move into this season of my life, how do I learn to grieve, and how do I learn to love?*

# CLARITY

## A. Grief

The twins of Grief and Love leave their mark through our lifetime. Former palliative care director in Toronto and writer Stephen Jenkinson says, "Grief is a way of loving that which has slipped from view and love is a way of grieving that which has not yet slipped from view."[i]

All of our human experience is mediated by loss. When there is no love, there is no grief.

Given a choice, during the summers of our lives, none of us will put up our hand for an assignment of learning to grieve. It's a lesson we rather not sit through, especially when things are going well.

Danish Philosopher Sven Brinkmann notes that "Grief tells us that we can never completely master life."[ii] Brinkmann argues that grief should be seen as a foundational emotion in an existential sense, which weaves into the fabric of our relationships. If we deny ourselves and others this central element of our being, we deny what it means to be human.

In the song "If We Were Vampires" by Jason Isbell and the 400 Unit, Isbell and his wife, Amanda Shires, sing,

> *Maybe we'll get 40 years together*
> *But one day, I'll be gone or one day, you'll be gone*
> *If we were vampires and death was a joke*
> *We'd go out on the sidewalk and smoke*
> *And laugh at all the lovers and their plans*
> *I wouldn't feel the need to hold your hand*
> *Maybe time running out is a gift*
> *I'll work hard 'til the end of my shift*
> *And give you every second I can find*

*And hope it isn't me who's left behind*
*It's knowing that this can't go on forever*
*Likely one of us will have to spend some days alone.*
*Maybe we'll get 40 years together*
*One day, I'll be gone, one day you'll be gone.*

It is not in our intuitive toolkit to comprehend that *"maybe time running out is a gift."*

Think of the loved ones in your life who have passed on.

I was thirteen years old when I experienced the first loss in my life. My maternal grandfather died of diabetes at age 74. Before that, one of his legs had to be amputated. Grandpa was an unusual character. I was told that he used to be a boxer. He inherited a fortune from his family, but he lost all of it through magical thinking and gambling. I remember my grandmother taking me on a bus ride to Robinson Road to meet Grandpa. I was told to walk up to a two-storey shop-house and fetch him, because no one else could get him out of the gambling den. I can still smell the choking scent of opium.

There was another side of Grandpa. He had a big heart for kids. You could tell. As far as I know, though he didn't have any biological kids of his own—including my mother—he adopted five of them.[1] I've also heard stories about him in the kampong (i.e., village) saying that he would set up grand fireworks for all the kids to enjoy. Grandpa holds a special place in my heart. I spent most of my primary school afternoons at his place while my parents were at work. He taught me how to skateboard, he bought me my first pair of leather boots, and he used to take me

---

1. In those days, families who were not financially able to raise their additional kids would "sell" them to those who could afford it.

window shopping at Centrepoint and indulged in my obsession with ninja-related movies at Kong Chian cinema in Toa Payoh.

When he was ill, I visited him in the hospital once or twice. I wish I had seen him more during that process, but I think the adults were protecting us kids from that uncomfortable situation of death and dying. Looking back, this was a mistake on their part. But perhaps they were also finding their own way of dealing with the pending loss.

After he died, unknown to anyone else, I would spend many afternoons of my youth after school, sitting by my Grandpa's side at the columbarium. I would write him letters and stuff them into the slots where flowers were supposed to go. I still think about Grandpa nearly every other day.

Grief needs a vessel. Without something to hold, grief will permeate until you attend to it.

When we feel the weight of love and joy of the people we care about, we begin to feel the full potential of grief—the price of love. A brokenhearted individual loses a part of themselves when they lose someone they love. Yet we would not have it any other way. Grief and love are twins.

## B. Love

The late Thich Nhat Hanh wrote in his concise book *How to Love* that **"To love without knowing how to love wounds the person we love."**[iii] Unfortunately, many of us don't know the art and practice of loving well.

Why do we inflict the most pain on the people closest to us?

Thầy noted,

> Your good intentions are not good enough; you have to be artful. We may be filled with goodwill; we may be motivated by the desire to make the other person happy; but out of our clumsi-

ness, we make them unhappy... Mindful living is an art, and each of us has to train to be an artist.[iv]

Without proper practice, our good intentions will not suffice.

One time, as we were wrapping up a session, a client asked me, "What is of the highest value in life?"

I was stumped by the suddenness and abstractness of his question. I had several immediate thoughts on this, but I babbled on about the importance of "self-determination," taking charge of our own lives, etc. In hindsight, I was unconsciously trying to give an answer that would be strategically helpful to him. My client nodded in agreement, but I knew the answer was not on par with the magnitude of the question he had raised.

The next day, the answer hit me. And how could I have not thought of this? It is even engraved on the inside of my wedding ring: "*...The greatest of these is love.*"

Pioneering family therapist Virginia Satir wrote the following poem:

> *I want to love you without clutching,*
> *appreciate you without judging,*
> *join you without invading,*
> *invite you without demanding,*
> *leave you without guilt,*
> *criticise you without blaming,*
> *and help you without insulting.*
> *If I can have the same from you,*
> *then we can truly meet and enrich each other.*

In a deep sense, **union is what we are seeking.** Between two individuals, with nature, with the community. While preserving our integrity without dominating another, to be part of something more than ourselves, and accepting each other for who we are.

Love is our greatest truth.

---

We are called to be practitioners of love and grief. In this time-limited mortal arrangement, if we do not learn how to love, and deny the invitations to grieve, we might inflict unnecessary grief on others and ourselves.

*In this season of your life, where do you need to be on the spectrum of Grief and Love? (Mark an '<', '>' or 'x' on the line below).*

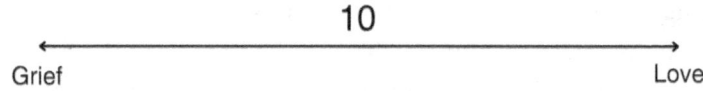

Grief                     10                     Love

## COUNSEL

### A. Grief

If you find yourself needing to make room for grief, here are some suggestions:

### 1. Grief Needs a Cup

If I have coffee, but no cup, I have nothing.

Grief needs a container in order to hold some of the overwhelm that spills into every aspect of our being.

In this liquid age, where nothing seems to hold, and everything is in a state of flux, we need to have "cups." Cups can be conceived as rituals.

Rituals require three things:

i. **Intention**
  ii. **Attention**
  iii. **Repetition**

Rituals play out in our everyday lives. How we say hello, and how we say goodbye. How we welcome a newborn baby, and how we mourn the loss of a loved one. Rituals exist in religious practices. We must also find our way to bring rituals into our everyday lives.

Without the presence of rituals in the face of what sociologists call "**liquid modernity**,"[2] we are left with no clear demarcation of the boundaries of life. Not that there aren't things to nourish us—too many in fact—but rather, we have no place to hold our intentions.

When there isn't a place to hold our intentions, our attention goes astray. Intentions must come from a place of will. But when they're forced upon someone, instead of creating solace, rituals become hell.

We create a psychological and spiritual container when we set aside regular time and space to intentionally place our attention on the loss of a loved one.

By setting apart space to grieve, we honour the relationship we have with the person who has passed on. To be clear, grief is not "containable." It's an unrelenting raging river. But creating time to hold and experience the waves of grief makes it more bearable.

Even if the word "ritual" doesn't sit well with you, an obvious sign that we yearn for structure is evident in the experience of a child's life. They want you to read *that* book before they go to bed. Yes, it's the fifteenth time they have read it, but they want *you* to

---

2. The term "liquid modernity" was coined by the Polish sociologist and philosopher Zygmunt Bauman. He used this term to describe the fluid and constantly changing nature of modern society.

read it with them. Their intention seeks for *your* attention to engage in the storytelling activity, and they intrinsically desire the rhythm of repetition.

Again, and again.

In these liquid times, we must protect our intentions.

Stop and ask yourself: How do you hold space for grief? Stephen Jenkinson notes in his book *Die Wise*, when we make a place for grief, "[we invite] human sorrow to the table as you would any guest unexpectedly appearing at your door at mealtime."[v]

This place, this vessel, is to behold the experience of what it means to be alive.

Practise intentionally creating space for grief through the use of rituals.

## 2. Re-membering Practices

People die, but relationships don't. Meaningful relationships permeate through our lives and beyond.[vi]

Despite their best efforts, nothing that the mental health multidisciplinary team did seemed to help. Jimmy was inconsolable. It has been two years since his wife died of cancer. She was someone he had entirely relied upon for his everyday and emotional needs. Most well-meaning friends, family, and healthcare professionals encouraged him to "move on." He would have, if he could. The truth was that he was afraid of "moving on." Not only did he fear forgetting about the precious memories they'd shared together, and as strange as it sounds, he also feared that taking care of himself would mean he no longer needed his wife, as he was previously dependent on her for nearly every aspect of daily living.

Finally, my colleague, Jimmy's treating psychologist, suggested that maybe he should take the pressure off "moving on." Instead, maybe he should make room to *re-member*[vii] his wife. Knowing that he was a practising Catholic, she suggested that he go to the nearby Church each morning to have a chat with his wife. Our fellow mental health practitioners weren't exactly sure about this suggestion, as it seemed paradoxical and might keep him stuck in his rut. Two weeks later, Jimmy returned for a follow-up appointment and was visibly more enlivened. He told my colleague, "I now get to spend some time talking with my wife. I know she's not replying, but I know she's there. And I feel her presence in that church, because we used to go there together every week for Mass."

In the small town of Otsuchi, on the coast of northern Japan, an old phone booth with a disconnected black rotary phone exists at the foot of a resident's garden. This phone booth, coined the "Wind Phone," became the place bereaved family members came to visit, to call those they lost when the tsunami hit in 2011. About 2,000 residents perished in that catastrophe.

A husband, left to care for his four kids, speaks to his wife on the Wind Phone.

> I told her that our daughters and I were looking for her for a long time," he said, "and we almost gave up.... On the last day, we went searching...we found [you]. I know you cannot come back, but I can go to you in the future." He told a reporter, "It's like when you close your eyes, [you] feel that someone is listening to you. I was so happy... so happy.[viii]

This might sound illogical to the rational mind. This does not necessarily mean that we need to find a phone booth to speak to the dead. Rather, we need to honour the fact that we yearn to make the abstract just a little more concrete, so that we can reorganise, reorient, and re-member the relationships we have in our lives. The push to "get on with life" and "move on" can sometimes feel like we are dismembering our relationship with our loved one. To re-member is to reconstitute our relationship with people who have passed away, but who continue to live on within us.

Practise re-membering the ones who have loved you into being, not dis-membering your relationship with them.

### 3. Grief is a Skill

We are called to be practitioners of grief. In a death-phobic culture, we do not see grief as something to apprentice ourselves to, even though it is a certainty that we will experience losses and our own demise. If we do not learn to die well, we do not learn to live well. If we try to evade, deny, or not talk about our mortality, such a bypass will affect those we leave behind.

The practice of grief is the *willingness* and the *exercise* of being part of something beyond yourself.

Why willingness and exercise? If we are willfully blind to it and conduct ourselves in a way that pretends this thing called death isn't there, we deny ourselves a wakefulness in our living. And if we don't exercise this mindful awareness, our mind forgets about the relationship between grief and love.

Here's how I do this: I installed a countdown timer app on my laptop. Its sole purpose is to countdown to one event: The day I'll die.[3]

Based on a simple Web search,[ix] as an Asian male who doesn't have significant bad habits or health issues, I estimated how long I might live (about 81.4 years), and then keyed in the rough date, and *voilà*, the day I'll die.

What was striking was how few days I may have left. When I started using this countdown timer, there were about 14,000 days left. At age 42, I assumed I would have a bit more time than that! At the time of this revision, at age 45, the timer says 13,314 days.

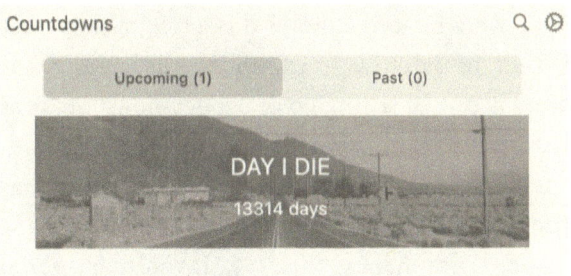

This timer wakes me up. We know we are going to die, but having an estimate of the number of days left puts things into perspective.

I told some people about what I did with this countdown timer. One person said, "That sounds a bit morbid." A youth I was working with said, "That sounds like a lot of time left." Talk about perspective.

Most people's exclamations about my countdown timer were

---

3. This idea was inspired by Kevin Kelly. See "My Life Countdown kk.org/ct2/my-life-countdown-1/

really about the implications for themselves. How many days do *you* have left? More importantly, how are you going to spend your limited lease in this life?

The second thing I do is to go to my kids' bedrooms and bless them each night when they are sound asleep. I kiss their foreheads. I remind myself that my kids are "guests" in my home. Henri Nouwen, a writer who has greatly impacted my life, wrote,

> Children are not properties to own and rule over, but gifts to cherish and care for. Our children are our most important guests, who enter into our home, ask for careful attention, stay for a while, and then leave to follow their own way. Children are strangers whom we have to get to know.

And before I leave their bedroom, I contemplate "what if?" What if they were no longer here? It is a tough question to reckon with. After all, to parent is to experience little daily deaths. This grief process is one of letting go of expectations, of "supposed to"s, of our assumptions of how kids and family life should be—and then being jolted into the present, which more often than not leads to an involuntary sense of gratitude that they are there in my life, and I am happy (See #3. Involuntary Gratitude, in Paradox 15. Surrender).

We may never fully master grief, but we can come to apprentice ourselves to this life-long learning process of living and dying.

Practise the mindful awareness of your mortal reality in order to fully engage in a life of love.

## B. Love

If you find yourself needing to learn how to love well, here are some suggestions:

## 1. "I See You"

When Rosanne was a preteen, she expressed a desire to do something important in her life. She wanted to write and be a musician. It wasn't just a passing feeling. But her mother was worried. To a degree, her concerns were warranted. Her mother wondered whether Rosanne would follow in her father's footsteps. Not only was he on the road most of the time, he also struggled with alcohol and substance abuse.

Her father was the cultural icon country singer Johnny Cash.

Rosanne was conflicted, because she saw how her father's addiction affected him. Still, she wanted to connect with him. "I remember when I was about twelve years of age, I wrote a letter to him," said Rosanne. "I said that I had things inside me I wanted to do. I was opening up, telling him I wanted to do important things, to write, and so on."

"He wrote me back, and said, 'I see that you see as I see.'" This meant the world to Rosanne. "I always held on to that."[x]

Being seen by another is truly powerful. Our task is not to change others, but to see who they really are, to **nurture their nature** and encourage them to find their own path to fully express their gifts.

Picture someone you care about. Take a moment to vivify this person in your mind's eye. Begin to see who that person really is on the inside, who they are as an individual, and imagine yourself embracing that as completely as you can. And then say, "I see you."[4]

Many times in our lives, we are unable to say to the person we love, "I see that you see as I see," because we simply see different things. That's ok. Our task, if love is our highest aim, is to be able to say, "I see you, and I love you."

---

4. Curiously, an African Zulu greeting is "*Sawubona*," which translates to mean "I see you." It has a long oral history, and it means more than our traditional "hello."

Call to mind others who "saw you" and encouraged more of you to come to the fore. Keep these people close in your memory.

Practise loving by nurturing the nature of others. Then you can say, "I see you."

## 2. Soften

Tenderness is not a weakness.

There is a deep fear that when we open up and soften down, we become woundable. There is a risk of getting hurt. Placing your heart in a glass bottle is a way to protect it from the wounds of living, but it makes it much harder for anything—much less love—to come in.

Trust requires risk. And *who* we trust matters. We can't just say, "learn to trust." We must think, "*Who* am I going to learn to trust?"

To work on things you care about requires you to exert a level of strength and focus on the task at hand. It requires you to fortify your will and discipline. To love the people you care about, on the other hand, requires you to do just the opposite, i.e., to soften (See #1. Strength and Warmth, in Paradox 6. Acceptance).

To soften is quite literally to loosen our muscular grip and to ease our body. Then it is to catch our breath and regulate our emotions. We don't need to stare with laser-like focus or squint with intensity. We can consciously soften our eyes.

On the inside, we begin to open and avail ourselves of others, to make room for the people you care about to inhabit in our heart. You might want to do this after a day's work, before you open the door to your home and say, "Hi kids."

We can only grow things when the ground is soft. We can only connect when our hearts are softened.

Practise softening your heart when you go home to the people you love.

## 3. Close the Gap Between Our Intentions and Its Effects

In his seminal book *The Art of Loving,* Erich Fromm writes, "People think that to love is simple, but that to find the right object to love—or to be loved by—is difficult."[xi]

If you are in any kind of long-term relationship, you know this to be true. Love is hard work.

Love is more than a noun. Love is a verb. It is asking for us to align our behaviour with our intent. What we need to do in perspective-getting is learn to ask questions in order to hear them and alter our perspective. (see Paradox 3, Outrospection).

*"What's on your mind?"*

Don't stop there, follow-up by asking, *"What else?"*

*"What is something missing that you need?"*

*"Help me to see what you see."*

*"What's happening for you that I might be unaware of?"*

Outrospection acts as a potential inoculation against our good intentions going bad. Yes, it is the thought that counts, but also the thought's **effects**. I can religiously water my plants on a daily basis, but if I'm not opening my eyes to the effects of overhydration on my green companions, it can kill some of them.

We can learn to understand the impact of our intentions through inquiring about the effects on the other. Your good intention of doing everything for your loved one may come from a place of love, but if you learn about its effects, you might find out that it robs the person of feeling like they have any self-agency. (See Paradox 8. Autonomy).

Love is an expansion, requiring you to look outside of yourself. By closing the gap between your intentions and its effects, you expand the size of your heart. "When our hearts are small ... We can't accept or tolerate others and their shortcomings, and we demand that they change," said Thich Nhat Hanh. "But when our hearts expand ... We accept others as they are, and then they have a chance to transform."

Practise checking the effects of your intentions, followed by the willingness to re-calibrate your actions.

## BROADEN YOUR NATURE

It is safe to say that all personality types will find Grief a difficult process. We are called to be practitioners of grief and love in this lifetime. Grief will be more pronounced when you experience major life shakes, and learning to love well can help us to be happy with each other.

If you are low in Agreeableness, you will benefit from "#3. Close the Gap Between Our Intentions and Its Effects". You may be a person others describe as "brutally honest," who speaks without mincing your words. But if you are to care enough about the person you are speaking to, an exercise of outrospection—how your words affect the other person—is worth contemplating.

---

*See Related Paradoxes: 1. Self-Care/Self-Forgetting, 3. Introspection/Outrospection, 6. Acceptance/Change, 8. Autonomy/Belonging, 15. Control/Surrender.*

# PART III: WELL-DOING

"The highest reward for man's toil is not what he gets for it, but what he becomes by it."

— *John Ruskin*

In the third and final section, we explore how "the happiness of pursuit" shapes our Well-Being and our Well-Belonging. We will look at the tension of opposites between the push for quality and quantity, the oscillation between recovery and stress, stillness and movement, our inputs and outputs, and the relationship between control and surrender.

# PARADOX 11. QUALITY/QUANTITY

**CONTRADICTION**

What is the approach to creating things of value? And why is it so hard to begin?
Do I need to learn to focus on making better or making more?

**CLARITY**

**A. Quantity**

A well-regarded ceramicist was invited to teach a class of 100 students. Given the size of the class, she randomly divided the class into two groups.

She moved Group A to one side of the class and told the 50 students that they would be graded on the quantity of pots they produced within an hour. That is, the more the better.

She moved Group B to the other side of the class and told them that all they had to do was channel their energy into making a single pot each in the next hour. That is, aim for quality.

So here's the thought experiment: Which group of students, A or B, are more likely to produce work of the highest calibre?

When I first read this story in the book *Art and Fear*,[i] I instinctively answered Group B. It makes sense, doesn't it? When you place all of your attention and channel your effort into a single thing, you should get better results than people who are just aiming for more, shouldn't you?

However, this is not the case. Group B, the group channelling all of their energy onto a single pot, was less likely to produce a beautiful piece of art. On the other hand, Group A, the cohort focused on making as many as possible within a time frame, was more likely to create something beautiful. Even more interesting for Group A, the pot they thought the least of was often judged by others as captivating. On the flipside, the product that they overvalued was not deemed as the highest quality.

There is a paradox at play. At the beginning, if you aim for quality, you miss the mark. Aim for quantity, and you are more likely to get quality. At the later stages of development, you need the opposite.

Why is this the case?

The contradictory relationship between quantity and quality is due to the fact that we are likely to **over-personalise** and **over-invest** in what we create. The product of my work says something about me. If it sucks, *I suck.*

When we are able to add some distance and detach from what we create, we are more likely to find ourselves unbound from the tight relationship between the creative act and our identity, and thus we feel more free to engage in the act of creating.

### Two Worlds in Our Minds

It's no secret that there are two hemispheres in our brain, not one. One is really good for creating, and the other for evaluating. In his book *The Master and His Emissary*, leading neuroscientist

Iain McGilchrist stretches beyond pop psychology and elaborates in great detail about the inner division we face based on the hemispheric differences in our brains. Most of us would think that the analytical and focused side of the left hemisphere to be the one in charge. Western civilisation has increasingly favoured the dominance of the left hemisphere's cognitive and perceptual style.

However, McGilchrist refers to the right hemisphere as the "master" and the left as the "emissary," i.e., the diplomatic manager. The right hemisphere is characterised by a more holistic and integrative function, recognising patterns, understanding context, and appreciating the whole. The left hemisphere, on the other hand, specialises in analytical and sequential processing, breaking down information into parts and stringing it with a sense of linear reasoning. To put it another way, "The conscious mind thinks it's the Oval Office," says Jonathan Haidt, "when in reality it's the press office."

The harmonious integration of the right and left hemispheres is needed for us to function. However, at the start of any creative endeavour, we would benefit from dampening our evaluative mind. Instead, we need to dial *up* and disinhibit the playful spirit, and be willing to let loose without the presence of judgement.

### Three Stages of Creating

The act of creating is not a linear process. In fact, it is quite often messy. But knowing which stage of the process you are in is helpful.[1] It is also encouraging because knowing where you are not only provides a sense of what's required of you, but also gives you a sense of direction of what's to come.

---

[1] You could be moving back and forth between these stages too. But for the first iteration, I would suggest that you go through a first pass of the three stages.

## Table 2. Stages of Creating

| Stages | Process | Paradox | Hemispheric Worlds |
|---|---|---|---|
| Seeding | Germinate and Experiment | Quantity | Master |
| Elaboration | Nurture and Incubate | Transition: Quantity to Quality | Bridge-Crossing (Corpus Callosum) |
| Evaluation | Prune and Implement | Quality | Emissary |

*i. Seeding*

At this first stage, you want to allow yourself full licence to lay down all ideas.

Brainstorm, mind-map, create an infinite list. Do whatever you need to do to put down all of your ideas.

Allow each idea to germinate, play around with each of the possibilities. See what you gravitate towards; allow that idea to move you viscerally. No need for explanations why one idea pulls you and why the other doesn't.

There's no need to judge. Remind your critical side that it has a role, just not at this stage. I sometimes refer to this early stage as **"For my eyes only."** I've come to accept that my first drafts of any writing projects are incredibly bad. At first, I used to think that it was because I'm not a "natural" writer. It also didn't help that my co-authors were brilliant writers who wrote well-crafted prose in their first drafts. But I've come to accept that that's not how I work. Most of us would benefit from permission to scatter some seeds of ideas first, without the constant evaluative mind judging whether this is anything worth its salt.

At the Seeding phase, go wide. Aim for Quantity.

*ii. Elaboration*

At the second stage, you want to take a nurturing attitude. Be the midwife to your ideas. Like a baby learning to crawl, encourage your ideas that resonate with you to take one extra step. Then another. Then try to stand. Then try to walk one step, two steps…. But don't push too hard. Allow yourself to sleep on it.

Return to the idea the next day. Incubation allows our default mode network (DMN) to do the active background synthesising work.[2] Maybe your third idea can be combined with idea number sixteen. Maybe thinking about all of your ideas the next day will nudge you to another idea.

Let your ideas grow. Your role at this stage is to cultivate them.

At the Elaboration phase, you transition from wide to narrow, focusing on the vital few ideas that pull you in. This crosses from aiming for Quantity into Quality.

## B. Quality

*iii. Evaluation*

Robert Fritz, author of T*he Path of Least Resistance,* says,

> The question, "What do I want?" is really a question about results. Perhaps a more precise way of asking that question is "What result do I want to create?" The question,"How do I get what I want?" Is really a question about process, not results.
>
> ...If you ask the "how" question before the "what" question, all you can ever hope to create are variations of what you already have... The process should always serve the result. Consider what you want [to achieve] independent of considerations of process.[iii]

At the final stage, you want to get critical. Prune, tweak, and refine your existing ideas. Ultimately, you want to see that you deliver what you are trying to create (See #1 What Do You Want to Create, in Paradox 2. Future).

At the evaluation phase, you go deep. Aim for Quality.

---

2. As mentioned in #1. Set Up Periodic Times to Retreat in Paradox 7, DMN refers to brain areas that are active when we are not engaged with the outside world, supporting processes like introspection and memory retrieval.

As you begin a life transition and create something new for yourself, aim for quantity. Do not become overly conscious, and don't over-evaluate what you are doing. It is only in the later stage that you will need to judge critically. Embrace the paradoxical relationship between "Quantity" and "Quality."

In this season of your life, where do you need to be on the spectrum of Quantity and Quality (Mark an '<', '>' or 'x' on the line below).

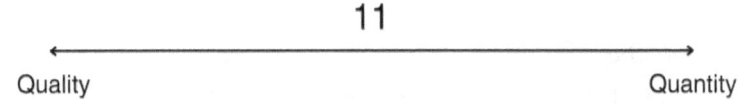

Quality                                                                 Quantity

## COUNSEL

### A. Quantity

If you find yourself needing to begin working on something complex, be it a creative work, a hard task, or any sort of project, here are some suggestions:

### 1. Aim for Ten Times More

When you are trying something new, like meeting new people, creating a work of art, or designing new innovations for your company, first aim for quantity, not quality.

If you need to write three verses for a song, write 30.

If you need an idea to propose to your boss, brainstorm ten ideas.

You'll begin to feel the stretch when you have reached five times the amount required. Don't relent at this point. Push for five more. Get someone to work through this with you, if required. Edging beyond what we think we are capable of reveals what we have at the fringes of our minds.

In the Seeding phase, we don't yet fully know what will grow out of our ideas. Thus, it's necessary to give yourself the full-blown permission to experiment, tinker and fiddle.

The key is not only to get the flow going in the act of creating, but also to become depersonalised to and de-invested in any specific idea or outcome. Becoming unwedded from your ideas and results helps at this stage. Especially because, if we are the creators, we are often bad judges of our own work.[iii]

Practise aiming for more than you need.

## 2. Cover Your Eyes

While I've referred to the Seeding phase as "For my eyes only," I'm going to suggest you learn to close your eyes.

As you aim for quantity in the Seeding phase, suspend judgement. Shut down the part of your brain that is trying to evaluate whether your work is any good, and just keep going. Evaluate *later*.

This is easy to say, but hard to do.

Take for example, the moment you open a Word document to begin writing. It feels as if that blinking cursor on the blank page is there for the sole purpose of cursing at you.[3]

Consider doing this: Take a blank piece of paper and cover the screen. Once you have everything set up, place your hands on the keyboard, and type away!

Forget about the formating and the spacing and the typos. Just go. Keep going. For every next idea, hit ENTER.

Practise producing work with your eyes closed.

---

3. Much of the process of writing this book was littered with wrestling matches between the cursor and me. I was probably the one doing most of the cursing.

## 3. Capture *All* of Your Ideas

Make it a practice to put down your ideas. Whenever I have a musical idea—especially if it sounds like a really good idea in my head—I'm convinced that, for sure, I will remember it.

And then, of course, I don't.

Thankfully, when it comes to writing, I've developed a habit of capturing most of my ideas. If a new idea is percolating, it often starts in my notebook. I scribble, sketch, mindmap, or type it up. And then, at a later stage, I scan these notes. I call the centralised location for all my ideas Personalised Learning System (PLS).

My PLS resides in a free piece of notetaking software called Obsidian. But for years, I was using another free application called Simplenote. The reason I made the switch to Obsidian was because of its ability to capture images and scanned documents (it does much more than that). Obsidian also has the crucial ability to create bidirectional links from one note to another. In other words, if I have an idea, I can create a link to a previous idea that I've made. Each note will show its relationship to the other. How cool is that?[4]

When you make it a discipline to commit your ideas to writing, this PLS becomes not so much as a "second brain" but an *extension* of your mind, a workshop space, allowing you to revisit, reflect, and retrieve your past ideas.

In the Elaboration phase, you might begin to hone in on existing ideas. Often, you'll also see connective tissues between seemingly disparate ideas that might turn out to be useful.

This is why I now rarely start any writing projects from a blank page. All I do is run a query search in my Obsidian vault, providing a few parameters (i.e., tags that I've labelled for each

---

[4]. If this piques your interest, I've made a series of videos on how I use Obsidian. See: bit.ly/darylobsidian

note), and then I can begin to string together the thoughts and ideas I have had in the past.[5]

Practise growing your own Personalised Learning System.

## B. Quality

If you find yourself needing to sharpen your work, here are some suggestions:

### 1. Be the Critic

Now, the Evaluation phase, is the time to formally invite your critical side to the decision-making boardroom. Let your critical side tear your idea to shreds.

Jerry Seinfeld has a system for his lifelong career as a stand-up comedian. He says that at the early stages of his writing process, he treats himself like an infant. "The key to writing is to treat yourself like a baby, very extremely nurturing and loving."[6]

In the editing stage, however, he would switch to being, in his words, a "hardass." Seinfeld says, "I'd then switch over to Lou Gossett in *Officer and a Gentleman* and just be a harsh prick, a ball-busting son of a bitch... 'That is just not good enough. That's got to come out,' or 'It's got to be redone or thrown away.'"[iv]

At the Evaluation phase, try not to sit in the same space as

---

5. In fact, much of the early seeds of this book were written in Obsidian.
6. Seinfeld's process is probably what makes him so good at his craft. In an interview on Lifehacker with a young up-and-coming comedian, he says that he writes every day. And to develop a writing streak, he says,

"[I have] a big wall calendar that has a whole year on one page and hangs on a prominent wall. The next step was to get a big red magic marker. For each day that I do my task of writing, I get to put a big red X over that day. After a few days you'll have a chain. Just keep at it and the chain will grow longer every day. You'll like seeing that chain, especially when you get a few weeks under your belt. Your only job is to not break the chain." See lifehacker.com/jerry-seinfelds-productivity-secret-281626 where you normally do your creative work. Dissociate from your creative side. Imagine that you are in a newsroom. The uptight editor-in-chief is seated in his glass office, away from the fray of the journalists and writers, banging frantically at their keyboards.

Practise being the editor-in-chief. Let it rip.

## 2. Gather a Feedback Group

Get others to give you feedback. Ask these people specific questions that you have doubts about.

In the process of writing this book, after being knee-deep in the manuscript for some time, I feel like I've lost objectivity to see it for what it is. So I send it off to a group of beta readers.

And even though I have drawn on my own roaring inner critic to edit the manuscript, I still have an external editor who takes a fine-toothed comb and forensically examines the writing as a whole, as well as on a line-by-line basis.[7]

Not all feedback is created equal. When you try to please everyone, you end up pleasing no one. So only pay attention to the feedback of people whose opinion you value.

Practise soliciting feedback and feed-it-forward to make the ideas better.

## 3. Deadline Before Death

Deadlines are less helpful at the Seeding and Elaboration phases, because during those early stages, we need coddling and gentleness and room for exploration. (Again, think of Seinfeld's idea of treating yourself like a baby.)

However, in the Evaluation phase, deadlines provide valuable pressure. If you don't have a boss to breathe down your neck, hold yourself accountable to complete the project by a certain

---

7. I can't thank each of you enough. See the Acknowledgements page.

timeline. Or ask a close friend to hold you accountable. Tell that person why this matters to you.

Remind yourself: What are you trying to create? (See #1 What Do You Want to Create, in Paradox 2. Future). Write your answer down.

As a commitment device for an important project, if you don't complete the task by your stipulated time, go so far as to agree to donate to an organisation that you hate.

One other reason for setting up a deadline at this final stage: It's tempting to keep refining and tweaking, in the name of trying to improve that finished piece of work. But the truth is, most things will feel like it's never "done." It's apt that an artist says that an album is "released." It's out there. It's no longer in your hands to keep tweaking. It's free—from you messing with it.

Celebrate when you're done. You are now free. Your work is *released*.

Practise using the pressure of deadlines at the Evaluation Phase.

## BROADEN YOUR NATURE

If you are high in Conscientiousness, you might be prone to wanting to do things perfectly and aim for quality right from the get-go. Conversely, if you are low in Conscientiousness combined with high Openness to Experience, you might be disorganised and easily pulled into a variety of different interests and rabbit holes, and not sequencing your creative process into stages. Watch out for both extremes. Use the suggestions in the Counsel section to guide you.

---

*See Related Paradoxes: 2. Present/Future, 12. Recovery/Stress, 13. Stillness/Movement, 14. Input/Output.*

# PARADOX 12. RECOVERY/STRESS

## CONTRADICTION

Most people seem to believe that high stress levels are the number one issue. But the inability to rest and recover from stress, no matter how much, is perhaps most insidious in our society.

*Do I need to learn how to rest, or do I need to learn how not to stretch myself too thinly?*

## CLARITY

### A. Recovery

Stress is not the problem; a lack of recovery is.

Physiologist Martin Moore-Ede presents an assessment of this modern-day conundrum:

> At the heart of the problem is a fundamental conflict between the demands of our man-made civilisation and the very design

of the human brain and body.... We (have become) machine-centred in our thinking—focused on the optimisation of technology and equipment—rather than **human-centred**—focused on the optimisation of human alertness and performance.[i]

We are misled to treat ourselves more as Machine and less as Flesh, and thus push ourselves into sheer exhaustion and burnout. As noted by Jim Loehr and Tony Schwartz, the authors of *The Power of Full Engagement*, "We have to learn to live our own lives as a series of sprints—fully engaging for a period of time, and then fully disengaging and seeking renewal before jumping back into the fray to face whatever challenges confront us."[ii]

A holiday in three months time is not the kind of recovery I'm referring to. By then, you will be too burned out to really enjoy the holiday. Besides, the lead-up to a big trip can be stressful in and of itself.

Loehr and Schwartz state that "our capacity to be fully engaged depends on our ability to periodically disengage."[iii] A vital principle is to appreciate and apply rhythmic breaks in your daily schedule. As it happens, our muscles grow not when we are exercising, but when we are resting.[1]

Recovery encompasses the process of healing and restoration following a physical or psychological challenge. An absence of recovery periods to interrupt prolonged stress leads to various adverse effects on the body and mind. Physically, it can weaken the immune system, elevate blood pressure, increase the risk of heart disease, disrupt sleep patterns, and contribute to conditions like headaches or gastrointestinal problems. Psychologically, it can lead to burnout, anxiety, depression, irritability, difficulty concentrating, and decreased overall well-being.

---

1. A contemporary field of study in exercise physiology has tapped into this important feature of stress and recovery, which is commonly called HIIT (High Intensity Interval Training, i.e., very short intense bursts of exercise paired with rest in-between). See Martin Gibala's book *The One-Minute Workout*.

## B. Stress

"Stress," said John O'Donahue, "is a perverted relationship with time."

The perversion is driven by pushing for more. To accomplish more, to be more productive, to expect more results in a given day. In other words, most of our stress manifests through our warped relationship with time.

On the other hand, avoiding stress is also not a way to live. Literally, the heart cannot be preserved by not exercising. Figuratively, the heart is weakened when we fortify ourselves against others for fear of getting hurt.

Stress-avoidance does not inoculate you from harm. This directly contradicts the science of hormesis. Greek for "to set in motion," "impel," and "urge on," hormesis is the phenomenon whereby exposure to low doses of a stressor induces beneficial effects in an organism.

Think of it this way: Machines are harmed by stressors, but living organisms are harmed by the *absence* of low-level stressors.[iv]

In other words, the intentional induction of a *chosen* pain can have beneficial effects on your dopamine system, which plays a crucial role in motivation, reward, pleasure, and regulating movement and emotional responses.[v] As most of us intuitively understand, the pursuit of pleasure does not lead to more pleasure. A hedonic lifestyle often leads to habituation, where repeated exposure to the same pleasurable thing can cause a decrease in its perceived enjoyment over time, requiring more or different stimuli in order to achieve the same level of satisfaction.

I met Sebastian in my practice when he was 17 years old. As a kid, Sebastian struggled to express his emotional side. His father, an immigrant from Italy, drummed into him what a man should and shouldn't be like ("You gotta be tough, or else they are gonna bully you," "Showing your emotions is weakness," "Don't be a crybaby."). On the inside, this view of masculinity was at odds for Sebastian. Meanwhile, his mother, meek and soft-spoken, seemed to know he had a more sensitive and creative side. She was stoic and took care of the household in spectacular fashion, without any complaints. Her love for and devotion to her family was communicated through her actions, and less through words.

Sebastian's mom could see that he was highly imaginative and less sporty than the other boys at school. He was reserved, but gravitated to literature and fine arts. She noticed how deeply absorbed he was when reading or drawing.

A week before Sebastian's sixteenth birthday, his mother was diagnosed with breast cancer. This hit the family hard, particularly Sebastian. He was overwhelmed by what was happening, as well as by the complex emotions he was experiencing. He dealt with his inner upheaval by staying out of the house as much as possible. He couldn't bear to face his mom, who was less than her usual self. Initially, when I asked about his reactions, Sebastian described himself as being "triggered" on a daily basis. "I feel overwhelmed and don't know what to do about it... I mean, there's nothing I can do to cure my mom. This is stressing me out," he said.

He hasn't lost his mom, but he is facing the uncertainty of what will happen when he does lose her. Family therapist and psychologist Pauline Boss calls this "ambiguous loss." This period of uncertainty mixed with layers of grief is also marked by guilt.

"I feel like shit about it," Sebastian told me.

Sensing an opportunity, I said, "You feel bad for your mom, but you also feel bad about the fact that you need to get out of the house, because it is confronting for you."

"Yeah."

"This stirs up a lot. Let's take a moment and think about this. What does your heart want you to do, even though it's hard?"

"I don't know..."

"Just take a moment... give this some room," I said.

Sebastian shifted his position in the chair and looked out the window. "I wanna sit beside my mom, and give her a hug." Tears well up. "I don't know. Why is this so hard?"

"I can hear that that's your intention. And most worthwhile intentions are hard..." I said.

Sebastian wrestled with his own conflict about this. "But this isn't exactly hard! I mean, I could just go up to my mom and have a chat, or see what kind of help she needs in the house."

Talking to a family member or lending a hand with the household chores doesn't necessarily classify as "hard stuff." However, many of the "hard" things we encounter are actually within (See #1. Approach the Internal Fear, in Paradox 7. Approach). In a difficult conversation, it might seem like the difficulty lies *between* two individuals, but actually, the difficulty we face is on the inside—what we are experiencing, the old stories that get stirred up, the challenges to our belief systems.

"I reckon that if you do connect with your mom, it speaks to who you really are, to the side that wants to come out more," I said.

"What do you mean?"

"You have a sensitive soul. I think you recognise that. You feel things deeply. You care about stuff more than you let others know. It's not a weakness; it's your superpower. It's who you are on the inside. Maybe it's time to let this river flow."

The journey that Sebastian had to take was not one of evading stress. Rather, it required getting closer to things he was avoiding, so that he could have a fighting chance to be true to his intentions.

---

There are times that we need to recoup, and there are times when we need to push ourselves to see what we are capable of.

*In this season of your life, where do you need to be on the spectrum of Recovery and Stress? (Mark an '<', '>' or 'x' on the line below).*

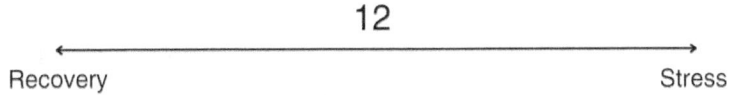

## COUNSEL

### A. Recovery

If you find yourself needing to learn how to rest and recover, here are some suggestions:

### 1. Rhythms of the Day

Learn to honour the daily rhythms of your body.

Why daily? Referred to as an internal biological clock, the circadian rhythm regulates various physiological processes in living organisms. This includes us humans. Our bodies are intricately linked to the circadian rhythm through a complex network involving the suprachiasmatic nucleus in the brain's hypothalamus (that's a mouthful of neuroscience), which serves as the master clock. This clock receives information from the eyes about light and darkness, helping to synchronise the body's internal processes with the external environment. We are highly influenced by the circadian rhythm, as it affects not only our sleep-wake cycle, but also hormone production, body temperature, metabolism, and cognitive functions.

In short, our bodies are in a musical relationship with the planet, interlocked with the rhythms presented to us from the cues of the external world.

Sure, there might be some days when you are in a mad rush to meet a deadline, or you might have a sick child to attend to, but generally speaking, not *all* days are like this. Respecting the rhythm of your body within the constraints of each day is akin to a musician playing a piece of music with an understanding that there is a tempo they are resting on. If we ignore the pulse of the song, we will be out of sync with the entire musical piece.

In a sense, when we fail to respect the rhythms of a day and behave like a caffeinated cotton-tail in response to whatever is thrown at us, we develop a sort of arrhythmia—we fall out of beat.

So what can we do to be in tune with our daily rhythm?

Start by designing your days.

You can do this at two levels: weekly and daily.

Before you begin each week, map out in your schedule your weekly rhythm of activities. Begin each day by reviewing your weekly schedule, and then zoom in on your intentions for the day. Why review your daily intention when you already have a weekly plan mapped out? Well, experience will tell you that things don't always go as planned. Plus, reviewing your daily intentions at the outset helps you focus your attention and calibrate your cognitive capacity to what lies ahead.

Nothing should stop you from planning monthly, quarterly, or yearly. However, when it comes to frontloading our minds and actively making execution plans for them, our working memory seems to do fine with plans for the week, and even better with plans for the day. This doesn't mean you shouldn't make longer-term plans. It simply means that we need to check in on a weekly and daily basis.

Given what we know about the circadian rhythm, here are some general suggestions on how to design your day:

- Whether you are a morning person or not, get some sun as soon as you wake up. Twenty minutes of direct

sunlight exposure sends a message to the pineal gland that it's daytime and reduces the production of melatonin, a sleep-hormone.[vi] This in turn promotes better sleep at night.
- Start each day with ten minutes of planning. Write your plan down on a piece of paper. Make clear to yourself what "done for the day" looks like for today.
- Block out two to three 60-minute chunks of undivided attention on activities that require focus. During these blocks, refrain from any "inputs"( i.e., messages, emails, social media).
- Block out one hour for a lunch break. This helps to break the day into halves, which makes it more manageable.
- Finally, each day, install periods of active recovery. (See next tip.)

If you don't plan for each day, your days will pass by default and not by design. (See #1. The Dailies, Strategies, Skills, Meals Framework, in Paradox 6. Change).

Practise designing your daily and weekly rhythms.

## 2. Active Recovery

Periods of recovery can look like one of the following:

- Short naps (Winston Churchill, Leonardo da Vinci, and top athletes take them; see Paradox 1. Self-Care).
- Walks (Henry Theoreau swears by this).
- Meditation (the great spiritual practitioners around the world prescribe this).
- A shower (everyone needs this).
- Listen to music (well, it's enjoyable).

The key is to make sure you schedule periods of recovery in a day. And given our hyper-productive lifestyle, I would encourage you to do any of these active recovery activities without the presence of your mobile device. Sure, you might need your phone to set the timer for a nap. Just don't engage in doomscrolling, thinking that it might help you fall asleep. The main principle for active recovery is to make it a *singular* activity. For instance, as a recovery activity, do not listen to music while reading the news. Listen to music with your eyes closed. Sing if you feel like singing. Dance if you feel like dancing. Let the music move you.

I recommend one recovery activity in the morning and one in the afternoon. (Recall the previous tip on scheduling your one-hour lunch break, in 1. Rhythms of the Day).

An important note: Most of us know that we need to rest, but many of us face serious difficulty allowing ourselves the space to rest and recover. We think we'll go all out Monday to Friday and then take a rest on the weekend. This is a deeply flawed gameplan.

I met David a year after he left a highly demanding managerial position in a mining company, which had required extensive travel. He was confounded by the fact he was experiencing bouts of anxiety, and that he couldn't "just chill" on the weekends and had to occupy himself with DIY projects or menial household chores. "If I become idle on weekends, I just fall asleep on the couch," he said. His wife was deeply concerned with his busy-bee disposition, and his kids could not get him to sit down and just play with them; he was too restless. It turned out that his new job, though less pressurising without the demanding travel requirements of his previous job, still pushed him hard from the moment he stepped into the office until the moment he left for home.

"Do you take a lunch break?" I asked.

"Nope," he replied without skipping a beat.

"Do you get out of your chair during the day, or take mini-breaks?"

"The only time I get away from my computer is to attend a meeting. And breaks? I used to smoke, so I would get a smoke break every now and then. But I've quit. Other breaks...hmm...To go to the bathroom?"

We ended up mapping out David's daily rhythm and began to implement active recovery periods throughout the day. Our aim was to break his schedule up with mini resets during the course of the day (see figure below). David was not keen on this idea at first, because he saw this as a hindrance to his productivity. Admittedly, David could see that he has a conscientious trait that could go to an extreme and manifest as workaholism. We processed his experience of anxiety, and decided that, if we treated anxiety as a signal and not the cause, perhaps we could reconfigure a more sustainable game plan.[2] It took him more than six weeks to implement this daily active-recovery strategy and to see its effects on his well-being. He first added a lunch break, and then he added some time to get away from his desk in the morning to meet other colleagues informally, and then he started to add a fifteen-minute walk each afternoon.

---

2. Some readers might suspect that David has ADHD, which could explain his restlessness and hyperactivity. He does not. These symptoms were not pervasive for him earlier in his life. In order to be diagnosed with ADHD, symptoms must be persistent and pervasive and cause impairment in two or more settings. Symptoms typically must have been present before the age of twelve.

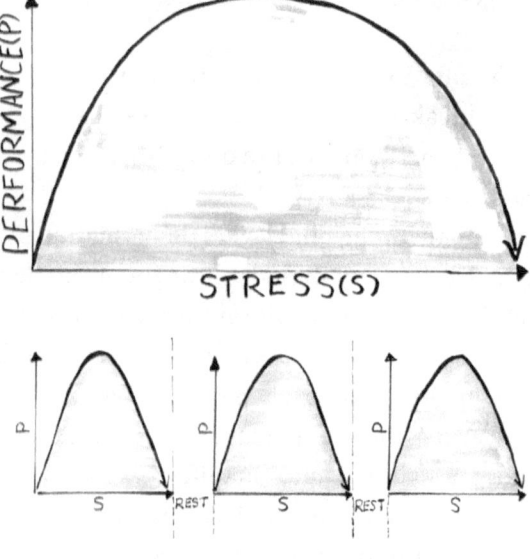

Practise the stress and recovery cycles on a daily level.

### 3. Give 80%, not 100%

In one of his newsletters, author Greg McKeown wrote,

> How many times have you heard the following phrases? No pain, no gain... Never stop grinding...Give it 110%.
> 
> These mantras, repeated over time, have led to two things: 1. A mass culture of burnout, especially among high achievers, and 2. People working harder and harder but getting worse results. Neither outcome is optimal.

His suggestion is counterintuitive, yet highly practical. The key is this: **Refrain from giving "maximum effort."**

This paradox is apparent when you examine the relationship between your daily and weekly life. On a daily level, you might be able to push hard to get stuff done while squeezing dry every available minute to tick off the items in your to-do list. Meanwhile, on a weekly level, you are depleted by the time the weekend arrives. You have things you want to do, but you are spent—there's little juice left in the tank. And then the cycle continues.

So what's the solution? McKeown suggests "working below your capacity."

Instead of pushing for 100% (or more) each day, set a compressed upper bound, say 75%, 80%, or 85%. Personally, I've stuck with 80%, just because I like the sound of it.

Here's how it plays out on a daily basis:

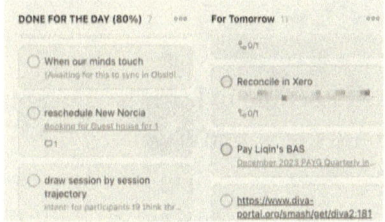

I kick off each day with my "Done for the Day (80%)" list. I add items to this list that I want to get done for today, and I might move items that I've previously parked in "For Tomorrow" (FT) into DD80. I might also move items from DD80 to FT that I thought could be tackled today, but realistically would go above my 80% Optimal Rule.

For me, the result of this practice has been profound. Not only am I planning and executing my clinical and work practices more intentionally, it also means that I do not go home on a daily basis giving my wife and kids leftover crumbs of myself.

To be clear, this does not mean that I do not give my 100% in what I do. The 80% Optimal Rule allows me to give my everything to what is in front of me, while managing how many things I give 100% to each day. For instance, I used to see seven or eight clients per day in my clinical practice. This was not sustainable. I would be totally worn out by the end of the day. Now, given what I know about my own capacity, I see six clients per day, with fifteen minutes gap between each person, plus a mandated block in my schedule at noon for lunch.

Some days, there is a temptation to do and achieve more, especially when I'm full of energy. The trick is not to fall for this temptation. Keep it at the 80% threshold. Plan ahead.

When we know how to plan for our days, we can plan for our years.

Practise giving 80%, not 100%, so that you can perform most optimally.

## B. Stress

If you find yourself needing to learn how to embrace purposeful stress, here are some suggestions:

### 1. Do Hard Things

The psychiatrist Annie Lembke was asked: If she could recommend only one thing that you can do to improve your mental health, what would that be? Her reply was, "**Do something that is hard.**"[vii]

This isn't a prescription for a miserable life. On the contrary, when we choose to exercise our free will and tackle something challenging, despite the obstacles and pains, we prove to ourselves we can do hard things. Dr. Lembke elaborates:

> Conventional wisdom tells us that when we are struggling, we should reward ourselves with some kind of treat: a nap, a piece of cake, a Netflix binge. But the truth is that the pursuit of pleasure leads to pain, and pain, in all its myriad forms, enhances our ability to feel pleasure.

There are some basic hard things everyone can do, as Lembke points out, "Move your body, take a cold shower, read a challenging book, write a thank-you note, clean out your closet, say you're sorry, order your coffee by talking to the barista rather than using the app." Note: Playing a challenging video game does not constitute doing a hard thing.

To get more specific on what hard things you can be engaging in, consult your Personal Paradoxical Profile. Depending on where you are and where you want to go, it should come as no surprise that the journey ahead will be filled with obstacles and challenges.

To know that we can get from A to B, and then from B to C, floods our nervous system with a cascade of neurological reward signals, such as the neurotransmitter dopamine. If we get easy hits of dopamine from passive activities and hedonic pleasures, though we get an initial spike of good feelings, with repeated use, our dopamine reward system enters into deficit. From an addiction perspective, we end up building tolerance. This neuroadaptation leads to users "chasing the high," which requires more and more of the stimulus. In her book *Dopamine Nation,* Lembke points out the paradox of hedonism: "The pursuit of pleasure for its own sake leads to *anhedonia,* which is the inability to enjoy pleasure of any kind."[viii]

Conversely, if we pay for our dopamine up front and actively work hard for it, not only will we build the resilience and robustness needed to strive for our personal goals, but the payoff and hard-earned pleasure will follow suit. When we seek dopamine for its own sake, we eventually pay the price. But when we work hard for our dopamine, we gain the rewards.

Renowned screenwriter, film producer, and director Aaron Sorkin keeps one equation in mind when writing his protagonists:

**Character = The Intentions + Obstacles**

Recall the meaning of the word "character," as mentioned in "Part I, What is Your Nature?". It's from the Greek word *kharakter*, meaning chisel. In a sense, when we move towards our intentions and face the inherent challenges along the way, our character is "chiselled" into being.

Pick one hard thing that is meaningful to you and do it. Don't worry about getting from A to Z. Focus on getting from A to B. This is how our character begins to grow, with its first step.

Practise doing hard things.

## 2. Circle of Development (COD)

One of my neighbours in Singapore used to say that our comfort zones can become our hell zones. The common trope is that we need to step out of our comfort zones... but where to exactly?

Our learning zones (LZs).

The space between our comfort zones and our learning zones is what Lev Vygotsky calls "the zone of proximal development."[ix]

Learning zones are not a comfortable territory to be in. When we stretch into the growth edge—from the comfort zone into the learning zone—we are moving from comfort to courage. Courage fuels action, and actions lead to new discoveries.

On the other hand, if we are not mindful of our limits, over-stretching our LZs can tip us into our panic zones (PZs). You know you are in your PZ when you are overwhelmed or flooded with strong emotions. If you are not cognisant of the impact of your history, being emotionally unregulated in the PZ can at times lead to re-traumatisation. Panic zone materials are usually either too far a stretch in terms of the content to be learned, or the topic at hand might have triggered ghosts of the past that have not been addressed.

The learning zone is the sweet spot between the comfort zone and the panic zone. Not too little, not too much.

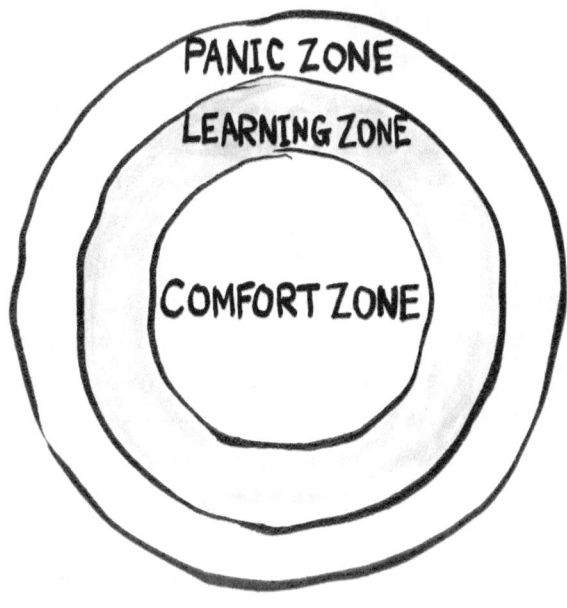

Take five minutes and ask yourself the following questions:

i. **Comfort Zone:** What are you used to doing on a daily basis without much effort?
ii. **Learning Zone:** If you are to work towards leading your life as best as you can, what do you need to learn to do? List them all down. Then rank them in terms of priority. Finally, circle the top three that will have the highest leverage in improving your life (See #3. Figure Out the What Before the How, in Paradox 8, Autonomy).
iii. **Panic Zone:** What is something you'd like to do but you know is too much of a stretch at this point in time?

Consider Nathan, a casually dressed, handsome-looking male in his early 30s who was dealing with a crippling level of social anxiety. Even though he would like to, he had struggled with hanging out with friends for the last five years. And now that he worked from home as a software engineer because of the COVID pandemic, he found himself even more reclusive. Being at home, tucked away from the social mingling of others and connecting with colleagues via video calls, was his "comfort zone," because there he was less confronted by his intense rumination on how others might be evaluating him. His family and friends suggest that he needed to "step out of his comfort zone" and connect more with others, that he needed to take a behavioural-exposure approach. But the issue was that the very thing that would be curative was also the thing that he feared. Working with Nathan, we needed to clarify his panic zone before proceeding to define his learning zone. "Everyone says I should go on a date... sign up for some dating app or something," he told me. "That's my panic zone at the moment." Labelling activities as panic-zone materials does not limit oneself. Instead, it serves as an intentional constraint. Constraints help us contain our efforts and stay focused on what's possible, and not get lost and overwhelmed by the "not yet possible."

Turning to his learning zone, Nathan felt he had wasted his young adulthood, living in fear of what others think of him. This has robbed him not only of a social life, but also of important experiences. After some back and forth, Nathan said, "I think my learning zone is to **learn to channel my focus on enjoying the moment, and less on trying to read others' minds.**" Nathan had tapped into a paradox: When we over-concern ourselves with what others are thinking, we neglect ourselves in that social situation. When we give credence to our comfort in a social context, we feel more at ease in our bodies while we are with others.

Two weeks later, Nathan decided to take up the invitation of an informal Friday-night office gathering. As he was getting ready to head out, his body was screaming "panic zone." But he knew this party was not exactly "too much" for him; it was just getting out of his comfort zone, which has become a hell zone for him.

At our next session, Nathan told me, "It didn't go as expected."

"What happened?" I asked.

"I realised that, actually, those people at work—as nice as they were—aren't my kind of people. I chatted with the main group a little. They were talking about politics and stuff, and then I found myself drifting off." I wondered whether this COD stuff was a write-off for Nathan, until he said, "The truth was, I was bored, and I wasn't enjoying myself." He shifted his attention to the musician that was playing. Thoroughly intrigued by this one-man band and his looping devices, he wandered closer to the stage. He bumped into two other colleagues, and they ended up chatting about how in awe they were of the performance, and later more about music in general.

"I had no idea those two fellas actually liked music as much as I did," Nathan said. "We made plans to catch up more regularly. We might go check out some vinyl down the road from our office. I think I should work from the office at least once a week. Might do me good."

Our COD is not static; it's dynamic. If there is movement and directionality in your development, what used to be learning zone material might evolve to into the domain of the comfort zone. Likewise, what was previously panic zone material can shapeshift into the realm of your learning zone.

What courageous step will you take?

Practise being cognisant of your circle of development and edging towards your learning zone.

## 3. No Substitution

When you are trying to do hard things, to stretch into your learning zone, the allure to do any *other* thing is very high.

For some people, being alone with their own thoughts and intentions can raise hell.

Timothy Wilson and colleagues conducted a series of experiments that showed people generally not only didn't like being with their own thoughts, they would rather get an electric shock than just spend time thinking.ˣ In one of the experiments, the researchers asked participants at the outset how much they would pay to avoid the shock during the thinking period. They concluded, "...What is striking is that simply being alone with their own thoughts for 15 min was apparently so aversive that it drove many participants to self-administer an electric shock that they had earlier said they would pay to avoid."[3]

Why are we so averse to being with our own thoughts? Perhaps it's because, as the researchers postulated, we have to be both the "scriptwriter" of what we are choosing to think and, at the same time, the "experiencer" of the meanderings of our thoughts.

We don't have to resort to shocking ourselves simply because we need to grapple with our own mind. One of the key ways to befriend our innerlife is to have a "no substitution" policy.

Let's say you are trying to write in your journal. It's relatively not a hard task, but it does require metabolic and cognitive resources. At this moment, strip away all possible substitutions. No checking your messages, no watching YouTube videos, no listening to your next podcast episode. Put your phone in another room. Eliminate everything else, except that one thing you intend to do. Write.

When you do not allow any kinds of substitution, procrastination will tempt you. At this point, please remember this suggestion once again: NO SUBSTITUTIONS. This also means not doing any other "productive" things. On many occasions while writing this book, I found myself visiting the front yard and mowing the lawn. Or I was tidying up the kitchen, or watering the plants. *I'll make my wife happy,* I'd say to myself. If I was

---

3. Specifically, 67% of the men and 25% of the women gave themselves at least one shock during the thinking period. The researchers posited that men tend to be higher in sensation-seeking, which led to higher rates of men shocking themselves.

outside writing at a cafe, my inbox was my go-to substitute for writing.

You and I have to refuse to let our attention get sidetracked. We have to move towards the direction of our intent.

Once you are out of the river of procrastination, you next have to face a *bug* that we have tried to eliminate in our modern lives, which actually turns out to be a *feature*: **Boredom**.

When you are trying to do something important and of value to you, procrastination might creep in. This is when boredom is your friend. *Sit in that chair.* Or as the author Steven Pressfield says, "Put your ass where your heart wants to be."[4] Guide your mind. Refrain from any other inputs (See_#2. Treat "More Planning and Learning" as Procrastination, in Paradox 14. Outputs).

Don't let boredom freak you out. It's ok. Boredom is the pain you avoid, but boredom is actually the antidote.

You are trying to do hard things. You are trying to grow in the direction you want to go. So let's go.

Practise putting your ass where your heart wants to be, with no substitutions.

## BROADEN YOUR NATURE

Every personality type needs periods of rest and recovery, but especially if you are high in Neuroticism, do not ignore the need for daily periods of recovery. When you burn yourself out, you are more likely to have negative emotional evaluations.

If you are low in Conscientiousness, make sure you take the time to plan out your schedule. Bake active periods of recovery into your routine. If you are highly Industrious—a facet of Conscientiousness—you might be highly driven, able to tolerate very stressful situations, and have no issues with "doing hard things." Still, know your upper limit of what done for the day

---

4. This is one of Steven Pressfield's book titles.

looks like (See Give 80%, not 100%). Be very cautious of not oversqueezing the day.

---

*See Related Paradoxes: 1. Self-Care/Self-Forgetting, 6. Acceptance/Change, 7. Approach/Retreat, 11. Quantity/Quality, 14. Inputs/Outputs.*

# PARADOX 13. STILLNESS/MOVEMENT

## CONTRADICTION

To see things clearly, we need stillness. To see what's ahead, we must keep moving.

Do I need to learn to be still, or do I need to learn to create more purposeful momentum in my life?

## CLARITY

### A. Stillness

Many of us have great difficulty being still. As mentioned in the previous Paradox. Stress, "#3 No Substitution," some would prefer an electric shock to being alone with nothing to do.

Stillness is closely related to Paradox 4. Solitude/Community. In the liminal space of change and loss, as you are Crossing Between Worlds, the practice of stillness helps you compose yourself, to see what is really in front of you instead of the projections that you overlay onto reality. "A good time to do nothing," says author Charles Eisenstein, "is any time you feel stuck." He adds,

> If we are stuck and do not choose to visit the empty place, eventually we will end up there anyway... The challenge in our culture is to allow yourself to be in that space, to trust that the next story will emerge when the time in between has ended, and that you will recognise it.... So please, if you are in the sacred space between stories, allow yourself to be there.[i]

When we allow ourselves to be still, our mind and body can catch up. When the waters are constantly disturbed by the movement of a passing boat, it is hard to see to the bottom of the lake.

A close cousin of stillness is silence. Silence has a purpose. "Silence is the mother of speech," wrote Thomas Merton[ii] One who speaks without the kinship of silence adds to the cacophony of noise. There is a wall of noise encircling us; most of its source is compactly tugged into that military-grade gadget you carry around with you. Its proper naming should no longer be a mobile phone. It should be called a hyper-information addiction machine.[1]

When we are still, when we are silent, when the dust has settled, finally, we get a chance to be present to the world around us, to the still, small voice inside of us, asking, requesting, and begging for us to listen.

But it can be hard to decipher the voices in our heads. Which ones are from the Ego, which ones are the internalised voices of other people's opinions, which ones are the ghosts from your past —which one should you heed?

Know this: you are not the voices in your head. You are the one hearing them.

---

1. A warning sticker should be added on the back of all phones, like those on cigarette boxes.

The first time I was at a one-day silent retreat, I felt like the chatter in my head was going to erupt. There was no escape from it. I was reminded to let the voice go and not get caught up in them; they were so loud I thought others would hear them. The next day, when I awoke, I felt a wave of calm. At the same time, it was as if my hearing and vision was sharpened. I felt more grounded and sensitised to the world around me.

When you are learning to be still, all sorts of mental constructions can creep up. Don't run away from them. This is a tunnel, not a cave. There is a way through. Stillness and silence, affords you the ability to see the inner and outer world with clarity.

## B. Movement

Our bodies are designed to move. If you go against this for too long, you'll pay a huge price.

We are not made to be sedentary.

Movement oxygenates the blood, and exercise strengthens our bodies, improves immune function, and reduces the chances of cardiovascular disease, hypertension, stroke, blood clots, frozen joints, impaired digestion, metabolic disease, and even skin problems.[iii] Mental health degrades with lack of movement. Seen in this light, compared to drugs, exercise can be seen as a "polypill," with fewer adverse effects, lower costs, and more preventative and multisystemic benefits to our health.[iv]

What is less obvious is that movement stimulates and challenges the brain by exposing it to unfamiliar environments. That is why moving in a natural environment is qualitatively different from running or walking on a treadmill, even though the physiological energy expenditure might be the same. We evolved to explore the world around us and to be stimulated by all that we see, hear, taste, smell, and experience.

When we don't move, we atrophy.

. . .

*Psychological Movement*

There is no doubt that we have a physiological need to move our bodies. We also have a need for *psychological* movement.

Psychological movement is a sense of making a series of autonomous progressive steps towards a desired goal, fuelled by curiosity and passion. Along the way, we develop a sense of mastery, and in turn, we experience one of the most engrossing neurochemical concoctions, called flow state.

The father of flow, Hungarian-American psychologist Mihaly Csikszentmihalyi (roughly pronounced as 'Cheek-Sent-Me-Ha-Yee') described active engagement in challenges as the following:

> The best moments in our lives are not the passive, receptive, relaxing times—although such experiences can also be enjoyable, if we have worked hard to attain them. The best moments usually occur when a person's body or mind is stretched to its limits in a voluntary effort to accomplish something difficult and worthwhile.
>
> Optimal experience is thus something that we make happen. For a child, it could be placing with trembling fingers the last block on a tower she has built, higher than any she has built so far; for a swimmer, it could be trying to beat his own record; for a violinist, mastering an intricate musical passage. For each person there are thousands of opportunities, challenges to **expand ourselves** [emphasis mine].[v]

Purposeful movement shapes us to become the person we can be.

One of the greatest struggles you will face as you are Crossing Between Worlds is creating a sense of self-directed psychological movement. It is most difficult at this point of your life simply because the path forward may not be obvious, as it can be fraught with ambiguity and doubt.

To feel like we are "moving" in the right direction reinforces what we are doing; it is an optimal experience to be engaged in life in this manner. To feel like we aren't making progress creates a negative loop that is hard to shake off. But by creating optimal experiences, we not only create a reinforcing positive pattern, we expand ourselves.

---

There are periods when we need to learn how to be still so as to see things clearly. And there are times when we need to move, in order to see what the future holds.

*In this season of your life, where do you need to be on the spectrum of Stillness and Movement? (Mark an '<', '>' or 'x' on the line below).*

13

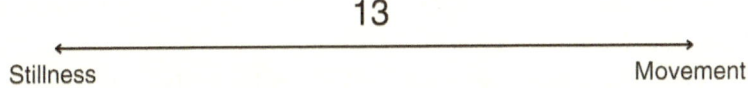

Stillness                                                              Movement

## COUNSEL

### A. Stillness

If you find yourself more on the side of needing to be still, here are a few ideas to tip you in the right direction:

### 1. Hearing Something New

Listen carefully to the world around you.

Pay attention to the natural environment you are in. Familiarity tempts us to switch off and not fully notice the ambient sounds around us. In his poem "Everything is Waiting for You,"

David Whyte writes, "Alertness is the hidden discipline of familiarity."[vi]

To be sure, noticing does not make you a master at stillness. But in order to notice the layers of sounds around you, you have to be still. (See #1. Sense, in Paradox 2. Present).

Practise the "hidden discipline" of noticing something new in the everyday, familiar world.

## 2. Writing

Some people write what they know. I encourage you to write *in order* to know.

Writing has a force-function: It slows you down. It's even slower if you write long-hand instead of typing on your computer.

It also makes you clarify what you are actually thinking and structure the heap of random thoughts bubbling inside into a (hopefully) coherent idea.

What to write? You could take a fully wide-open practice suggested by the famed author Julia Cameron called "Morning Pages" (i.e., "The first thing you do when you wake up, write whatever comes to mind in your stream of consciousness"),[vii] or you can use a guided approach. The latter strategy could involve writing based on a question that you pose to yourself (e.g., "What am I really afraid of if I leave this job?").

Questions are quests that you can go on. A good question invites us to explore areas of our lives we take for granted. If you are struggling with coming up with questions, ask yourself,

> "What has been on my mind lately?"
> "Why has this been on my mind?"
> "What are the inner struggles that I am facing?"
> "What is missing in my life right now that I need?"
> "How would I name the current season I am in?"

*"What is life asking of me?"*
*"What am I unwilling to feel?"*
*"What makes me come alive?"*
*When you write, you are still.*

Practise writing in order to know.

## 3. Meditation and Contemplation

The terms meditation and contemplation are often used interchangeably. There are many similarities between them, but it might be helpful to tease them apart.

I like to think of meditation as an active focusing of the mind. And contemplation is the more passive and receptive experience of opening the heart and mind. Meditation is an exercise of the mind, while contemplation means to empty it and avail oneself to stillness, remaining open and willing to be moved (see Willful vs. Willing). Meditation is to train the mind to "see" with a zoomed-in lens, while contemplation is to see with a wide-angle lens.

It's ok if the distinction doesn't make a lot of practical sense just yet. Let's take a step further.

*Meditation:*

Start by training your mind to focus at will on what you choose. Maybe it's mindful breathing, or focusing on a lit candle, or on the ambient sounds in your environment. This sounds simple, but it's not easy. When you are still and focused for a period of time, you will find your mind wandering like a goldfish. That's ok. As the Zen Buddhist priest Ruth Ozeki would suggest, "Return." Gather your focus once again. Come back to the practice.

*Contemplation:*

Considered to be one of his "Buddhist brothers" by the Dalai Lama, Catholic Trappist monk Thomas Merton was steeped in an interdisciplinary approach to spirituality, exploring various faiths such as Buddhism, Taoism, Hinduism, and Sufism. Merton said,

> Contemplation is the highest expression of man's intellectual and spiritual life…It is spiritual wonder. It is spontaneous awe at the sacredness of life, of being. It is a vivid realisation of the fact that life and being in us proceed from an invisible, transcendent, and infinitely abundant source. Contemplation is, above all, awareness of the reality of that source.[viii]

So how do I practise contemplation? Among others, Merton has written extensively on this subject.[ix] Here is my take on contemplation:

**Open yourself to all that is in front of you with no expectations, no goal, no agenda, no outcome. Allow yourself to be touched, moved, and inspired.**

This might sound a little new-agey, but it's not easy to arrive at this stage of mind. Our minds are often entrained by a goal that we are pursuing, even if it's just a to-do list for groceries. Either that, or our minds are *entranced* by our screens and we get sucked in.

Which is why meditation is required. Meditation is like a pathway leading to the door of the house. We have to guide our minds to get there. When we do, we let go and allow ourselves to be fully immersed in and experience this "spiritual wonder." No goal, no agenda, no outcome.

Spend five to ten minutes meditating i.e., using whichever exercise you prefer to focus your mind (zoomed-in lens). Then spend another five to ten minutes contemplating, i.e., letting go of control and opening up your focus (wide-angle lens).

Practise actively guiding your mind through meditation, and practice letting your mind experience contemplation.

## B. Movement

If you find yourself more on the side of needing to add movement in your life, consider the following:

### 1. Walk, Saunter, and Walk-and-Talk

We are made to move.

Go for walks or jogs out in nature. Every walk that you take in the park or in the bush requires you to make scores of micro-adjustments to foot pressure, angle, and pace—without even thinking about it. Along with honing our sense of navigation and our memory systems, these adjustments, author Daniel Levitin notes, "stimulate the neural circuitry of your brain in the precise way that it evolved to be used." Exercise stimulates the hippocampus, critical to memory formation and retrieval. "This is why so many studies show that memory is enhanced by physical activity," says Levitin.[x]

Note: Walking on a treadmill is not the same as walking in the natural world.

You might also want to engage in a specific type of walking: Sauntering. To *saunter* is to walk in a leisurely manner, without a specific destination or goal in mind. This can also be a kind of mindful walking, where you pay attention to your surroundings. This can be relaxing.

Finally, the next time you schedule a one-on-one meeting with a colleague or a chat with a friend, instead of conversing at a cafe, try having a walk-and-talk meeting.

Daniel Kahneman and Amos Tversky, two prominent psychologists known for their groundbreaking work and close partnership in behavioural economics, decision-making, and cognitive biases, often engaged in a practice they called "walking and talking." This involved taking long walks together while discussing their research ideas and findings.

There is an art to walking, advocated by Henry David Thoreau. He said, "Me thinks that the moment my legs begin to move, my thoughts begin to flow."

Practise the art of walking, and of thinking with your feet.

## 2. Psychological Movement: The Vitality of Going Somewhere.

There are three questions to guide you as you engage in psychological movement, especially when you are making significant changes during these crossroads:

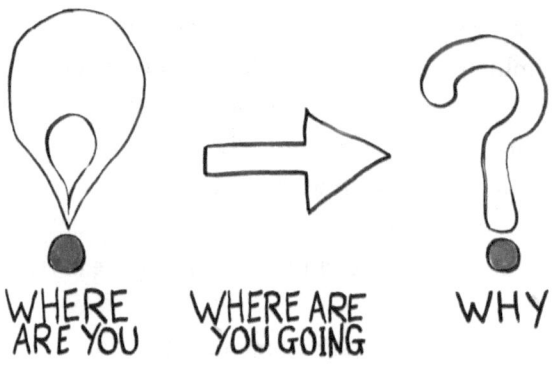

### i. Where Are You?

Thankfully, if you have worked through the Personal Paradoxical Profile, you have already answered this question, "What Is the Current Season of Your Life?"

This is synonymous with figuring out "Where Are You?" Before figuring out where you need to go, knowing where you are is vital. Before the advent of Google Maps, if a friend asked for directions to your home, you would first need to find out where he was coming from.

. . .

## ii. Where Are You Going?

*Alice: "Would you tell me, please, which way I ought to go from here?"*
*Cheshire Cat: "That depends a good deal on where you want to get to."*
*Alice: "I don't much care where—"*
*Cheshire Cat: "Then it doesn't matter which way you go."*

— *Lewis Carroll, Alice's Adventures in Wonderland.*

"Where Are You Going" is not just about goals. This is about what you want to be different in your life, what needs to change, what you need to let go of, and who you want to become. It's somewhat cliche to say that we are all on a "journey," but the truth is we are all moving and going somewhere. The real question is, are you going where you want to go?

Sometimes the changes you make will take you to an actual different geographical location. But more often than not, where you are "going" is more a psychological experience.

Kenneth knew that filing for a divorce was inevitable. He could not see how their relationship could go on after his wife cheated on him. They tried couples therapy. He saw his part in the breakdown of their marriage too. He was hardly present at home, caught up in his new business and justifying it by saying he was providing for the family. He could not imagine being single. Worse, he could not imagine being away from his seven-year-old son. He made a commitment to himself that after the divorce, he was going to spend twice the amount of time he had been with his son, and half the amount of time at work. He would have to break up with his wife, but not with his son. He knew that his son found it hard to make that distinction, but Kenneth realised he was in a season of separation, and where he wanted to go was to turn things around and be an active and present father; unlike his workaholic father.

. . .

### iii. Why Are You Going There?

> "If you have your why for life, you can get by with almost any how."
>
> — *Friedrich Nietzsche*[2]

Knowing your Why is the foundational force that will propel you forward. Without a Why, no matter how clear the first two factors of "Where Are You?" and "Where Are You Going?" are, you will not be able to sustain your efforts. Simon Sinek says, "Working hard for something we don't care about is called stress; working hard for something we love is called passion."[xi]

Here's one way to think about your Why. Suppose you decided to plant a lemon tree. There are the physical materials, the genetic blueprint, and the natural processes that enable the growth of the tree. Aristotle would label these the Material Cause (i.e., soil, water, nutrients, sunlight), Formal Cause (i.e., DNA, which determines the tree's species, structure, and growth patterns), and Efficient Cause (i.e., photosynthesis). The fourth and last Cause, which Aristotle calls the Final Cause, meaning "What is it ultimately for?," could be many different things.[xii] One person could have planted the lemon tree to simply grow lemons to use for cooking, another could have planted it simply to fill an area in the garden, and another person could have planted it in commemoration of a relative who has passed on.

Aristotle's Final Cause can serve to guide you as you are

---

2. This quote has been with me for many years since reading Viktor Frankl's seminal book *Man's Search for Meaning*. I later learned that the original quote was from Friedrich Nietzsche's *Twilight of the Idols*. Curiously, the full aphorism was less inspirational, and more of a jab at the English. It read, "If you have your why for life, you can get by with almost any how—. Humanity does not strive for happiness; only the English do" Nevertheless, the application of this phrase is still useful.

Crossing Between Worlds. Final Cause is not just the end result—it's the end, the beginning, and the process of your transition. Final Cause is not just your goals. It's the purpose behind your goals—it's the reason you make goals in the first place; it's your ultimate Why.

The questions you need to ask yourself are:

*Why do I want to make this change?*

*Why does this matter to me in a deep and personal way?*

The reason I like Aristotle's philosophy of the Final Cause is because it asks, at bottom, **what is the Why *behind* the Why?**

Clarifying your Final Cause is an important exercise. Here's my suggestion, taking it sequentially: First, map out your storyline. Second, construct your final cause.

*a. Map Out Your Storyline:*

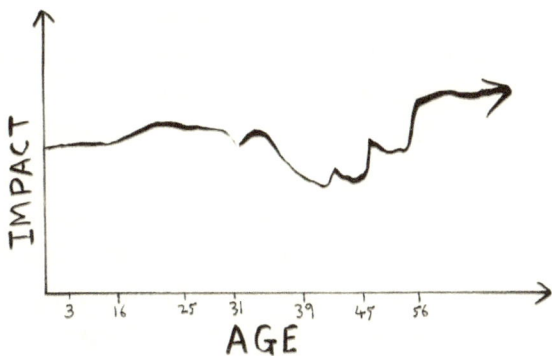

- Take a piece of paper, draw a Graph. The X-axis is your age, and Y-axis is the degree of impact an event has on you (i.e., positive impact will be marked higher, and negative impact lower. The horizontal middle will be neutral).
- Dig into your memory. Recall significant events from your history. Start as young as you can remember.

- Think of three kinds of events: **High Points, Low Points,** and **Turning Points.** High Points will be plotted higher on the Y-axis, Low Points will be scored lower on the Y-axis, and Turning Points could be anywhere on the graph, subjected to your personal evaluation of the experiences. Turning points can sometimes feel terrible in the moment, but have a positive impact in retrospect.

Turning Points could also be thought of as "transformational moments," that is, incidents that changed your belief about yourself and/or the world. These significant moments can also come from someone who said something surprising about you.

In my all-boys secondary school, Mr. Crawshaw read a composition to the entire class. After he was done, he said, "This writer is poetic." The class burst into a mocking fit of laughter.[3] He called my name to pick up the composition from him, and I suddenly realised it was my work he had been reading. The flood of embarrassment lasted for days, and the teasing from my classmates continued. But years later, Mr. Crawshaw's remark changed how I felt about myself. Even though I wasn't doing well academically in secondary school, I internalised the possibility that, actually, I can write. For me, this moment was a turning point.

Now, why should you map out your storyline? Simon Sinek, David Mead, and Peter Docker write, "Discovering your WHY is like panning for gold in the river of the past: the gold is there, lost in the debris of the river, hidden by rushing water."[xiii] In short, your past can reveal a lot to you.

### b. Construct Your Final Cause

Now that you are done with your storyline, take a moment to zoom out and look at the bigger picture. Do you notice any

---

3. In case you are wondering why they were laughing, boys at that age behave differently when it's *all* boys only. We make a ruckus at nearly everything possible.

patterns, any recurring themes? Share your storyline with someone you trust. Talking about it helps to clarify your thoughts.

Next, start to draft your Why. Sinek and colleagues suggest a useful format:

"To _____, So That _____."

The first blank is about contribution, and the second is about impact.

Looking back at my storyline and reflecting on where I was, after a couple of iterations, I wrote the following:

"To *touch, move, and inspire others as others have done for me*, so that *they will feel a piece of heaven, come alive, and in turn share that with others*."

A few things to note. Your Final Cause—your Why—should not be self-serving; it should be others-focused. If your Why is not contributive to others, it's probably self-serving. I once worked with a musician who was suffering from severe stage anxiety before her performances. As we explored her Why, she said she wasn't in it for the money. However, after some discussion, she admitted that all that mattered to her was how well-liked and adored her music was. She was a little perturbed when I told her that wasn't a good Final Cause. "That's also the reason your anxiety is flaring up," I added. Her Final Cause had to be about her fans, not about her (see Paradox 1. Self-Forgetting). She got caught up in how she was perceived to be and lost track of the experience of the people who go to her performances. She returned some weeks later and said, "Here's my Why: I want to bring joy to others." This was not just a shift of perspective; it was a shift of reason, motivation, and direction. Her focus is now on each person in the crowd. Her stage anxiety dissipated, because she's no longer hyper-conscious of herself.[xiv]

Your Why is not domain-specific. It will permeate across the personal and professional sides of your life. Even though you might be working through changes in specific areas of your life (i.e., personal, relational, or work), your Why cuts across the board. Given the generalisibility of this exercise, give yourself ample time to work through it. You need not finish it in one sitting.

Practise articulating and refining where you are, where you are going, and your Why. Share them with those you trust. This three-part structure will be the life-blood that takes you forward as you are Crossing Between Worlds.

### 3. Improving vs. Improvising

To improve is to work on something and "push" hard to get better. To improve is to keep trying your best. Trying your best tightens you up, and you become inflexible and rigid. Besides, what really is your best anyway?

To *improvise*, on the other hand, is to open yourself to emergent possibilities, allowing yourself to be "pulled" by what is "not yet seen ahead of time," which is the meaning behind the Latin *improvisus*. To improvise is to *not* try your best. To improvise is to open yourself to the surprises ahead and allow yourself to be altered. (See Paradox 5. Yes).

Kevin Kelly suggests, "Rather than steering your life to avoid surprises, aim directly for them."[xv]

Unlike a classical musical notation, there is no "fixed" score to the road as you are Crossing Between Worlds. Even if there were cookie-cutter recommended paths ahead, you still might want to create your own road.

## Paradox 13. Stillness/Movement

The path of least resistance might not be the prescribed path.[xvi]

The only way to make progress is by taking steps forward, one foot at a time. Years ago, before we got married, my wife and I were driving in the rural areas of Queensland. This was the first time I had driven somewhere without streetlamps on the road; it was pitch black. I turned on the car's floodlights, but I couldn't keep them on due to traffic in the opposite direction. I was beginning to panic. "I can't see far..." I said. And then my wife said to me, "The only way to see further is to keep moving. Just go slower." (See #3. Act Before You Think, in Paradox 5. Yes).

Said in another way, to improvise is **less "think before you act" and more "act in order to know."**

At times, attempts to improve and engage in purposeful movement towards a goal can paradoxically impede progress (see Paradox 11. Quantity). Our efforts start to get in the way of real progress.

When you are trying to improvise, be less in Defense Mode

and more in Discovery Mode. When you are in Defense Mode, you scan for dangers and threats, you fixate on what you might lose, and your focus is on safety. When you are in Discovery Mode, you scan for opportunities, you think about what you might gain, and your focus is on what you might find.[xvii]

Here's a list of things you can do to flex your improvisational skills:

*i. Self:*

- Sing an impromptu song about your Monday blues (see #4. Sing, in Paradox 2. Present).
- Do something unplanned. Stop by a restaurant that you've never gone to before (don't look up the reviews). Go to that beach spot that you drive by all the time.
- Take a different route home. Notice what surprises you in your surroundings. (see #3. Involuntary Gratitude, in Paradox 15. Surrender).

*ii. Relationships:*

- Have an agenda-less conversation with someone. Treat it like a game of ping-pong. Keep the ball going (See #2. Say "Yes! And…," in Paradox 5. Yes).
- Do something spontaneous with your family this weekend (see #3. Invitation to Play Together, in Paradox 8. Belonging).
- Go along with what your partner likes. Stop "Yes…but-ing" them. Let go of your own plans (see #2. Say "Yes! And…, in Paradox 5. Yes).

*iii. Work:*

- Sequence a brainstorming session with colleagues by first allowing each person to think through on their

own, followed by a group discussion. See every idea, big or small, as a gift. Allow experimentation of ideas .
- For a specific task, swap roles with a coworker from a different department.
- When something doesn't go quite as planned, say to yourself, "This is exactly what I need." Adapt. Learn. Let go of your expectations (see Paradox 15. Surrender).

Here's the disposition you want to have: **Prepare like an accountant, but engage like a jazz musician.** Open yourself to the myriad of possibilities, try every possible option on for size before you make up your mind. You are learning to discover more about you and what's calling out to you.

To be clear, there is some risk involved in this approach. It might not yield immediate results. That's OK if you are not in Defense Mode and are willing to learn and let go of controlling every outcome (see Paradox 15. Surrender). Even when you hit a dead end, that's ok. There is always something to learn if you are in Discovery Mode.

Practice improvising to get you moving, so that you can discover the land of possibilities in front of you.

## BROADEN YOUR NATURE

If you are highly enthusiastic, restless, and Extroverted, you might find Stillness challenging at first. On top of that, if you are also high in Neuroticism, Stillness might raise significant discomfort in you. Start by practising Stillness in smaller doses, or take mindful walks with a friend. Gradually increase the time and level of focus. You might also benefit from a guide to help you find the types of practices that suit you best.

If you are low in Openness to Experience, you might find the ideas in #3. Improving vs. Improvising somewhat of a challenge at first. The ideas aren't difficult, but the shift in perspective might be unusual for you. Allow yourself to be playful.

---

*See Related Paradoxes: 1. Self-Care/Self-Forgetting, 2. Present/Future, 4. Solitude/Community, 5. Yes/No, 11. Quantity/Quality, 15. Control/Surrender.*

# PARADOX 14. INPUT/OUTPUT

## CONTRADICTION

It is easy to get stuck on "feeding" yourself with inputs without risking yourself by putting out your creations. Meanwhile, no one is going to take care of the quality of your inputs.

Do I need to intentionally curate my inputs, or do I need to learn to produce more?

## CLARITY

Artists are familiar with this paradox. And most of us feel the pressure of the outside world, which measures us on the quality of our output.

### A. Input

Food is information. And information is food.

More than ever before, we are nudged to become consumers of low-grade information. This constant hijacking our attention has turned us into dull-witted procrastinators.

As mentioned in "#1. The Dailies, Strategies, Skills, Meals (DSSM) Framework" (Paradox 6. Change), for better or for worse, **you are what you feed.**

If information is food, we have become a society that is on a diet of coke and double-cheeseburger type of content.

**Your well-being is highly dependent on your well-doing.** Your job and your self-improvement efforts are dependent on what you feed your mind. If you exclusively feed your mind a diet of cute Instagram memes and short clickbait videos, you are training it to focus like a squirrel. We have become a society of shallow thinkers.[i]

This might sound like an exaggeration. At the time of this writing, in the early 2020s, many of us have lost the ability to hold our attention on one task for more than ten minutes. Do you find yourself reaching for your phone while watching a movie? Cognitive science indicates that, after we switch tasks, we need about 20 minutes to focus on the new task. If we want to reach a flow state, we must train our focus. Flow follows focus.[ii]

The cost of a scattered mind is high. It isn't just that we are habituating ourselves to inattentiveness, or even self-inducing attention deficit hyperactivity disorder (ADHD), but we're also losing the ability to hone in on what is worth our attention, what is important, what we care about, what matters most in this mortal life. In short, it's not just our attention that is lost. Our *intention* is also thwarted (See How Tech Is Trapping Us Between Worlds, in Part I: The Framework).

For better or for worse, *no one* is going to take care of your inputs. If we do not take care of what we feed our minds, we become not only easily distracted, but also addicted to the stimuli served up by the dopamine cartel of Silicon Valley and its ilk. Instead of watching a movie, reading a book, or even listening to a three-minute song, we are now lured to become junkies of fifteen-second Shorts and Reels, lifeless and reductionist book summaries, and 24-second TikTok sugar-coated pop melodies.

This pursuit of the next dopamine hit, something new and interesting to give us a quick buzz, puts us on an endless and aimless cycle. As mentioned in "#1. Do Hard Things" (Paradox 12. Stress), this pursuit of pleasure actually leads us to less pleasure.

This, dear reader, is a **drug-seeking cycle.** Behind every web experience, social media feed, and infinite pit of digital inputs, legends of software engineers are designing and tweaking their platforms to turn you, a "user," into a junkie.[1] Don't be fooled just because they aren't using pills and needles to get you hooked. These companies have gotten so big that even government bodies around the world have a hard time stopping them.

In an interview with economist Tyler Cowen, prolific music writer Ted Gioia was asked what advice he had for others. Here's what Gioia said:

> In your life, you will be evaluated on your output. Your boss will evaluate you on your output. If you're a writer like me, the audience will evaluate you on your output.
>
> But your input is just as important. If you don't have good input, you cannot maintain good output. The problem is no one manages your input. The boss never cares about your input. The boss doesn't care about what books you read. Your boss doesn't ask you what newspapers you read. The boss doesn't ask you what movies you saw or what TV shows or what ideas you consumed.[iii]

## B. Output

Even if you become a knowledge junky (e.g., read a lot, listen to

---

[1]. On another level, these companies are also getting you hooked on being one of their dealers. This is called being an "influencer." Author Simon Sinek calls the influencer not a boss of their own, but a freelance employee of the Algorithm. The Algorithm is their boss.

podcasts, attend all kinds of workshops and conferences), all that wisdom is only worth what you contribute to the world.

An overconsumption of inputs can sometimes be a tactic of procrastination—something I'm prone to.

To create something and release it—be it an idea at a board meeting, a piece of art, a music composition—is a bold act. Outputting from a place of generosity is an act of gracious self-forgetting (see Paradox 1. Self-Forgetting), which entails a sort of gift-giving of what's inside you. "Here. This is what I have to give, and I hope you find it valuable." Seen in this light, *outputs are gifts to the world.*

But what exactly are your valuable outputs as you are Crossing Between Worlds? Valuable outputs are not just a think-aloud of our rambling thoughts. Valuable outputs first germinate in the consideration between what I have to offer and what's going to be valuable to others. And what I have to offer is dependent on the juxtaposition of our gifts and the minglings of high-quality inputs.

Wisdom-hoarding does not build culture. Wisdom-sharing is an invitation to bring the gift of stories. We all need a diet of soul-quality stories. Not only do others benefit from this, but when we teach it, we are the ones that learn it best.

Ultimately, the aim of this book is to help you bring forth your true gifts and contribute to the world around you. **Your gifts are meant to be given away.** "Is it too much to ask, to live in a world where our human gifts go toward the benefit of all?" says Charles Eisenstein.[iv]

**The project of our lives is not about self-improvement.** Rather, it is more about going back to our original self, figuring out our gifts, what's natural to each of us, and to allow that to come forth more intimately so that you become more fully alive.

As stated at the outset of this book, our Nature is designed to be nurtured, informed by our needs. Without this nurturance, even motivated individuals will end up on the hamster-wheel of constant addictive self-improvement cycle.

Sr Joan Chittister points out, "Life is not meant to be a burden. Life is not a problem to be solved. It is a blessing to be celebrated."[v]

Discover and celebrate your gifts. Our generous gift-giving then has the potential of becoming high-grade inputs for others, which just might touch, move and inspire others to be part of the circle of gift-giving (see #3 Vocalising Appreciation, in Paradox 9. Receiving Care).

---

The quality of our outputs depend heavily on the quality of our inputs. Nevertheless, at different junctures, you need to pay more attention to one or the other.

*In this season of your life, where are you needing to be on this spectrum of Input and Output? (Mark an '<', '>' or 'x' on the line below).*

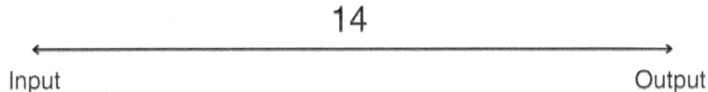

## COUNSEL

### A. Inputs

If you find yourself more on the side of needing to take care of your inputs, consider the following:

## 1. Protect Time and Attention with High-Quality Inputs

Our minds are like LEGOs. Clarity of thought is cultivated one brick at a time, one on top of the other. The outcome of this LEGO play is a LEGO house (or a castle, or a plane—you get to pick).

Engaging in a ceaseless form of content consumption is like all the LEGO pieces that you need (and more), and none are stacked upon each other. The outcome of this type of LEGO play is a heap of mess.

So what do we do instead? Rather than fish from the contaminated pond, cast your rod in the ocean of high-quality inputs. What are high-quality inputs? Instead of relying on algorithms to determine the type of content you consume, develop a habit of picking what *you* would like as a source of input. High-quality inputs are content that hold the possibility of enriching you, matching your growth edges, that speak to the needs of the current season that you are in. These are often long-form, timeless pieces, and not bite-size quotes or summaries of ideas.

For instance, instead of reading blogs or Web articles, read a book or listen to an audiobook. Think of this as "stretching" your attentional muscles to think deeply. In order to develop a sensibility needed to navigate the challenges of Crossing Between Worlds, we need to train our minds to go further than we are used to.

As you engage in high-quality inputs, safeguard your intentions by protecting your attention. You need to manage your attention when you decide to sit down and engage in a book. Many would advise putting your phone in another room. I would take it a step further: Install a blocker on all of your devices. Set it to designated times to disallow you to open specific applications and websites.

The guiding principle behind this is to **make a big decision**

**to avoid small decisions** (see_#3. Make a Big Decision to Avoid Small Decisions, in Paradox 5, No).

One of my downfalls is Email. I love my Inbox. I love hearing from people. To me, I treat my emails like precious old-school letters. I do my best to respond to people who write to me, which could be from people I consult and supervise, or related to my writings for "Frontiers of Psychotherapist Development" or my other blog site, "Full Circles: Reflections on the Inner and Outer Life."

But most of us end up using email as an instant messaging platform. A large part of the daily workflow was that I kept my email app open and checked it every now and then. It is as if I interrupt my task and walk to the letterbox every 30 mins to see if "I've got mail."

If you are like me, reflexively checking your emails when you really don't need to, use an app blocker like Freedom or Cold Turkey. I've made a pre-commitment not to check my Inbox between 11pm to 12pm the next day. I have no access to it when I go to bed and in the mornings. In addition, when I am working on something that requires my full attention, I turn on Freedom to block access to my emails, in case my monkey-mind acts on its own. It sounds absurd that I would be trying to jailbreak into my inbox when I clearly set out not to touch it in the first place, but it has happened several times.

Your pitfall could be other things like Facebook, news feed, Youtube, porn, or online-shopping. Make a big decision to avoid small decisions and put a lock on it, especially for times when you are really trying to nourish yourself.

Another straightforward step you can take: Turn off notifications on *all* of your devices. You could simply turn to Airplane or "Do Not Disturb" mode on your phone when you are trying to focus. Again, if you were to "make a big decision to avoid small decisions," batch all of your non-urgent notifications into a scheduled notification setting. In other words, instead of getting alerts and bings whenever a feed comes in at random, you get them all at a predetermined time. This makes a huge difference on your ability to experience flow states. It's worth repeating: flow follows focus.

While short-form content feeds us with a quick-release of dopamine which doesn't last, high quality long-form content nourishes us for a slow-release of reward that is much more fulfilling—and beneficial.

Practise entraining your mind to consume longer-form content, like a book or a movie. Take care of your inputs.

## 2. Active Engagement with the Content

> "Gunpowder destroys itself along with its victim, while a book can keep on exploding for centuries."
>
> — *Christopher Morley, author of* The Haunted Bookshop.

I love books.

Growing up, I wasn't really a book lover. Not until Rachel, my maths tutor, gave me Sue Townsend's book, *The Secret Diary of Adrian Mole*. Even though it was fiction, there was a truth (and humour) that shook me up. I was 13–14 years old, and it was such a revelation to learn about someone's inner-life.

If thought is a monologue, reading a book is a kind of dialogue. It's a conversation with someone who has thought about a single topic for a very long time.

Fiction is not made up of lies. Good fiction provides truth told through archetypal stories.

Non-fiction is (often, not always) made up of facts. Non-fiction provides information that can serve you as a rough map to the territory that you are embarking on. Wanna improve family life? Read Bruce Feiler's *The Secrets of Happy Families*. Wanna improve your sex life? Read Laura Richardson's *Slow Sex*. Wanna learn to be productive? Read Cal Newport's *Deep Work*... the list goes on.[2]

Now that you are engaged in long-form content, like reading a book, here's my suggestions:

*Fiction:*

Sometimes you are reading fiction for leisure, and that's fine. But if you picked up this book, you are likely at some sort of crossroads in your life. This is a special period of bridge-crossing. It would be useful to be in good company—even if it was in the form of books.

Consider the following recommendations when you read fiction:

i. **Characters**: Which of the characters do you relate to the most and why?
ii. **Challenges**: What conflicts did the characters face? How were those difficulties resolved? How did those challenges shape them? (See Part I, What is Your Nature?).
iii. **Resources**: What inner and outer resources did the characters tapped into? How did specific relationships shape them?
iv. **Resonance**: What are parts of the story that resonated with you the most? What moved you?

*Non-Fiction:*

Read non-fiction with the intention of nourishment, not information. **Information is not transformation.** What you will need at this stage is fuel for fire, to not only help you sustain through difficult times, but also "cook" up some useful thoughts

---

2. See my website for a smorgasbord of book recommendations organised by topics: darylchow.com/recommendations

that will aid your transition from an old world to a new world that is awaiting for you.

Once you've picked a non-fiction book that speaks to your needs, here's three suggestions to improve the process of reading non-fiction:

i. **Pre-Test:** With book in hand, scan through the Table of Contents, back cover and the Index Page. Before you begin, test yourself. What do you already know about this topic? Quickly mind-map or list it out on one of the starting blank pages within the book, write it out in your notebook, type it in your note-taking app of choice, or simply take a small piece of paper and insert it into the front pages once you are done.

ii. Why do this? Turns out that we learn better when we connect with our prior knowledge, and when we are surprised by what we learn—especially when the new knowledge is counterintuitive.

iii. **Key Ideas:** Next, at the end of each chapter, take a pause and reflect. Note down the key ideas that resonate with you. Limit these to no more than 3-5 points. Once again, either write this down at the end of each chapter, or slip in a small piece of paper. If you are reading on a digital device, you can simply highlight and add a note to the start of the chapter. If you are listening to this as an audiobook, you can add bookmarks, create a note for each chapter.

iv. **Key Actions:** Now that you have the Key Ideas, take one final step and note down what you do about these Key Ideas. Key actions are basically your personalised "call to action." This is what you will actually think or do differently. Key Actions is where alchemy happens. It's actually quite challenging as you are doing this at a chapter-by-chapter level. (See Appendix D for a template for reading non-fiction).

For example, in Jonathan Haidt's book, *Anxious Generation*, though I had Key Ideas that I grafted from Chapter 1, there wasn't much I could add to Key Actions as he laid the foundations of the research as an introduction. Here's what I noted down for Chapter 2:

**Key Idea:**

*1. Thought Experiment: 2007 back to the future in 2024*
*#thoughtexperiment*

"...*you wake up 10 years later and look around. The physical world looks largely the same to you, but people are behaving strangely. Nearly all of them are clutching a small glass and metal rectangle, and anytime they stop moving, they assume a hunched position and stare at it.*"

*2. Our kids grow fast, then slow, then fast.*

*- unlike chimpanzees*

"*They grow rapidly for the first two years, slow down for the next seven to 10, and then undergo a rapid growth spurt during puberty before coming to a halt a few years later.*"

*- learning via play and the "social electricity" of attunement.*

*3. Smartphones and tablets in the hands of children as experience blockers.*

*4. Social media are conformist bias and prestige bias.*

*- Conformist Bias: Follow the tribe*

*- Prestige Bias: Follow the influencer*

*5. Peak Periods:*

"*For those in the peak years of puberty, which comes a bit earlier for girls...For girls, the worst years for using social media were 11 to 13; for boys, it was 14 to 15.*"

**Key Action:**
*#keyaction*

*1. Let my kids play with other kids, synchronously and with attunement. i.e., not to coddle, overprotect, overly-organise or intervene with them too much.*[3]

If you are engaging in the three aspects of Pre-Testing, Key Ideas, and Key Actions, you are now effectively reading *actively*,[4] not passively. You can also use these suggestions when you listen to an audiobook or a podcast or watch an online course.

One could argue for the more efficient case of reading book summaries instead. To me, the difference between book summaries and actually engaging with a full-length book is like viewing photos of Japan versus actually touring the streets of Tokyo. Perhaps book summaries are useful when you want an appetiser of the book before you fully invest in it. Otherwise, experience the book yourself.

Practise having a deep and active engagement with your input. Seek to learn. Learning is ultimately about changing your mind. To be learnable is to be changeable.

### 3. Have a Conversation with a Wise Person

Find a guiding light in others.

Seek out people you admire, respect, or look up to. These could be your peers or your seniors. They may or may not have gone through a similar situation as yours. We need to be in touch with embodied wisdom, someone who has perspective and a caring heart.

Because you are on the horizon to making key transitions in life, open up to them and talk it through with them. Set up a time to have a deep conversation.

---

3. You might notice the hashtags that are used in. These are tags that I use for my note-taking in a free app called Obsidian. I call this way of note-taking a Personalised Learning System (PLS). For more on this, check out my Obsidian video series: bit.ly/darylobsidian

4. For more on how to develop a reading practice, listen to this podcast episode, bit.ly/intentionalreading

Conversation is one of the highest art-form. It's something that we do all day, but to have a beautiful conversation with someone is a real gift. This is why musicians call a good performance a "great conversation." Legendary saxophonist Stan Getz said, "A good quartet is like a good conversation among friends interacting to each other's ideas." We find ourselves and each other through the emergent reality of conversation.

Some of the best conversations happen when we can hear ourselves clearly. Because the person in conversation with you has been an active participant with you each step of the way through deep listening, asking questions, and having this back-and-forth with you. Thus, we are listened to into speech. When someone trustworthy listens intently, you start to unveil the unspokens; not just the "will say"s, but also the "won't say"s, and the "can't say"s.[vi]

If you have a deep conversation with someone who embodies wisdom, you can't help but be changed.

What if we don't know people who could be our guiding light? First, think it through carefully. Think about all of the people you have met, from teachers, sport coaches, friends, extended family members, colleagues, people you might have chanced across at a conference, etc. Is there anyone that you can reach out to? You'd be surprised how honoured someone would feel if you said to them that you'd like to pick their brain on something that you are working through, and you tell them why you'd value their input (e.g., "Because I really respect the way you handle your work and personal life... and you seem to provide very useful perspective at meetings").

Some of you might find the benefits of entering into therapy with a licensed professional. After all, the majority of the work that therapists do is not just to reduce symptoms such as anxiety and depression. We aim to help people make positive changes so as to become who they really are and feel fully alive.

Practise engaging in deep conversation with others who embody wisdom. Put your ego aside and reach out.

**B. Outputs**

If you find yourself more on the side of needing to focus on your outputs, consider the following:

**1. Have You Been Faithful to Your Gifts?**

The question you need to ask between worlds: Have you been faithful to your gifts?

What are your gifts? Gifts typically reside in the intersection between what's valuable to you and what's valuable to others.

What's valuable to you are things you think about even when you don't have to because you can't help yourself; that's where your mind goes. You enjoy them, and you are good at them. These are the native skills, talents, natural abilities, and interests that you have unearthed or cultivated since you were a child.

What's valuable to others, on the other hand, is based on

their needs, wants, and desires and the problems they encounter that need addressing in the real world.

Therefore, Gifts are where these two factors meet.

You might have put aside your interests in the old world. In the new world, I urge you to consider resurrecting the gifts that live within you.

Lewis Hyde, the author of *The Gift,* whom I mentioned in "#3. Vocalising Appreciation" (Paradox 9. Receiving Care), argues that the true value of a gift lies not in its possession but in its circulation and exchange. Seen in this light, **a gift is only a Gift when it meets a need.**

Create a Venn diagram like the one above (See Appendix E for a template). Think big. Think audaciously. If you are stuck, think about the problems in this world you'd like to solve. Peter Diamondis and Steven Kottler call this "Massively Transformative Purpose" (MTP).[vii]

Identify items that overlap in the Venn diagram. Granted, not everything you are obsessed with directly becomes a gift to others. Think laterally.

Now that you've identified areas that are in the intersection between What's Valuable to You and What's Valuable to Others, chances are they fall into one of three new categories. Imagine we double-click on the centre of the two-circle Venn diagram, and it opens up to a new triple Venn diagram called **True, Useful, and Beautiful.**

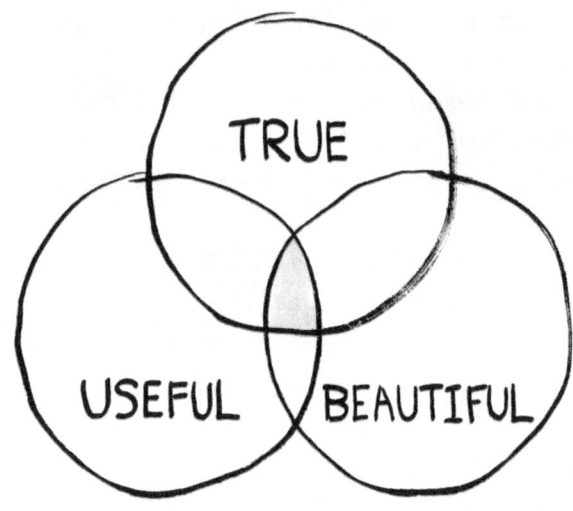

**True:** Someone who values truth will be inclined towards domains related to justice, philosophy, science, and the pursuit of what accurately represents the world and the way it ought to be. (Think of lawyers, social activists, journalists, research scientists, etc.)

**Useful:** Someone who values usefulness will gravitate towards work that helps others, adds value, and makes the world a better place. (Think of social workers, nurses, doctors, people in the helping profession, etc.)

**Beautiful:** Someone who values beauty is moved by aesthetics and wants to create and bring that experience to others. (Think of artists, musicians, designers, architects.)

Lucky are the ones who have one or two overlaps. A medical professional who pursues scientific truth and desires to help others stands at the intersection of True and Useful. An art teacher who uses art as a medium to reach kids as well as inspire them through creative endeavours navigates the space between Useful and Beautiful. A mathematician who values the rigorous truth of mathematical logic and the aesthetic pleasure of elegant solutions resides in the blended worlds of True and Beautiful.

Rare are the ones who have all three domains overlapping. One person comes to mind. Vietnamese-born Australian Ahn Do is an author, actor, comedian, and painter.[viii] Do and his family came to Australia as refugees in 1980. He earned a Business Law degree but opted to do stand-up comedy instead. He was known for his sharp and relatable humour. He later transitioned into visual arts full time, coming in as a finalist for the Archibald Prize in 2014, 2017, and 2019. Do dabbled in acting and later published his memoir, *The Happiest Refugee,* an account of his family's escape from Vietnam. He is also a national bestseller in children's books.

What's most moving for me is watching his television series *Anh's Brush with Fame,* where he paints prominent figures while engaging each of them in a deep conversation. In one episode, Gill Hicks, a peace advocate who survived but lost her legs in the London terrorist bombings on July 7, 2005, said that "Anh captures the life within me... that's the greatest thing that can come out in a painting." Consolidating his outputs within the framework of **True, Useful, and Beautiful**, Anh Do is able to help draw out his interviewees' lived experiences and untold stories, as well as tell his own story in his autobiography (i.e., True), creating an emotional and even therapeutic experience not only for interviewees like Hicks, but for viewers as well (i.e., Useful), and painting visually captivating portraits of each of his subjects (i.e., Beautiful).

Where do your gifts reside in the **True, Useful, and Beautiful** framework?

Regardless of where your gifts lie in the Venn diagram, your task is to share them. We all have a part to play in the world.

As you contemplate your gifts, do appreciate the following paradox: blisters from the past can actually be blissful gifts for the future. Josh Shipp, who went from being an at-risk foster kid to a Harvard graduate, and now a keynote speaker and best-selling author, says, "Annoyances are assets in disguise." Take some time to dig for gold in your past (see #2. Psychological Movement: Map Out Your Storyline_and revisit your Why, The Final Cause, in Paradox 13. Movement).

For as long as she could remember, Bernadette was thought of as "too sensitive." She would cry easily as a child, and she was quickly overwhelmed by her external environment. One time, her mother found her in tears in her bed. "What's wrong, honey?" Her mom asked.

"Did you hear that?" Bernadette replied.

"Hear what?"

"That song that just played."

"Not really. Why?" her mom asked.

"It's so moving."

Her parents encouraged her to go out more and play with the kids in the neighbourhood. But her proclivity seemed to indicate that she enjoyed her own company.

Now, as an adult, Bernadette is an artist—a very good one. She is also studying to be a counsellor. Bernadette is not just a "highly emotional person," she is what psychologist Elaine Aron would call a "highly sensitive person (HSP)."[5]

Take another example. Ellis, who struggled with school. He

---

5. Carl Jung was the first to suggest this sensitivity trait back in 1913. He said, *"This excessive sensitiveness very often brings an enrichment of the personality.... Only, when difficult and unusual situations arise, the advantage frequently turns into a very great disadvantage, since calm consideration is then disturbed by untimely affects. Nothing could be more mistaken, though, than to regard this excessive sensitiveness as in itself a pathological character component. If that were really so, we should have to rate about one quarter of humanity as pathological."* Jung was roughly accurate about the prevalence of the sensitive trait. In the general population, Elaine Aron estimates that one out of every five persons is an HSP. This sensitive trait is not exclusive to humans and can be found in animals as well. However, while about 20% of the general population has this trait, in clinical practice, Aron reckons the actual occurrence rate is closer to 50%.

As a crude estimate, I reviewed my clinical caseloads over a period of a few weeks. Out of 36 people, at least thirteen (36%) of them match the working definitions of HSP. That's not quite half of the people at my practice, but certainly more than 25%.

was disorganised, often inattentive in class. He was diagnosed with ADHD. Teachers did everything they could to help him sit in his chair and stay focused on the lesson. By and large, their efforts were futile.

I later learned from the existing research that, based on a cross-sectional study of more than 9,000 individuals, there is a positive connection between clinical ADHD and entrepreneurial intentions and action. There is potential self-selection inclination towards those with ADHD starting their own ventures (though does not suggest anything about the performance of their entrepreneurship).[ix] In another study, compared to non-ADHD peers in a college-student sample, students with ADHD scored higher in originality, novelty, and flexibility.[x] Finally, a third study suggests that compared to the control group, adults with ADHD reported more real-world creative achievements.[xi] From a personality-trait perspective, individuals with ADHD are more likely to be high in Openness to Experience, low in Conscientiousness and to a lesser extent Neuroticism.[xii] The hyperactivity-impulsivity trait is related to low Agreeableness[xiii] and high Extraversion.[xiv]

Now, as an adult, Ellis is finding his footing and is a highly driven entrepreneur. He has a patent for an invention under his name. A few more patents are in the oven.[6]

Practise panning for the gold that is hiding in your history. These are your gifts, even if they were previously seen as annoyances. As Rumi wrote, "What hurts you, blesses you."[xv]

---

If you think you are an HSP, I recommend Aron's book *The Highly Sensitive Person*.
6. To be clear, this is not to suggest that there isn't a downside. Impulsivity, difficulty in corralling attention on a given task, hyper-focusing, and time blindness can be debilitating.

## 2. Treat "More Planning and Learning" as Procrastination

"Are you sharpening pencils, or are you creating art?"

— *Richie Norton*

Jordan started off the day with a clear intention: to make some illustrations in the ProCreate app on his iPad. First, he spent some time setting up his table, tidying his room, and organising his to-do list on his iPhone. Then he watched some YouTube how-to videos, and then he clicked on some more videos about some other app that could help with his drawing. The next thing he knew, three hours had passed. By now, he was feeling tired, uninspired, and deflated. He had to leave for his 1 p.m. work shift soon.

Jordan is not alone on this slippery road of lost time.

Planning and learning can easily morph into procrastination.

The act of engaging in more planning and trying to learn more in order to know more is a form of psychological trickery, derailing you from actually doing the thing you are trying to do in the first place. You'll feel active and busy with goal-setting and gathering more "useful" information, but actually, you are just procrastinating.

Sure, there might be gaps in your knowledge. But do not replace the act of engaging in your creative endeavour with more preparation and acquiring new knowledge.

Boredom is the antidote to this trap. Learn to befriend it. Sit with the tension, and don't fill your attention with substitutes. (See #3. No Substitution, in Paradox 12. Stress).

Refrain from chasing more inputs. As the pioneering cognitive scientist Herbert Simon said, "A wealth of information creates a poverty of attention."

Push yourself to the edge of what you can do without any

research.[7] Note some things you might want to learn more about *later*. Visit them after you have nurtured your existing ideas to their fullest based on your current limitations.

**Make First, Then Manage**

You might be thinking, *But I still need to get stuff managed and organised.* In 2009, Paul Graham, cofounder of the influential seed-capital firm Y-Combinator, published a highly talked-about blog post called "Maker's Schedule, Manager's Schedule." Graham argues that we need to distinguish between two different hats that we wear when working, that of a "Maker" and that of a "Manager."[xvi]

The Manager's schedule is divided into short time blocks, typically one hour long or less, filled with meetings, phone calls, and other tasks. This schedule is optimised for quick decision-making and coordination. In contrast, the Maker's schedule requires long, uninterrupted blocks of time, typically several hours, to reach a state of deep focus and productivity.

Who typically wears the Manager's hat most of the time? Graham states, "Most powerful people are on the Manager's schedule. It's the schedule of command."

On the importance of the Maker's hat, Graham asks, "Don't your spirits rise at the thought of having an entire day free to work, with no appointments at all?"

While you might be in a situation where others who wear the Manager's hat will impose on your work as a Maker, you also need to manage your own work (i.e., scheduling tasks, organising your priorities). Likewise, even if you typically wear the Manag-

---

7. To students trying to write essays, I would advise that you do not begin the writing process with "research." Instead, begin writing based on what you already know. Elaborate as far as you can based on your current knowledge. *Then,* when you reach your limits, go do some research. By doing it this way, you have already begun. The next step is to substantiate or correct what you got wrong based on the existing literature.

hat in your work, you too need to park aside some time to be a Maker (i.e., to write, think, reflect, and create).

When it comes to Output though, the rule should be this: **Make First, Then Manage.**

Don the Maker's hat as soon as you hit the ground running. Schedule time to switch to the Manager's hat and get organised later on. Why? As mentioned earlier, planning can morph into a form of procrastination. By training your mind to default to being a Maker first, you'll start to realise how much you can get done in a limited period of time—and you'll feel great the rest of the day now that you've created something from the get-go.

Practise creating your output as soon as you get started for the day. Everything else is procrastination.

**3. Serial, Not Parallel.**

If you are in a season of your life that is about Outputs, I highly suggest you take a "Serial, Not Parallel" approach.

A Serial approach is one where you work on one project at a time before moving on to the next. A Parallel approach is where you work on a couple things at the same time.

```
        SERIAL              PARALLEL
         ┌─┐
         │A│
         └─┘
          +
         ┌─┐                  ┌─┐   ┌─┐   ┌─┐
    ⇨   │B│    vs    ⇨      │A│→│B│→│C│
         └─┘                  └─┘   └─┘   └─┘
          +
         ┌─┐
         │C│
         └─┘
```

I used to work on several things at any given moment. I would even be fastidious with "batching" similar work together (e.g., writing, clinical practice and supervision, research, online courses, speaking engagements, admin tasks). When a new research project came in, I would add that to the schedule and manage my time around it. This became a problem when my commitments started to balloon. I was getting overwhelmed and becoming scatter-brained.

In part, this was an issue of saying Yes to too many projects (See Paradox 5. No). On the other hand, it was also due to a lack not just of time management, but also of attention and energy management. I simply couldn't handle all of it at a given point in time.

That was when I started to zoom out and extend my timeline perspective. Instead of looking at my work from a day-to-day, and week-to-week schedule, I started to plan on a month-by-month and quarter-by-quarter basis. "Okay, I can't commit to this research project this month, because my caseload is full right now. But I can fully commit to it next month."

In a fit of frustration, I pasted a huge piece of butcher paper on the wall and drew a thick horizontal line across it. Next, I indicated each month of the year as a node on that line. Then I listed all my major projects on one Post-It note each. Finally, I limit one primary Post-It note to each month. I called this **The Snake Chart.**

This does not mean that you should simply drop the ball on all other stuff that requires your management (see previous point, "Make First, Then Manage").

As I looked at the Post-It notes scattered on the floor, waiting to go on the Snake Chart, I started to realise, "Holy cow, these can't all be done, even within a year."

This is where I slid into a familiar cognitive bias: the planning fallacy. I started to think that I could squeeze in two instead of one primary project for a particular month (*See* #1. Loosen the

Trappings of Busyness, One Day at a Time, in Paradox 1. Self-Care).

Resist the temptation to pack in more than one primary project per month. We are very bad at estimating how long tasks will take us to complete. Whether it is the construction of the Sydney Opera House or your humble kitchen renovation, most things will take longer than one envisions.[8] That's because, when it comes to our plans, we tend to see things through an optimistic lens. "Yeah, that's doable. I can smash that out in a day."

However, I still couldn't dampen that optimistic side of me. Here's what I did to circum-navigate this dilemma: I added another set of different-coloured Post-It notes to the Snake Chart, called "Secondary Projects." If the Secondary Project does not take significant cognitive resources, I might put it in there for the month (e.g., as I write this, completing this manuscript is my Primary Project for the month, and my Secondary Project is to open the fourth cohort of an online course that I conduct for therapists.) If the Secondary Project takes more resources out of me, I will attend to it only after I complete the Primary Project. For example, next month, my Primary Project is to record the audio version of this book, and my Secondary Project is to complete a very rough draft of another book that has been germinating for more than a year. Since I have already some of the outline for that done, I am optimistic about completing it. That said, I am prone to planning fallacies, so that is why I've listed it as a Secondary, and not a Primary, Project.

Practise stacking up your projects serially, not in parallel. As you do this, you'll start to zoom out and take a longer-term perspective. Your future self will thank you.

---

8. This book is a fine example of the planning fallacy. I thought I would get this done in a year. It has taken me more than three and a half years.

## BROADEN YOUR NATURE

If you are high in Openness to Experience, be careful not to go down too many rabbit holes at the same time. Many things can appeal to you, so you will have to pay careful attention to the amount of Inputs you take in and the depths you get yourself into.

If you are low in Conscientiousness, you might find that these suggestions stretch you a fair bit. This may be required as you are trying to organise not only how you spend your time, but how you engage in your well-doing so that it not only improves your well-being, but ultimately help you in this critical period of Crossing Between Worlds.

---

*See Related Paradoxes: 1. Self-Care/Self-Forgetting, 5. Yes/No, 6. Acceptance/Change, 9. Caregiving/Receiving Care, 12. Recovery/Stress, 13. Stillness/Movement.*

# PARADOX 15. CONTROL/SURRENDER

## CONTRADICTION

There are many things we can do to regain a sense of control in our personal and professional lives. We assume that to surrender is to resign ourselves to fate, when in actuality, learning to surrender is a practice of appreciation and letting others in.

Do I need to learn to put my hands on the steering wheel and be more responsible, or do I need to learn the art of surrender?

## CLARITY

### A. Control

Moving towards the life you want, the person you want to become, is an exercise in the degrees of freedom at your disposal. As stated in the Introduction, to move in accordance with our intentions is to resist the pitfall of becoming victims to our circumstances. To move is to exert strength that propels motion in a specific direction.

Think of it this way: The boat is the mother of nurturance, providing you a basis of care and support to stay afloat. The sail, on the other hand, is the father of leadership, offering you guidance and helping you move where you need to go.[1]

If you are on a boat, it's quite easy to stay afloat. What we are trying to do is to catch the wind to sail the craft. This takes skill and intention. If we stick with this metaphor, there are three phases that we have to go through when embarking on moving this sailboat. In **The Arc of Life** (see figure below), the journey entails the following: **Freedom, Responsibility, Adventure.**

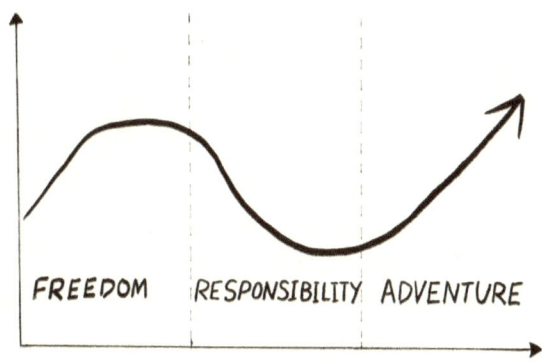

---

1. To be clear, though related, I'm not necessarily talking about the literal roles of mothers and fathers. Single mothers can provide both maternal nurturance and paternal guidance. Conversely, there are also fathers who are the providers of emotional support. Ultimately, we need both nurturance and guidance.

. . .

Similar to the Arc of Life, Franciscan Friar Richard Rohr describes a related process of spiritual development. He called it the journey from

"Yes, to No, to Yes."[i]

Elsewhere, he describes the path of transformation as the unfolding of

"Order, Disorder, Reorder."

Rohr notes that most traditions try to keep you in the first box of "Order," even when it doesn't fit reality.[ii] This stunts any kind of real transformation and development. We have to go through states of "disorder" in order to come out the other end of "reorder."

The Arc of Life is not a prescriptive formula, but rather, it serves as a "form," a structure to help you think through the stages of development as you cross between worlds.

Let's go through each of the three phases.

*Freedom*

"Chemical elements do not choose which way to combine. Genes do not make decisions," wrote the late Rabbi Jonathan Sacks. "But we are free; we do choose. We do make decisions ... [Freedom is] God's most fraught and fateful gift."[iii]

When we embark on this voyage of leaving our old world behind, we are exercising the gift of freedom. The *freedom from* the past that binds us, as well as the *freedom to* engage in the choices we make. What a liberating feeling to be free from limiting beliefs, old narratives, and fears that held us back. Fear is no longer a headwind but a tailwind.

Most of us are familiar with the Statue of Liberty, a gift

from France to America in 1886, commemorating the two nations' friendship and shared love of freedom. But have you ever noticed that she isn't standing still? The statue's right foot is actually lifted, as if in mid-stride, as if to say, "Liberty is on the move."[iv] Paradoxically, as noted by German psychoanalyst Erich Fromm, the fear of freedom can sometimes grip us. Nevertheless, we are invited to exercise our freedom for play, our freedom to explore and discover the world within and without.

*Responsibility*

As we come of age and reckon with the freedom at our disposal, we enter into a new phase. At this arc of the journey, we begin to comprehend that liberty begets responsibility. With the choices that we make—willingly—we learn that the territory of responsibility comes with sacrifice. You can't have it all. You can pursue *anything* you want, but not everything. Freedom asks for the partnership of responsibility. This means to take on the obligations of self-control and regard for others.

When we think about these two phases of Freedom and Responsibility, as author Ryan Holiday incisively points out, "We don't have a freedom problem: we have a responsibility problem." What Holiday is saying is that we have overinflated the value of freedom at the expense of responsibility. "Responsibility is understanding yourself as belonging to something larger than yourself."[v] Our responsibility is to see beyond just individual good, but the common good of all, shifting the lens from "I" to "we."[vi]

Austrian psychiatrist and Holocaust survivor Viktor Frankl said,

> When we look upon human life without the blinkers of preconception, we must conclude that both consciousness and responsibleness play the basic roles in the drama of existence...Being human means being conscious and being responsible.[vii]

Curiously, 75 years after the Statue of Liberty was inaugurated in New York Harbour on the East Coast, another statue was proposed to be erected on the West Coast. It was to be called the Statue of Responsibility, symbolising the flipside of America's prized virtue.[viii] This statue was the brainchild of Frankl. He said,

> Freedom, however, is not the last word. Freedom is only part of the story and half of the truth. Freedom is but the negative aspect of the whole phenomenon whose positive aspect is responsibleness. In fact, freedom is in danger of degenerating into mere arbitrariness unless it is lived in terms of responsibleness. That is why I recommend that the Statue of Liberty on the East Coast be supplemented by a Statue of Responsibility on the West Coast.[ix]

Features of Responsibility include sacrifice, pain, and suffering. Ask any parent, and they will tell you about the heartaches and headaches of Responsibility. In the amateur sport of parenting, the moment you think you've turned pro, the rules change.[x] Bearing a personal cross inevitably demands certain sacrifices. When you become a parent, you instinctively sacrifice your own needs. Your attention turns to the cute and helpless baby (and sometimes pint-size dictator) in your arms.

The road of Responsibility is difficult. Yet pain is a teacher. The right-size dose of stressors produces a beneficial effect.. This is why self-imposed stressors of doing something challenging (e.g., lifting weights, running, taking a cold shower, confronting your fears, learning a new skill) helps us grow. As we like to say, "No pain, no gain."

As mentioned in "Paradox 12. Stress", hormesis is Greek for "to set in motion." The feeling of being in motion, pushing forward in the right direction, not only remoralises and re-energises you, but the "effort equal to reward" also dampens the pain. Pain specialist and paediatric emergency physician Amy Baxter notes that motion is effective at "shutting the gate" on sharp pain. She adds, "Choosing what to focus on increases control. Fear and control are the volume knobs for pain."[xi] Although Baxter is speaking about physical pain, I suspect this is also true for psychological pain.

If we take up the cross of responsibility, where does it lead us in the arc of life?

*Adventure*

When we hoist the sail and face our responsibilities head-on, the adventure of our lives awaits us.

When we look back at the journey we have undertaken, meaning comes to us *retroactively*. Things start to make a bit more sense. In this third phase, an adventure is calling out to you. It is unclear what the path will look like exactly, but the same is true of a holiday trip to Europe. You know roughly where you'll go and what you'll do—but not precisely. That's the point of an adventure: to go somewhere new.

There are those who think they can get from Freedom to Adventure by making a spiritual and emotional bypass from the country of Responsibility. But by doing so, one forfeits the chance to really discover what they are made of. Prematurely hunting for an "adventure," without a deep experience of what it means to be a responsible person predisposes the individual to occupy the passenger seat, with a lack of control of where life is going. Not only are their hands not on the steering wheel, they will be prone to see themselves as victims of circumstances. Recall Rohr's process of development, from "Yes, to No, to Yes." He says, "You can't have all Yeses and no Nos."

Conversely, an individual who hasn't fully experienced the Freedom to play and explore and go forth with their own ideas and interests, and too quickly jumps into the world of Responsibility, might find themselves needing to renegotiate the direction they're heading in.

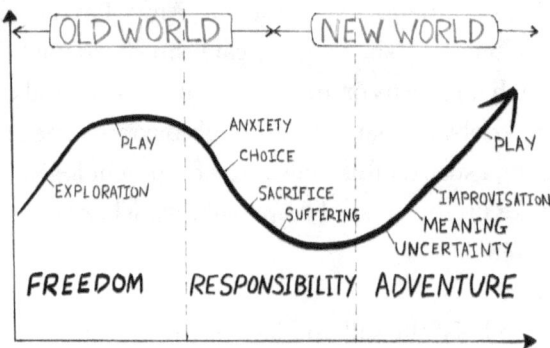

Consider Asher, who in his mid-40s decided to leave a mining-related business he'd led for fifteen years. This decision didn't come easy. It was fraught with fear, especially due to the possible loss of financial security. A recent car accident had shaken him, leaving him in an "existential crisis," as he described it. The incident gave him pause, which morphed into a sort of angst. "How the heck have fifteen years passed just like that? What have I been doing with my life?" Seeing his son, who's a year younger than his business, mature and become independent has been striking. "I only went into this business because I was cashing in. My mate and I were offered the opportunity to take over the business from his father, who was retiring, and we thought it was a great way to create financial security in our lives."

And it was. Asher noted, "I've learned so much in this period, but something in me feels neglected and unchecked. It's as if I've forgotten a part of me that has always been there ... but I don't know what it is." Looking back, Asher realised he hadn't gone through a full-fledged development at the stage of Freedom to explore. He'd rushed into the world of Responsibility. Being the oldest of three siblings, he fell into the role of being a "responsible" parentified child for his siblings when his father left when he was a pre-teen.

## Paradox 15. Control/Surrender | 293

He could have continued the venture with his business partner and had a comfortable retirement. But something was gnawing at him. He said, "I don't want my son to see me do the things I have to do, at the expense of doing the things that make me come alive."

Naturally, I asked, "What makes you come alive?"

"I have no idea!"

Not having a sense of a better alternative does not mean you should not give it space and time to percolate. With the support of his wife, Asher took two months off to give it some thought. Never had he taken a vacation longer than two weeks. This was foreign territory for him. During this period, instead of brushing it off as a typical mid-life crisis, Asher noted that he had always valued both the "human-caring" side of work, as he described it, as well as the world of art and aesthetics (See #1. Have You Been Faithful to Your Gifts, in Paradox 14. Output). These were missing in his life. The things he valued were providing emotional support to his employees and being a mentor to them. In one of our therapy sessions, he said to me, "In fact, I want to do more of what you are doing!"

Asher's love of art had been entirely relegated to the backseat for most of his adult life. As a child, he remembered having a deep interest in painting and poetry, both of which were shelved due the responsibilities and mental energy he gave to the upkeep of his business. It was palpable that he had missed this side of him, the side that yearns for aesthetics, beauty, and creativity. Not long after our meeting, for the first time in a long time, he picked up his paintbrush once again.

Fred Rogers once told the story of a sculptor consigned to do his craft in a school:

> There was a man who would come every week to sculpt in front of the kids. The director said, "I don't want you to teach sculpting. I want you to do what you do and love it in front of the chil-

dren." During that year, clay was never used more imaginatively, before or after.... A great gift of any adult to a child, it seems to me, is to **love what you do in front of the child** [emphasis mine]. I mean, if you love to bicycle, if you love to repair things, do that in front of the children. Let them catch the attitude that that's fun. Because you know, attitudes are caught, not taught.[xii]

The greatest gift we can give is to do what makes us come alive and allow others to witness us.

Meanwhile, Asher found a natural fit for himself in his work life. He contacted other firms, putting out feelers, and companies began to hire him to coach and mentor other executives. This resonated with him, because he had recognised a deep desire in himself to help others on an individual level. Had he not pulled the reins and took a pause in his life, he would have simply continued in the world that he was in, one that was undoubtedly comfortable, familiar, and secure. Crossing to this new territory gave him anxiety, but at the same time, it opened new doors of possibility. Of course, exercising his freedom to do what life called him to do meant he would have to take on new responsibilities and make new sacrifices. (see graph above). All of this will also impact his wife and kids. However, for the first time in his life, he is now opening up to Adventure in his life. Not only is he gaining meaning, he gets to do what makes him come truly alive, and his family gets to witness it. This can't be taught to his kids; they can only be "caught."

In the Arc of Life, take control of what scares you.

## B. Surrender

> "We must be willing to let go of the life we planned so as to have the life that is waiting for us."
>
> — *Joseph Campbell*

You do not need to have everything figured out.

And yet, you can still move forward. How? By allowing yourself to be moved.

In *A Field Guide to Getting Lost*, author Rebecca Solnit writes,

> Worry is a way to pretend that you have knowledge or control over what you don't—and it surprises me, even in myself, how much we prefer ugly scenarios to the pure unknown.[xiii]

Ambient musician and producer Brian Eno has observed that our culture tends to over-glorify people who seem to have everything under control, and undervalue people who learn the art of surrender.[xiv]

Yet the art of surrender is not at all a passive activity. It is not being "Willful," as described in Part I: Framework ("Willful vs. Willing"), and it is also not about exerting force and control. As you are Crossing Between Worlds, to Surrender is to avail yourself of the following equation:

. . .

### Surrender = A Practice of Appreciation + Learning to Let In - Ego

Let's look at each of these three facets of surrender in detail.

*A Practice of Appreciation*

The practice of appreciation is to take a perspective that **nothing goes to waste**. When we were little, my grandmother had a tradition of making a blanket for each of us. This blanket was weaved together from pieces of cloth she had kept over the years while she was sewing other garments. Not one blanket was the same. Mine became a security blanket that I kept for years.

A jazz musician is like a bricolage maker. They take what is presented in the improvisational act of music creation, they listen attentively to what's unfolding, and then they build on that. Meanwhile, their fellow musicians respond to what is being played in the jam session, and then...something is created out of nothing.

Of course, a professional jazz musician does not come onto the stage without a body of musical wisdom acquired through years of practice and tinkering.[xv] But unlike a classical music performance, which attempts to execute a piece of notated music with fidelity, a jazz musician must surrender their conscious striving and take an intuitive leap.

Ted Gioia writes,

> The improviser may be unable to look ahead at what he is going to play, but he can look behind at what he has just played, thus each new musical phrase can be shaped with relation to what has gone before. He creates his form retrospectively.[xvi]

What if you applied the principles from bricolage and improvisation to your life, especially when you are Crossing Between

Worlds? (See #3. Improving vs. Improvising, Paradox 13. Movement).

### Learning to Let In

To surrender is to let in. Not only do we have to be utterly open to the experience of what's ahead of us, we also have to detach ourselves from specific outcomes. This is not easy. The reason it's not easy is because we are goal-fixated creatures.

A friend of mine, Iggy Tan, wrote a book called *Stop Craving Happiness*. He walked me through a practice he suggests in the book. It goes something like this:

- State what you expect ("I expect to help my clients today," "I expect myself to be a good son to my parents," "I expect to end work on time and get home and be a good father and husband," etc.).
- And then add, "And I let this go...."

The first time I did this, Iggy encouraged me to gesture with my hands as I spoke the above. He suggested I move my hands as if I was sweeping into my head while saying "I expect," and then sweeping out when I said "And I let this go." It was a little odd, especially since we were having this conversation in a cafe.

But doing this exercise, I was struck by how much tightness I held in my body when I listed my expectations. The experience of specifying each of my expectations and then releasing them was akin to an acupuncturist placing a needle on my skin and releasing a pressure point.

This does not mean that I'm now going to be careless with my clients, forget about my parents, and get home late and ignore my family. Rather, it allowed me to "let in." **When we let go of our expectations, we open ourselves to experiences.** When we are open to experiences in the here and now, we are more likely to connect with others. When we take an appreciative stance, coupled with an openness to "let in," we are no longer wedded to specific outcomes. Instead, everything becomes a gift.

### Minus Ego

The final piece in the Surrender equation is the humility to gracefully not think about yourself (see Paradox 1: Self-Forgetting). Besides, a good sense of self is not preoccupied with its sense of self.

When we let go of our egos, we let go of an illusion that we keep of ourselves. This false self, as Thomas Merton calls it, has its adaptive functions. It keeps a certain story alive. It keeps a certain image we would like others to see of us. But soon enough, the attempted solution of the Ego becomes a problem. Instead of allowing you to feel and experience the world around you, it binds and restricts you, only caring about maintaining itself, the Ego.

A while back, a former client, Mika, reconnected with me for a consultation. I hadn't seen him for some years. He had become highly-driven and was making significant strides in his work life. I first knew him during his youth. He'd come from a tumultuous and unstable family background. Before we closed, I said to him, "Remember, you have nothing to prove."

"What do you mean?" he asked.

"I mean, you have nothing to prove."

"Don't go all Mr. Miyagi on me. I have everything to prove!"

"I'm not trying to, Mika. I want you to feel free, to do what is life-giving for you, and to not fall into the trap of needing to prove anything to anyone."

"Hmm... I'll have to sit on that one," he relented.

I'm not implying that Mika was ego-tripping on his achievements, but it's a subtle tripwire to over-identify with our successes and accolades, especially if we came from a place of lack and then worked hard to achieve results in our career. Perhaps my timing wasn't the best, but given where Mika was previously, I'd sensed that he was coming to a new turning point in his life.

Combined with the practice of appreciation and learning to let in, the tempering of our Ego ultimately frees us to expand our sense of self in the world, and to take in the beauty and life that has been around us all this time.

---

During the COVID-19 pandemic, you might have experienced situations that were utterly beyond your control.

An elderly parent of a friend of mine had to be taken to the city's hospital without anyone allowed to accompany him due to safety regulations. His children, living overseas, were not able to get on a flight to visit him. Another friend lost his sister to cancer. He and his parents had to attend the funeral virtually, because they were unable to get on a plane due to travel restrictions.

Powerlessness can give rise to anxiety. Afterall, anxiety feeds on the desire for certainty that can never be quenched completely by more certainty. In fact, the antidote to anxiety is not more certainty, but rather it is increasing our ability to make room for uncertainty.

Various ancient traditions suggest that the choice isn't between absolute control and surrendering to fate. This capacity to hold "both/and" in a non-dualistic way allows us to embrace the world. As Havelock Ellis puts it, "All the art of living lies in a fine mingling of letting go and holding on."

When things are ultimately beyond our immediate control, we are faced with angst at being rendered useless. These are the times when life insists we learn to surrender, to not throw punches in the air, to let go of specific outcomes, to let go of our expectations, to sit in the darkness of our solitude, draw on all of the fortitude within and around us, and turn everything into a prayer.

"You do not have to sit outside in the dark. If, however, you want to look at the stars, you will find that darkness is necessary. But the stars neither require nor demand it."

— *Annie Dillard*[xvii]

---

There are times we need to reign it in and take charge of our lives, and there are other times when we need to learn the art of surrender.

*In this season of your life, where do you need to be on the spectrum of Control and Surrender? (Mark an '<', '>' or 'x' on the line below).*

15

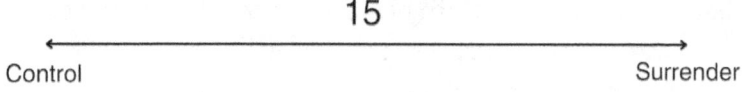

Control                                                             Surrender

## COUNSEL

### A. Control

If you find yourself on the side of needing to be more in control, here are a few questions to ask in order to orient yourself in the right direction:

### 1. The Exercise of Freedom

Take another look at the Arc of Life graph. Let's start with the first phase: Freedom.

Reflect and write your response to the following questions:

*Do you feel free to exercise your will?*
*Are there areas where you need to free yourself from old stories, bad habits and addictions, and limiting patterns of behaviour?*
*Are there areas from which you need to free yourself in order to see a possible world, explore new facets of life, or revisit people and things you've taken for granted?*

Or perhaps, like Asher, you haven't really had a chance to fully experience a sense of freedom to play and explore. Do not simply dismiss the issue as a quarter-life or midlife crisis. Entertain its visitation at least.

Practise the use of your liberty.

## 2. Take on Responsibilities

In an interview with Dia Chakravarty, Jordan Peterson said, "If you're looking for meaning, take on responsibility."

Peterson adds,

> There's no difference between voluntary responsibility and meaning. They're the same thing. And boy, that's a secret worth knowing... Take responsibility for yourself, take responsibility for your mate and for your children. And then expand that responsibility outward, envelope as much as you can, as you become more skilled...

Similarly, the late Rabbi Jonathan Sacks said, "The ethics of responsibility is the best answer I know to the meaning and meaningfulness of a life."[xviii]

There is something powerful about the volitional choice of taking on the mantle of responsibility. It is acting upon your free will to do something about where you want to take your life.

Therein lies the second phase of the Arc of Life.

Reflect and write your response to the following questions:

> *What responsibilities have you been evading?*
> *As you are at the crossroads, what areas are beckoning you to figure out, to learn, to go to the edge of your current ability?*
> *What sacrifices are you willing to make in the process? What pains and "dis-orders" will you have to endure?*
> *What do you have to leave behind in order to move forward?*
> *Finally, ask yourself, **"Have I been faithful to my gifts?"** (see #1. Have You Been Faithful to Your Gifts?, in Paradox 14. Outputs)*

Practise volitionally taking on responsibilities in order to lead a meaningful life.

### 3. Call to Adventure

As you exercise your freedom and take on the mantle of Responsibility through the developmental process, a road of Adventure awaits you. You can reject the call to move forward into a new and unknown world and remain in the comforts of the familiar world, or you can embrace the Adventure. The choice is yours. The burden of Responsibility can crush your spirit. But if you persist, you may uncover a new life.

Renowned mythologist Joseph Campbell begins the Hero's Journey with the "Call to Adventure," a pivotal moment where one is beckoned to embark on a transformative quest. For some, the word "Calling" seems out of step in this secular age. To answer a call can be seen in a religious and nonreligious light. It could manifest as responding to God's call to a life of service, or it can also mean responding to a prompting within a particular vocation. However you think of "Calling," not only will circumstances and things change, *you* will be changed.

This "Call" disrupts the hero's ordinary world and is followed by a series of challenges and ordeals that propel the individual into the unknown, but if the hero persists through the trials and tribulations, a new world opens up as they undergo profound transformation.[2]

A call needs a response. It requires the meeting of freedom and responsibility, free will and choice, even in the face of uncertainty.

Reflect and write your response to the following questions:

> *Where is life calling you?*
> *What really matters to you?*
> *What do you want to create?*
> *Are you willing to be altered and "re-ordered" by your experience?*
> *Do you like who you are becoming?*

Practise embracing the uncertainty that comes from the Call to Adventure as you take steps forward.

## B. Surrender

If you find yourself more on the side of needing to learn how to surrender, consider the following:

---

[2]. Stories from various cultures that follow the Hero's Journey framework resonate with people, as it provides a universal structure that reflects the human experience of growth, challenges, and self-discovery. Examples include, *The Lord of the Rings* by J.R.R. Tolkien, *Star Wars* by George Lucas, the *Harry Potter* series by J. K. Rowling, and *The Odyssey* by Homer.

## 1. The Door to Openness

One of the biggest questions we need to ask ourselves from moment to moment is **"How open is my heart?"**

How open am I to the experiences on the outside, which stirs up feelings and memories through my embodied sensations?

Openness is a precondition for the art of surrender. When we stay open, our curiosity can proceed forward. Suspend what you know, and take things in as if for the first time. Can you move from being willful to willing? (See Willful vs. Willing, in Part I: The Framework).

When we are open, we raise the odds of being moved, being affected in a way that inspires living (see Bridge-Crossing, in Part I: The Framework).

Begin the day by asking yourself, "How open is my heart?" Don't force the answer, but wait for a sense of where you are. Gradually open your hands; don't clasp them. If you are the praying kind, pray with open hands. "Is there anything that I am holding on to with a clenched fist?'

> "You only become a person when you are capable of standing open to all the gifts which are prepared for you."
>
> — *Henri Nouwen*[xix]

Practise rending your heart wide open.

## 2. Stop Fighting

"When we laugh," says Peter Kreft, "We lose control."[xx]

Stop the prideful fight inside yourself. Stop insisting on a certain self-image. Let go of your titles, your public image, and the persona that you're trying to upkeep. Let go of trying to have everything under control, or even thinking of yourself as good and loving. Learn to laugh at the absurdity of this game we play.

When you can see how much you are at war with yourself by trying to keep up with this positive image, you can learn to stop fighting and take yourself less seriously. The word humour is etymologically related to "humble" and "humus," which means earth. Kreft says, "Humility is usually misunderstood. It's not a low opinion of yourself; it's no opinion of yourself... Humility is the deflator of pride." When we carry a touch of levity, we can let ourselves go a little bit more. This brings us back to earth.

Next, stop insisting on the "Book of Supposed To."[xxi] The Book of Supposed To consists of a litany of expectations and ought-to-bes. The grievance we experience is the gap between the "supposed to" and how things are. Carrying this book around in our lives weighs us down and keeps us from experiencing the life that is actually in front of us.

When we carry this Book of Supposed To with us wherever we go, we end up trying to convince other people instead of understanding them. **The opposite of understanding is convincing.**[xxii] When we put down this Book of Supposed To, we begin to learn that there are multiple perspectives, and two things can be true at once. Instead of being convicted by our own convictions, we can expand and connect with each other. When we put down this Book of Supposed To, we can let go of past resentments and the need for a certain future.

When the inner battle stops, we allow the heart to ease in and become less divided and more understanding.

Practise letting go of your expectations.

### 3. Involuntary Gratitude

We can't control many things, but we can learn to cultivate what we are grateful for.

There is a lot of press about gratitude exercises. There are good reasons for this, but an effective gratitude exercise is more than simply listing things that you are grateful for. A colleague of mine told me that every Friday afternoon, her boss insists that each coworker in the office has to tell the group what they are grateful for. You can only imagine the cringe factor for most of them doing this. The moment you try to manufacture gratitude, it blows up in your face.

Gratitude springs forth from where our attention is. When we learn to guide our attention and slow down, we can't help but *be moved* by a sense of gratefulness for what's there. A wakefulness starts to come to you as you notice the tree by your street, your exuberant child at the playground, or the taste of the meal your spouse prepared.

Here's a suggestion: Instead of keeping a gratitude journal (or hosting a Friday gratitude meeting), keep a **noticing journal**. Start each day by picking one person, one thing, or one event to focus on. Take one minute and focus your attention on what you have chosen. You don't have to force "gratitude" into the equation. Allow yourself to be moved by the object, person, or event. Stay with it for a minute. Then go write it down. This method prioritises deep emotional engagement over simple enumeration, and each entry should be concise—no more than 100 words.

If you are using a digital device, you might want to write the things you noticed that led to involuntary gratitudes all placed in one folder or in the same note so that you have a running list you can easily go back to. Just make sure you add the date, and number each entry. The numbers create a feeling of continuity and motivation to keep going.

Finally, some days you might find yourself wanting to add more than a single person, item, or event to your entry. Still, pick just one, and leave the others for the next day. This will build momentum and prevent you from being overwhelmed.

After she left Singapore for Australia, my eldest sister left behind a poster that I placed on the back of my bedroom door:

"Lord, you have given me so much. Please give me one more thing: A grateful heart."

Practise letting yourself be moved by gratitude.

## BROADEN YOUR NATURE

If you are high in Conscientiousness and low in Openness to Experience, you are likely to face an internal conflict with the idea of letting go of control. This is because you'd much prefer some semblance of orderliness and predictability. Don't be disheartened by the challenge of Surrender. There are parts of your life that you have to gain Control over, and others where you have to relinquish the tight grip that chokeholds the possibility of Adventure. Listen to this changing season of your life and what it asks of you. May you be willing to be moved into Adventure.

---

*See Related Paradoxes: 5. Yes/No, 6. Acceptance/Change, 8. Autonomy/Belonging, 9. Grief/Love, 12 Recovery/Stress, 13. Stillness/Movement.*

# CONCLUSION

# PERSONAL PARADOXICAL PROFILE (P3) REDUX

Now that you've completed all of the fifteen paradoxes, it's time to revisit your Personal Paradoxical Profile. What does your P3 look like? What are some key ideas that stand out to you?

Maybe you are at a different place in your life as you near the end of this book. Given the current seasonality of your life, are there areas that need recalibration in your P3?

Once you've reviewed your P3, make sure to place it somewhere highly visible to you. Pin it to your wall, or keep it as a bookmark in your notebook. In addition, I suggest you take a picture of your P3 and save it in the photo library on your mobile device. Refer to it every now and then (See A Gift For You). The most important thing is to be reminded of what is the most important thing.

Finally, to bulletproof your efforts, it is now time to complete the **Course of Action** (see Appendix F). This is critical. It's where ideas turn into action. Don't skip this final step.

If you are rereading this book at a different season of your life, know this: Where you were previously tilted towards in the fifteen items of the P3 might be the total opposite in this current new chapter. As you might recall, different seasons have different needs.

Across your life, as mentioned in "Part I: The Framework" (see Bridge-Crossing), you are likely to face a handful of significant life quakes. During these different shakeups, you are likely going to need to move towards different ends of each of the fifteen spectrums in P3. In one new season, you may need something new. And in subsequent seasons, you may long for a thing you had before. Life progresses in a circle, not a straight line. So don't get distracted by trying to find the "right" formula. As the saying goes, "What got you here, won't get you there."[i]

In the scheme of things, you have to learn to hold onto these polarities during the course of your lifetime. Life is not an either/or situation; it's both/and. *You breathe in, you breathe out.* I mean, you can't say, "I'm a 'breathing in' kind of person; breathing out is not my thing."[ii] You are going to need to do both.

---

One last step: Complete Appendix F.

Nature → Nurture → Needs → Naming the Season → Complete the P3 → Read the 15 Paradoxes → Revisit Your P3 → Course of Action

# A CALL TO BECOME A GIFT TO OTHERS

A king once summoned all of his wise men and asked them,

"Is there a mantra, a suggestion, or a line I should remember that will apply in every situation and every circumstance, in every sorrow and in every joy? Tell me, what would it be?"

All the wise men were perplexed. They became worried, because they couldn't come up with a response to such a strange request. They pondered a long time without any progress. Finally, a soft-spoken elder said he had an answer, but he requested he be allowed to write it on a piece of paper, and that the king was not to see it immediately.

Only in a time of extreme danger, when the king found himself alone and there seemed to be no way out, only then was he to see it. The King put the paper in his diamond ring.

Years passed, and then the kingdom came under attack. The king's army fought bravely, but defeat was inevitable given the strength and size of the enemy. The king fled on his horse. He looked back and saw the ruins that were his kingdom. As he stopped his horse, sobbing in defeat, he noticed the diamond ring shining in the sun, and he remembered the piece of paper hidden within it. He opened the diamond and read the message.

It said: "This too shall pass."

The King read the message again and again. Suddenly it struck him. "Indeed. This, too, will pass. Only a few days ago, I was enjoying my kingdom. I was the mightiest of all the kings. Yet today, the kingdom and all its pleasure have gone. I am here trying to escape my enemies. Like those days of luxury have gone, this day of danger too will pass."

A calm came over his face. He stood there for a long time. Suddenly, the road where he was standing was full of natural beauty. He had never known that such a beautiful place was part of his kingdom. It was as if the king was seeing with new eyes. After he recaptured his kingdom, struck by the message of the ring, once again, solemnity entered his heart. This time, his true purpose revealed itself.

Courage entered his heart. He reorganised his remaining army and fought again. He defeated the enemy and regained his empire. When he returned after victory, he was received with much fanfare. The whole capital was rejoicing in the victory. Everyone was in a festive mood. Flowers were being showered on the king from every house, from every corner. People were dancing and singing.

In that moment, The King said to himself, "I am one of the bravest and greatest kings. It is not easy to defeat me. See how I overcame defeat." But then the diamond of his ring flashed in the sunlight and reminded him of the message. He opened it and read it again: "This too shall pass".

His face fell flat. He gazed at the crowd and looked at his people, men, women, and children, young and old. He realised deep in his bones that, regardless of good or bad times, his true purpose was ultimately to serve his people well.

For the first time, the king felt truly alive.

As you are Crossing Between Worlds, remember that this

period is an invitation to a life that is waiting for you. Remember the paradoxes discussed throughout this book: The more you give, the more you get. The more you learn to accept yourself, the more you have the ability to change. The more you know how to grieve, the more you know how to love.

You are called to be faithful to your gifts. Your true gifts will be of value to others. After all, a gift is only a gift when it serves a need. As you embark on this path, you will not only be aiming for new goals, you will also reckon with the differences between your true and false selves.

> "[Virtue] is not just about what we do but also about the kind of person we are called on to become."
>
> — *Jonathan Sacks*[i]

"What are your goals in life?" is different from the question "Who do you want to become?" I have yet to meet anyone who said, "I want to become my false self."

What is a false self? Conversely, what is a true self? Thomas Merton, a Cistersian monk whose writings have been a deep well of inspiration for me, described the false self as "shadowed by an illusory person."[ii] Elsewhere, he wrote, "Many poets are not poets for the same reason that many religious men are not saints: they never succeed in being themselves. ... They waste their years in vain efforts to be some other poet, some other saint. ... There can be an intense egoism in following everybody else."[iii]

The false self is catalysed by the delusions and speed of mass culture, largely dictated by the Algorithm of whichever Silicon Valley organisation is at the helm, amplifying the worst sides of ourselves. It is hard to come into contact with our true self, because we are constantly being nudged to consume content at a breakneck pace. But we can get to know our true and quieter self when we travel at the speed of life, not at the speed of light. Merton noted, "Hurry ruins saints as well as artists."[iv]

On the other hand, relating to the discovery of the true self, Merton said, "To find our true self, we must peel away the layers of the false self crafted by societal expectations and personal illusions." But this process is fraught with slippery slopes. "You can never be sure," Merton warned, "whether you are being true to your true self or only building up a defence for the false personality that is the creature of your own appetite for esteem."

To be clear, the false self is not our bad self. Rather, it is the outward beefed-up layer we portray to others and ourselves. It is the pretence, the facade, the arrogance, and the smarts. It's mostly based on the false stories we tell ourselves. As Richard Rohr points out, "If a person keeps growing, their various false selves usually die in exposure to greater light."[v] The false self is a thwarting of what was originally meant to be good. The true self is, in essence, the original goodness. Buried by all the layers of falsehood that we carry, underneath the rough, is the diamond.

Do not underestimate the fact that you are a visionary. The sheer act of reading this book suggests that you are in the act of shaping who you are becoming. You have the ability to imagine a possible future. I'm not saying you can manifest your $10 million dollar wish by simply thinking about it. I'm saying that if you open yourself up to nurturing and give your gifts to others who need them, you will move—and be moved—to become who you really are.

There is no predetermined plot. You will "grow" your own road.

And you will be inspired to help others who are Crossing Between Worlds, too. When you are able to tap into your unique gifts, you will call out the unique gifts in others. The more you nurture your unique gifts, the more you are able to seek them in others. Reach out to those people in your life who are taking steps for change. You can become their guide, their mentor, their counsel at times when they need you most. Be a witness to their significant period of transformation so that they will be inspired to make a similar journey to the one you have. They may need different things compared to what you needed (i.e., their P3 might look different), but they can still learn from your experience.

In the three main sections of this book, I've attempted to weave the inter-relationship between well-being, well-belonging, and well-doing. Much of our well-being is dependent on who we relate to and the tasks we take upon ourselves to pursue.

My hope in writing this book is that as you are making life transitions, you seize this opportunity of heightened awareness on the inside and sharing that gift with the world on the outside. As you are Crossing Between Worlds, may you peel away and undercut the illusions of the false self and come to discover a true self that is waiting for you to come alive.

When you come alive, others will be exposed to greater light.

> *Let everything happen to you: beauty and terror.*
> *Just keep going. No feeling is final.*
> *Don't let yourself lose me.*
> *Nearby is the country they call life.*
> *You will know it by its seriousness.*
> *Give me your hand.*
>
> — Rainer Maria Rilke (1875-1926)

# A GIFT FOR YOU

Thank you for coming all the way to the end. I don't take for granted the privilege I have to walk with you through these 15 Paradoxes.

As my gift to you, I want to offer a set of materials to help sustain your efforts through this period of change and transition. These consist of

- A downloadable **Pocket Guide** containing the key points of the 15 Paradoxes and tips.
- Templates of the exercises.
- Entirely **free access** to the audiobook (I don't believe you should pay twice for the same content).
- And more!

Go to **darylchow.com/seasons** to download the resources. Email me if you have questions at info@darylchow.com.

# ACKNOWLEDGEMENTS

To Carol Morgan, Emily Di Palma, John Sync, Rachel Moore, the beta-readers from the Frontiers of Psychotherapist Development (FPD) community, and my colleague Sharon Lu, all of whom put up their hand up to read the early versions of this half-baked idea back in 2021. It means a lot to me that I got to hear your inputs. In the midst of my self-doubts, you helped shape this book and made me pull my socks up. I hope I've done you proud.

To Shawn Mihalik, my editor. You are a true maestro with words. I took copious notes on all the stuff I learned from you in our previous collaboration on *The First Kiss* book, and I took more copious notes on all the stuff I learned from you in this book. Your love of the craft (and fountain pens) is inspiring. You amaze me.

To John Adrian Olid, thank you for your assistance through these months. I appreciate your help in these mad times, especially in the later stages of finishing up this manuscript. Your family is lucky to have you, a hardworking man of God.

To Joel Louie, my longtime friend and designer of this book's cover. This is the first time in my experience of book projects that the initial round of mockups was right on the money! You chose to help me even though this was a demanding period in your life. It means a lot to me. Your friendship is one of the handful that I really treasure. Keep the music alive.

To my clients and the people I supervise/coach, it is you I seek to serve. I've received a gift of life from working with you. Sometimes I've missed the mark, and I've tried, as far as I can, to learn as quickly as possible. Your stories are in me; I don't own them. They are *your* stories. They have shaped me in profound ways. For this, I am eternally grateful for your trust.

To my friend and longtime mentor, Juliana Toh. Your voice is often in my head. I hear them as these words form in the book. You remind me of the perennial truths I often forget. For this, I am deeply thankful.

To Edmond Nixon, C.S.s.R, our cuppas together mean a lot to me. Your wisdom, humour and appreciation for the beauty that surrounds us are infectious.

To all my instrumental mentors, who wrote the books that I loved, sitting on the shelf next to me. You don't know me personally, but your words have touched, moved, and inspired me. Thank you for putting down in words what has been in your hearts and minds.

Finally, to my wife and kids. I made a promise to myself to be less of a Grouch during the process of writing this book from 2021 to 2024. I've failed pretty often. Forgive me. Pray for me—to make things easier, for us to play and laugh together more, and to bring a piece of Heaven here for each other—and for others in need.

# APPENDICES

# Appendix A: The Personal Paradoxical Profile (P3)

As mentioned in Instructions to the Personal Paradoxical Profile (P3), here is a copy for your reference. For a printable version of the P3, go to **darylchow.com/seasons**.

# PERSONAL PARADOXICAL PROFILE (P3)

Name: _____  Date: _____

Age: _____  Review Date: _____

Instructions:
1. *Reflect on your current circumstances and describe the season of your life using either a single word or a sentence.*
2. *Mark an '<', '>' or 'X' on each of the 15 lines below. Where you demarcate on the line is based on **where you are now**, and the symbol you use will depend on **where you need to go**. Each of these three symbols represent a marking of your current situation and the direction you need to take in this season. For further elaboration, see the book Crossing Between Worlds, How to Begin section.*

**Q. What is the current season of my life?**

_____

## I. WELLBEING

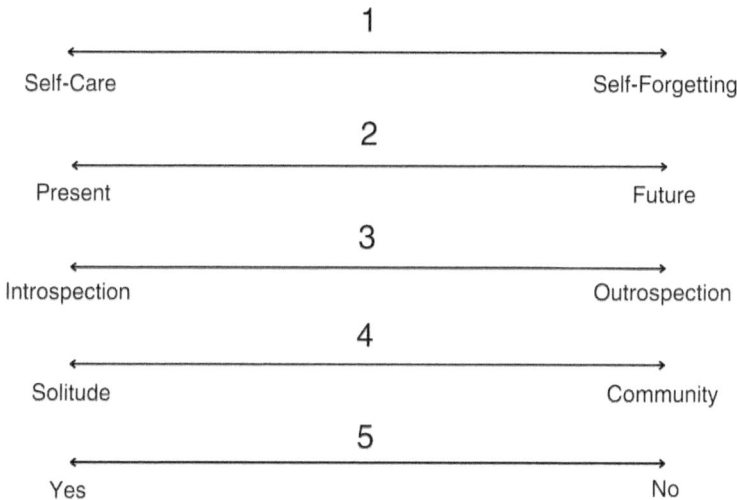

*For strategies to navigate this period of your life, read Crossing Between Worlds, darylchow.com/cbw*

## II. WELL-BELONGING

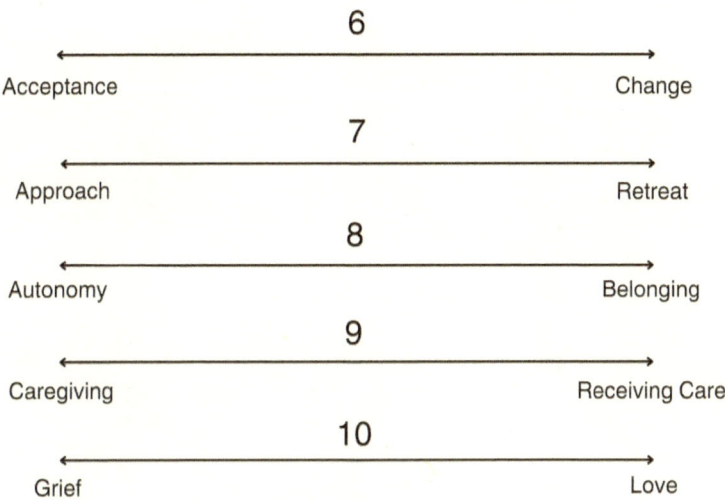

## III. WELL-DOING

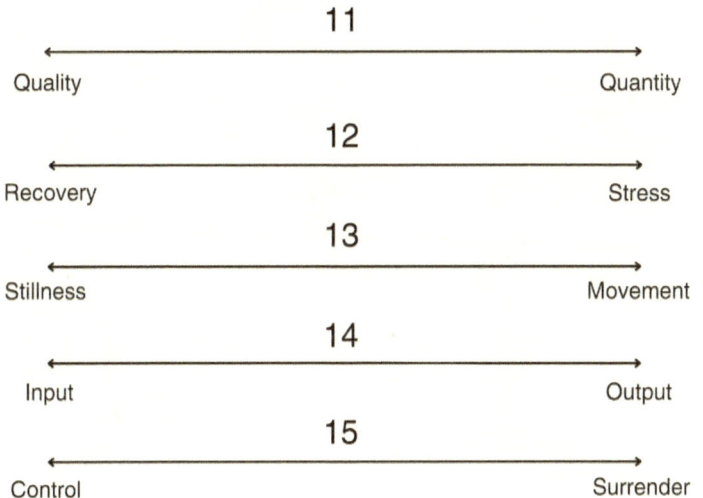

*For strategies to navigate this period of your life, read Crossing Between Worlds: darylchow.com/cbw*

## Appendix B: The Big Five Personality Construct

As mentioned in "Part I, What is Your Nature", here are three options to figure out your temperament using the Big Five Personality Construct.

### 1. Rough-and-Ready:

This is the quickest way to get started. There are three steps. First, review the table and its description and rate each of the ten sub-scales within the Big Five factors (i.e., two subscales within each of the five) from a -2 to a +2 (i.e., -2 = very low and +2 = very high; 0 = neutral). For example, on *Openness to Experience,* rate how high you are on interests in *Intellectual* ideas and openness to *Aesthetics* and creative pursuits. Revisit the details about the Big Five Personality Construct in What is Your Nature.

Second, after you are done with each of the 10 sub-scales, average each of the pairs. For example, if you self-rated *Intellect* as +1 and *Aesthetics* as +2, your *Openness to Experience* will be +1.5 (i.e., $(1 + 2)/2 = +1.5$.).

Third, get someone who knows you well to rate you as well. Before telling them how you self-rated on the Big Five Personality Construct, let them rate you independently on each of the 10 sub-scales. Thereafter, you can share and discuss the ratings. You can also get a friend or family member to rate themselves, and you in turn rate them. This can spark some interesting conversations.

Granted, this is a quick-and-dirty approach and not precise. That said, it is useful, especially if you combine your self-rating and collateral rating from others who know you well.

## Scoring:

| -2 | -1 | 0 | +1 | +2 |
|---|---|---|---|---|
| Very Low | Low | Neutral | High | Very High |

| BIG FIVE PERSONALITY CONSTRUCT | | | |
|---|---|---|---|
| 5 Main Factors | 10 Sub-Factors | Ratings (-2 to +2) | Main 5 Scores (average each of the pairs) |
| Openness to Experience | Intellect | | |
| | Aesthetics | | |
| Conscientiousness | Industrious | | |
| | Orderly | | |
| Extraversion | Enthusiasm | | |
| | Assertiveness | | |
| Agreeableness | Politeness | | |
| | Compassion | | |
| Neuroticism | Volatility | | |
| | Withdrawal | | |

## 2. Free and Reliable Version:

There are countless free online personality tests, though some are dubious, and several are not empirically validated. However, Spencer Greenberg and his team at Clearer Thinking have made a version of their personality test freely available online. Their "Ultimate Personality Test" combines the three most popular personality frameworks in one—you'll receive a personalised report with your Big Five traits, your Enneagram, and your Jungian Type (inspired by MBTI). If you take this option, zoom in on the Big Five aspect of the report.

Here is the link: clearerthinking.org/post/we-re-launching-the-ultimate-personality-test.

## 3. Comprehensive Paid Version:

For $9.95, the Understand Myself website has one of the most comprehensive and useful paid versions that I know of (understandmyself.com). The personalised report created by co-authors Drs. Jordan Peterson, Daniel Higgins, and Robert Pihl are detailed and useful. A noteworthy mention is that this version breaks down the two subscales of each of the Big Five Personality traits. In other words, based on your responses to the 100-item questionnaire, you get a percentile rating on ten sub-scales instead of just five.

As you learn more about your personality traits, keep in mind that we have a tendency to under-value traits that are unlike our own. The next time you are at dinner with extended family and a political discussion ensues, pay careful attention to others who have different views from yours. As you might recall from the book (see What's in Your Nature in Part I, The Framework), Haidt notes that people's political beliefs are influenced by their moral intuitions, which are in turn shaped by their personality traits. For instance, conservatives tend to score higher on measures of psychological traits such as conscientiousness, traditionalism, and respect for authority, while liberals tend to score higher on measures of openness to experience, empathy, and tolerance for ambiguity. This, in turn, leads to moral polarisation, in which individuals on opposite ends of the political spectrum perceive each other as morally and ideologically opposed. This polarisation is driven in part by differences in personality traits and moral intuitions, which can lead individuals to interpret the same events or issues in divergent ways.[i]

## Appendix C: Dailies, Strategies, Skills, and Meals (DSSM) Framework

As mentioned in "Paradox 6. Change", here is a quick rundown on each of the four factors of the DSSM framework, as well as a template for your use.

**Definitions:**

**Dailies:** What you do regularly.
**Strategies:** A set of guiding principles or rules of thumb. (See **Counsel** sections for each of the 15 Paradoxes for examples).
**Skills:** Things you can learn and get better at.
**Meals:** What you nourish your mind and body with. This applies to content you consume, as well as food you eat.

*Note:* Your DSSM Framework is context-dependent. Based on what you indicated in your P3, write down the season you are in at the top of the table.

# Template:

| Name The Season You Are In: _____ | | | |
|---|---|---|---|
| **Dailies** | **Strategies** | **Skills** | **Meals** |
| | | | |

## Appendix D: Reading Non-Fiction

Reading non-fiction is often like going through a cookbook—not just for pleasure, but to actually cook up a meal." As mentioned "#2. Active Engagement in Contact in Paradox 14. Input", here is a table to document your pre-test (i.e., what you think you know about the topic before reading the book), key ideas (i.e., main points) and key actions (i.e., actionable steps) for each chapter of a book you are reading:

| Book Title: | | Date: |
|---|---|---|
| Pre-Test: | | |
| Chapter | Key Ideas | Key Actions |
| 1 | | |
| 2 | | |

## Appendix E: Have You Been Faithful to Your Gifts?

As mentioned in "Paradox 14. Outputs", here is a template to help you identify your Gifts.

First, list What's Valuable to You on the left circle. Second, list What's Valuable to Others on the right circle, i.e., what you wish to bestow onto others and the world at large. Finally, look for items that sit at the intersection between the two circles.

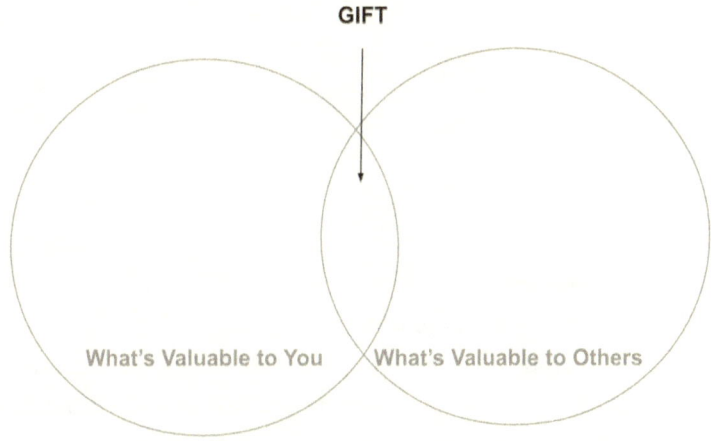

Now that you've identified areas that are in the intersection between What's Valuable to You and What's Valuable to Others, chances are they fall into one of three new categories. Imagine we double-click on the centre of the two-circle Venn diagram, and it opens up to a new triple Venn diagram called **True, Useful, and Beautiful.**

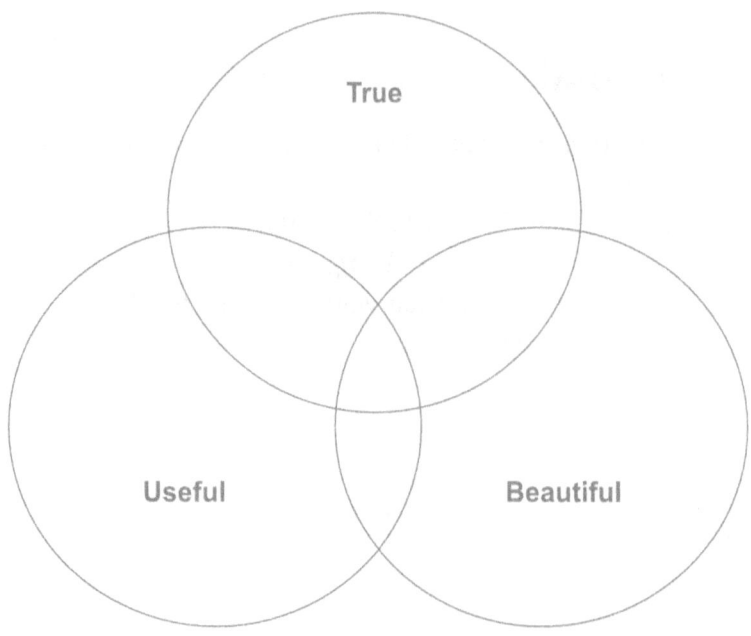

Take a moment to fill in the template above at where you think you might reside in the venn diagram.

**True:** Someone who values truth will be inclined towards domains related to justice, philosophy, science, and the pursuit of what accurately represents the world and the way it ought to be. (Think of lawyers, social activists, journalists, research scientists, etc.)

**Useful:** Someone who values usefulness will gravitate towards work that helps others, adds value, and makes the world a better place. (Think of social workers, nurses, doctors, people in the helping profession, etc.)

**Beautiful:** Someone who values beauty is moved by aesthetics and wants to create and bring that experience to others. (Think of artists, musicians, designers, architects.)

## Appendix F: Course of Action

This is where we take the universal ideas and convert them into personal actions.

There are a total of 7 steps to make sure your course of action plan has the highest chance of success.

**1. Review**

Flip through this book once again. Revisit how you've answered your Personal Paradoxical Profile in accordance to the way you've identified the current season of your life.

**2. Each Domain**

In each of the three domains, *Well-Being, Well-Belonging,* and *Well-Doing*, identify **one key area** in each that will help you make the necessary adjustments to go in the direction you need to take. Revisit the ideas provided in the *Counsel* section of each of the 15 Paradoxes (Or use the Pocket Guide for a concise summary. See **A Gift For You**).

You might have more than one thing to do in each of these areas. Try your best to narrow down to just one.

Here's what I need to do for each of the three domains:

**Well-Being:**

_____
_____
_____

**Well-Belonging:**

_____
_____
_____

**Well-Doing:**

_____
_____
_____

## 3. The One Thing

The distance between A to B is not the same as B to C, or C to D. Figuring out and acting upon the first step of A to B is *the* most important course of action you can make to beat procrastination.

Even though each of the three domains are important in their own right, **pick one area** that will have the greatest leverage. Sometimes this might be the one with the greatest impact, or one that is the easiest one to begin with.

**The one thing I can begin doing is**

_____

_____

_____

## 4. Crystal Ball to Barriers

In the next six months, imagine the worst thing that can derail your best made plans. Vivify them as much as possible in your mind, and then list them down below.[1]

_____

_____

_____

Casting your eyes into where you might falter is a great way to pre-emptively deal with potential pitfalls.

## 5. Design a System, Not a Goal

The amateurs have goals.

The pros have a system.

In the words of famous cartoonist, Scott Adams,

"Goal-oriented people exist in a state of continuous pre-success failure at best, and permanent failure at worst if things never work out. Systems people succeed every time they apply

---

[1]. I first learned this idea of a Pre-mortem exercise from the work of Gary Klein. Credit should also go to the Stoics (see Ryan Holiday's book, *The Obstacle is the Way*).

their systems, in the sense that they did what they intended to do. The goals people are fighting the feeling of discouragement at each turn. The systems people are feeling good every time they apply their system. That's a big difference in terms of maintaining your personal energy in the right direction."[i]

You might have identified in #3. *The One Thing* to be "more present" (2. Present / Future Paradox). While this might be a good goal to have, it is not a system.

A system is something you do daily, weekly, or at least in a consistent rhythm. As long as you keep at your system that you've designed, every move that you make is in the step of the right direction.

In the example of wanting to "be more present," a system might look like

- Every Friday, 5pm, take a meditative walk for 15 mins at the local park (see #1. Sense, in Paradox 2. Present).
- Commit to eating food without the phone present on the table at mealtimes and savour the food. (see #2. Savour, in Paradox 2. Present).

## 6. Anti-Goals

Inversions are a powerful way to get clear on what's needed to be focused on.

Identify what you should *not* be focusing on. Make a list of your Anti-Goals; things that you should not focus on as you work on #3. **The One Thing:**

_____
_____
_____

## 7. Pick a Review Date

Finally, pick a specific date in the future to review your Course of Action. Schedule it as a meeting in your calendar.

Not only would you review your Course of Action plan, you would also assess "**What is the Current Season of Your Life?**" And re-calibrate your Personal Paradoxical Profile (P3; see Appendix A).

I suggest a review date to be typically between 1 to 3 months time.

Review Date: _____

---

Here's where we are at:

**Nature** → **Nurture** → **Needs** → **Naming the Season** → **Complete the P3** → **Read the 15 Paradoxes** → **Revisit Your P3** → **Course of Action**

*Congratulations for making it all the way to the end!*

# NOTES

## PART I: THE FRAMEWORK

i. *A Joseph Campbell Companion: Reflections on the Art of Living* by Joseph Campbell.

### 2. Bridge-Crossing

i. *Life Is in the Transition* by Bruce Feiler.
ii. Janis H. Zickfeld, Thomas W. Schubert, Beate Seibt, & Alan P. Fiske. (2019). *Moving Through the Literature: What Is the Emotion Often Denoted Being Moved?*: Emotion Review, 1–17. https://doi.org/10.1177_1754073918820126
iii. *Steal Like An Artist* by Austin Kleon.

### 3. Nurture Your Nature

i. marketplace.org/2018/10/30/myers-briggs-system-evaluate-employees/
ii. Morgeson, F. P., Campion, M. A., Dipboye, R. L., Hollenbeck, J. R., Murphy, K., & Schmitt, N. (2007). Reconsidering the Use of Personality Tests in Personnel Selection Contexts, *Personnel Psychology, 60*(3), 683–729. [https://doi.org/10.1111/j.1744-6570.2007.00089.x](https://doi.org/10.1111/j.1744-6570.2007.00089.x)
iii. Taken from *Personality Isn't Permanent* by Benjamin Hardy.
iv. See also You are a Multitude. fullcircles.substack.com/p/multitude
v. *How to Live* by Derek Sivers, p. 87.

### 4. Why Needs?

i. *Transcend* by Scott Barry Kaufman.
ii. *Impro: Improvisation and the Theatre* by Keith Johnstone.

### 5. Why Seasons?

i. *Imagine If...* by Ken Robinson and Kate Robinson.
ii. Ford, B. Q., Mauss, I. B., & Gruber, J. (2015). *Valuing happiness is associated with bipolar disorder. Emotion, 15*(2), 211–222. https://doi.org/10.1037/emo0000048

If you are actually reading this, the items used to measure the Extreme Valuing of Happiness scale (Mauss et al., 2011) might be of interest to you:

(1) How happy I am at any given moment says a lot about how worthwhile my life is.
(2) If I don't feel happy. Maybe there is something wrong with me.
(3) I value things in life only to the extent that they influence my personal happiness.
(4) I would like to be happier than I generally am.
(5) Feeling happy is extremely important to me.
(6) I am concerned about my happiness even when I feel happy.
(7) To have a meaningful life, I need to feel happy most of the time.

iii. Genesis 3:8-12.
iv. For a useful visual summary on the Fourth Turning, watch this video youtu.be/xeVyfiPocLk
v. Watch Jack Grapes interview, youtube.com/watch?v=V7yTb-k1ju4&feature=share
vi. *Mere Christianity* by C.S. Lewis, pp. 32-33.
vii. *Standing at the Edge* by Joan Halifax.
viii. *Will and Spirit* by Gerald May.
ix. An interview with Stephen Jenkinson, "A Generation's Worth: Spirit Work While the Crisis Reigns" (Orphan Wisdom, 2021). play.anghami.com/episode/1029889755.

## 7. How to Begin

i. *The Dignity of Difference* by Jonathan Sacks, pp. 56-57.

## 8. What Not to Do When Crossing Between Worlds

i. I've borrowed this analogy from Alok Kanojia, a.k.a. Dr. K.

## 9. Structure of the Book

i. Lambert, M. J., Burlingame, G. M., Umphress, V., Hansen, N. B., Vermeersch, D. A., Clouse, G. C., & Yanchar, S. C. (1996). The reliability and validity of the Outcome Questionnaire. *Clinical Psychology & Psychotherapy*, 3(4), 249-258. The Outcome Questionnaire, a measure of well-being, consists of three subscales: symptom distress, inter-personal relations, and social role

## PART II: Well-Being

i. *On Becoming a Person* by Carl Rogers, pp. 186-187.

## Paradox 1: Self-Care/Self-Forgetting

 i. *Consolations* by David Whyte.
 ii. For more on this, see this blog post "The Speed of Life." darylchow.com/fullcircles/the-speed-of-life/
 iii. en.wikipedia.org/wiki/Karoshi
 iv. *Lead Yourself First* by Raymond Kethledge and Micheal Erwin.
 v. See this article: darylchow.com/frontiers/the-60-hour-rule/
 vi. *Anam Cara* by John O'Donohue, p. 28.
 vii. *Quit* by Annie Duke.
 viii. Duckworth, A.L., Peterson, C., Matthews, M.D., & Kelly, D.R. (2007). Grit: Perseverance and passion for long-term goals. *Journal of Personality and Social Psychology, 9*, 1087-1101.
 ix. This quadrant is largely inspired by a podcast interview with Annie Duke, freakonomics.com/podcast/annie-duke-thinks-you-should-quit/
 x. See the body of work by Mihaly Csikszentmihalyi, such as *Flow: The Psychology of Optimal Experience*, *Finding Flow: The Psychology of Engagement with Everyday Life*
 xi. *The Purpose-Driven Life*, in Day 19, "Cultivating Community, by Rick Warren.
 xii. See Austin Kleon's excellent blog, austinkleon.com/2021/08/09/surprise-is-an-enabler-of-seeing
 xiii. I watched YouTube channels like Stephen Travis Art, Sketching Scottie and Future Condos to help get me started.

## Paradox 2. Present/Future

 i. *Composing a Further Life* by Mary Catherine Bateson, as cited in *The Good Ancestor*, p.22.
 ii. *How Emotions are Made* by Lisa Fieldman Barrett.
 iii. *The Environment that Shapes Us* by Lily Bernheimer.
 iv. This question was inspired from the book, *The Path of Least Resistance* by Robert Fritz.
 v. Klein, R. J., Jacobson, N. C., & Robinson, M. D. (2023). A psychological flexibility perspective on well-being: Emotional reactivity, adaptive choices, and daily experiences. *Emotion, 23*(4), 911–924. doi.org/10.1037/emo0001159
 vi. onbeing.org/program/michael-longley-the-vitality-of-ordinary-things/9022
 vii. *The Good Ancestor* by Roman Krznaric.

## Paradox 3. Introspection/Outrospection

 i. *Missing Out* by Adam Philips, p. 4.
 ii. *Mindwise* by Nicholas Epley.

## Paradox 4. Solitude/Community

i. Read this article by social psychologist Jonathan Haidt, *Why the Past 10 Years of American Life Have Been Uniquely Stupid*, theatlantic.com/magazine/archive/2022/05/social-media-democracy-trust-babel/629369/
ii. *No Man is an Island* by Thomas Merton, p. 127.
iii. *Consolations by* David Whyte.
iv. *Dopamine Nation* by Anna Lembke.
v. *No Man is an Island* by Thomas Merton, p. 85.

## Paradox 5. Yes/No

i. Poem by Mary Oliver *"Wild Geese."*

## Part III: Well-Belonging

i. *The Phenomena of Man* by Pierre Teilhard de Chardin, p. 263.
    Note: The translated version I have is worded differently from jcfj.ie/article/ireland-europe-and-catholic-social-teaching-shared-values. "The peak of ourselves, the acme of our originality, is not our individuality but our person; and according to the evolutionary structure of the world, we can only find our person by uniting together. There is no mind without synthesis."

## Paradox 6. Acceptance/Change

i. This was from an audio recording of a panel discussion at The Evolution of Psychotherapy Conference.
ii. This phrase is attributed to organisational theorist Steve Spear.
iii. From *The Sermon on the Mount* audiobook, Chapter 5 by Richard Rohr.
iv. *A Way Of Being* by Carl Rogers, pp.22-23.
v. *Impro for Storytellers* by Keith Johnstone, p. 59.
vi. For a comprehensive discussion on the topic of Comparison, see fullcircles.substack.com/p/comparison
vii. I did not come up with this phrase. I believe I first heard it either from David Whyte or John O'Donohue. Both are poets and close friends with each other.
viii. This newsletter is for people in the helping profession, called *Frontiers Friday* darylchow.substack.com
ix. For more on the impact of alcohol, check out Andrew Huberman's podcast episode on "What Alcohol Does to Your Body, Brain, and Health."
x. For more on food and nutrition, I recommend reading Mark Hyman's book *Food: What the Heck Should I Eat.*

xi. See research from Adams, G. S., Converse, B. A., Hales, A. H., & Klotz, L. E. (2021). *People systematically overlook subtractive changes. Nature,* 592(7853), 258–261. doi.org/10.1038/s41586-021-03380-y

xii. *Drunk Tank Pink by Adam Alter.*

xiii. Based on Bruce Alexander's research, Johann Hari proposes another reason why the majority of the veterans didn't develop heroin addiction: They reconnected with people in their lives when they returned home.

xiv. Kammrath, L. K., McCarthy, M. H., Cortes, K., & Friesen, C. (2015). Picking One's Battles: How assertiveness and unassertiveness abilities are associated with extraversion and agreeableness. *Social Psychological and Personality Science,* 6(6), 622–629. https://doi.org/10.1177/1948550615572635](https://doi.org/10.1177/1948550615572635

## Paradox 7. Approach/Retreat

i. *Improv Wisdom* by Patricia Madson, p. 104.
ii. *Wintering* by Katherine May.
iii. Adapted from David Whyte's audiobook *What to Remember When Waking.*
iv. *The Screwtape Letters* by C.S. Lewis, p. 161.

## Paradox 8. Autonomy/Belonging

i. From *Riverflow,* "House of Belonging" by David Whyte, p. 8.
ii. *Choice Theory: A New Psychology of Personal Freedom, by* William Glasser.
iii. *The Courage to be Disliked* by Ichiro Kishimi and Fumitake Koga,, p. 210.
iv. I'm not quoting the exact words here, as I can't seem to find the particular episode that I saw.
v. *Play* by Stuart Brown.
vi. From Letters from Esther #53: Novelty Is A Powerful Aphrodisiac. Here's How To Have More. estherperel.com/blog
vii. See Netflix documentary, *Abstract.*

## Paradox 9. Caregiving/Receiving Care

i. *Gravity and Grace* by Simone Weil.
ii. Conjectures of a Guilty Bystander by Thomas Merton
iii. wcspeakers.com/speaker/john-p-foppe/
iv. *The Undivided Life* by Parker Palmer.
v. From Richard Rohr, *The Art of Letting Go* audio series. This is also attributed to Martin Buber's writing on I-Thou relationship. The Minimalists also have a book, *Love People, Use Things.*
vi. *Dignity* by Donna Hicks.
vii. rosalynncarter.org
viii. *Life of the Beloved* by Henri Nouwen, p. 25.

## Paradox 10. Grief/Love

i. This quote by Stephen Jenkinson was cited from one of his interviews. See https://youtu.be/SIN3erN9uoI?si=plHO_JJ74bGbYVv.
ii. *Grief* by Sven Brinkmann, p. 3.
iii. *How to Love* by Thich Nhat Hanh, p. 39.
iv. *Ibid* p. 68.
v. *Diewise* by Stephen Jenkinson,, p. 168.
vi. *Tuesdays with Morrie* by Mitch Albom.
vii. Much of what I've learned about the concept of re-membering practices, I owe it to the work of Lorraine Hedtke and John Winslade. I highly recommend their book, *Re-Membering Lives*.
viii. Listen to this BBC podcast: Heart and Soul - The wind phone: http://www.bbc.co.uk/programmes/w3csz4jr
ix. worlddata.info/life-expectancy.php
x. This story was taken from *Freakonomics Radio* episode. 355. "Where Does Creativity Come From (and Why Do Schools Kill It Off)?" freakonomics.com/podcast/creativity-2/
xi. *The Art of Loving* by Erich Fromm,, p.2.

## Paradox 11. Quality/Quantity

i. *Art and Fear* by David Bayles and Ted Orland.
ii. *The Path of Least Resistance* by Robert Fritz, pp. 70-73, and p. 135.
iii. Berg, J. M. (2016). Balancing on the Creative Highwire: Forecasting the Success of Novel Ideas in Organisations. *Administrative Science Quarterly*, 61(3), 433–468. https://doi.org/10.1177/0001839216642211
iv. Taken from Tim Ferriss podcast interview with Jerry Seinfeld tim.blog/2020/12/08/jerry-seinfeld/

## Paradox 12. Recovery/Stress

i. As cited in the book, *The Power of Full Engagement by* Jim Loehr and Tony Schwartz.
ii. *The Power of Full Engagement* by Jim Loehr and Tony Schwartz, p. 12.
iii. *Ibid.*, p. 38
iv. *Antifragile by* Nassim Taleb.
v. *Dopamine Nation* by Anna Lembke.
vi. For more on sun exposure and vitamin D, read *Energize* by Michael Breus and Stacey Griffith, and *The Vitamin D Solution* by Michael Holick.
vii. stylist.co.uk/health/mental-health/one-good-thing-dopamine-hard-things-reset/791433.
viii. *Dopamine Nation*, by Anne Lembke.
ix. *Mind in Society: The Development of Higher Psychological Processes* by Leo Vygotsky.

Notes | 351

x. Wilson, T. D., Reinhard, D. A., Westgate, E. C., Gilbert, D. T., Ellerbeck, N., Hahn, C., Brown, C. L., & Shaked, A. (2014). Just think: The challenges of the disengaged mind. *Science, 345*(6192), 75–77. https://doi.org/10.1126/science.1250830

## Paradox 13. Stillness/Movement

i. *A More Beautiful World Our Hearts Know Is Possible* by Charles Eisenstein, pp. 121-122.
ii. *No Man Is an Island* by Thomas Merton, p. 258.
iii. Stults-Kolehmainen, M. A. (2023). Humans have a basic physical and psychological need to move the body: Physical activity as a primary drive. *Frontiers in Psychology, 14*, 1134049. https://doi.org/10.3389/fpsyg.2023.1134049
iv. Fiuza-Luces, C., Garatachea, N., Berger, N. A., & Lucia, A. (2013). Exercise is the Real Polypill. *Physiology, 28*(5), 330–358. https://doi.org/10.1152/physiol.00019.2013
v. *Flow: The Psychology of Optimal Experience* by Mihaly Csikszentmihalyi.
vi. "Everything is Waiting for You," *in River Flow* by David Whyte.
vii. *The Artist's Way* by Julia Cameron.
viii. *New Seeds of Contemplation,* by Thomas Merton, p.1.
ix. Among the many, Merton's two books *New Seeds of Contemplation,* and *No Man Is An Island* are worth reading.
x. The *Changing Mind* by Daviel Levitin, p. 282.
xi. See *Start With Why* by Simon Sinek.
xii. I first learned about Aristotle's Four Causes in Richie Norton's book *Anti-Time Management.*
xiii. *Find Your Why* by Simon Sinek, David Mead, and Peter Docker, p. 17.
xiv. See also "Graceful Self-Forgetting" darylchow.substack.com/p/ff183
xv. "103 Bits of Advice I Wish I Had Known" by Kevin Kelly kk.org/thetechnium/103-bits-of-advice-i-wish-i-had-known/
xvi. *Image from* https://en.wikipedia.org/wiki/Path_of_least_resistance
xvii. The phrase Defense Mode and Discovery Mode was coined by Jonathan Haidt in his book *Anxious Generation.*

## Paradox 14. Input/Output

i. *Deep Work* by Cal Newport.
ii. *The Art of Impossible* by Steven Kotler.
iii. medium.com/conversations-with-tyler/tyler-cowen-ted-gioia-music-history-jazz-9a042d13b268
iv. *The More Beautiful World Our Hearts Know Is Possible* by Charles Eisenstein, p. 12.
v. *The Breath of the Soul: Reflections on Prayer* by Joan Chittister.
vi. "Listening into Speech," /darylchow.com/frontiers/listeningintospeech/

vii. See Peter Diamondis' and Steven Kottler's books *Bold* and *The Art of Impossible*.
viii. en.wikipedia.org/wiki/Anh_Do
ix. Lerner, D.A., Verheul, I. & Thurik, R. Entrepreneurship and attention deficit/hyperactivity disorder: a large-scale study involving the clinical condition of ADHD. *Small Bus Econ* 53, 381–392 (2019). https://doi.org/10.1007/s11187-018-0061-1
x. White, H. A., & Shah, P. (2016). Scope of Semantic Activation and Innovative Thinking in College Students with ADHD. *Creativity Research Journal*, 28(3), 275–282. https://doi.org/10.1080/10400419.2016.1195655
xi. Boot, N., Nevicka, B., & Baas, M. (2020). Creativity in ADHD: Goal-Directed Motivation and Domain Specificity. *Journal of Attention Disorders*, 24(13), 1857–1866. https://doi.org/10.1177/1087054717727352
xii. Van Dijk, F. E., Mostert, J., Glennon, J., Onnink, M., Dammers, J., Vasquez, A. A., Kan, C., Verkes, R. J., Hoogman, M., Franke, B., & Buitelaar, J. K. (2017). Five factor model personality traits relate to adult attention-deficit/hyperactivity disorder but not to their distinct neurocognitive profiles. *Psychiatry Research*, 258, 255–261. https://doi.org/10.1016/j.psychres.2017.08.037
xiii. Nigg, J. T., John, O. P., Blaskey, L. G., Huang-Pollock, C. L., Willcutt, E. G., Hinshaw, S. P., & Pennington, B. (2002). Big Five dimensions and ADHD symptoms: Links between personality traits and clinical symptoms. *Journal of Personality and Social Psychology*, 83(2), 451–469. https://doi.org/10.1037/0022-3514.83.2.451
xiv. The existing evidence between ADHD and Extraversion appears mixed. However, some evidence suggests that Extraversion is a significant predictor of hyperactive-impulsive ADHD symptoms, but not so for inattentive symptoms. See Parker, J. D. A., Majeski, S. A., & Collin, V. T. (2004). ADHD symptoms and personality: Relationships with the five-factor model. *Personality and Individual Differences*, 36(4), 977–987. https://doi.org/10.1016/S0191-8869(03)00166-1
xv. From "Enough Words?" in *The Essential Rumi* by Rumi, p. 20.
xvi. I highly recommend reading Paul Graham's blog post, "Maker's Schedule, Manager's Schedule." https://paulgraham.com/makersschedule.html

## Paradox 15. Control/Surrender

i. From *The Art of Letting Go* audio series by Richard Rohr.
ii. Listen to the *On Being* podcast interview with Richard Rohr (onbeing.org/programs/richard-rohr-growing-up-men/), and read his book *Wisdom Pattern*.
iii. *The Great Partnership* by Jonathan Sacks, p. 71.
iv. wbur.org/hereandnow/2017/09/20/dave-eggers-her-right-foot#
v. ryanholiday.net/why-we-need-a-statue-of-responsibility
vi. See *Morality* by Jonathan Sacks.

vii. *The Doctor and the Soul* by Viktor Frankl, p. 24.
viii. ryanholiday.net/why-we-need-a-statue-of-responsibility
ix. *Man's Search for Meaning* by Viktor Frankl, 4th edition.
x. See darylchow.com/fullcircles/parenting-is/ and darylchow.com/fullcircles/45learnings/
xi. ted.com/talks/amy_baxter_how_to_hack_your_brain_when_you_re_in_pain
xii. See this Charlie Rose interview: youtu.be/BDojoOiKLuc?si=U7L7vBkT2ePB2QNs
xiii. *A Field Guide to Getting Lost* by Rebecca Solnit, p. 88.
xiv. See this video Exploring Creativity by Brian Eno. youtube.com/watch?v=JUL8kNYmgsA&feature=share
xv. Listen to this *99% Invisible* podcast episode that talks about how a bootlegged book of jazz standards, called *The Real Book*, shaped and influenced countless jazz musicians. 99percentinvisible.org/episode/the-real-book/
xvi. *The History of Jazz* by Ted Gioia, p. 61.
xvii. *Teaching a Stone to Talk* by Annie Dillard, *p. 38.*
xviii. *Healing a Fractured World* by Jonathan Sacks, p. 6.
xix. *With Open Hands* by Henri Nouwen, *p. 53.*
xx. From *Ha!* by Peter Kreft.
xxi. This phrase is borrowed from Stephen Jenkinson.
xxii. Adapted from Becky Kennedy's book on parenting, *Good Inside.*

## Personal Paradoxical Profile (P3) Redux

i. This is the title of a business book by Marshall Goldsmith.
ii. This sentence was inspired from a live conversation between Parker Palmer and Courtney Martin. onbeing.org/programs/parker-palmer-courtney-martin-the-inner-life-of-rebellion/

## A Call to Become a Gift to Others

i. *Healing a Fractured World by Jonathan Sacks,* p. 242.
ii. *New Seeds of Contemplation* by Thomas Merton, p.34.
iii. *Ibid*, p. 98.
iv. *Ibid*, p. 98.
v. cac.org/daily-meditations/letting-go-of-the-false-self-2023-08-09/

## Appendix B: The Big Five Personality Construct

i. *The Righteous Mind* by Jonathan Haidt.

## Appendix F: Course of Action

i. *How to Fail at Almost Everything and Still Win Big* by Scott Adams.

# ALSO BY DARYL CHOW

**THE FIRST KISS**

Undoing the Intake Model
and Igniting the First Sessions
in Psychotherapy

DARYL CHOW, Ph.D.

Mind This Voice:
**The Write to Recovery**

Personal stories and lessons about recovery
from mental health concerns

Edited by
Patricia Yap    Daryl Chow
Sharon Lu       Brenda Lee

# BETTER RESULTS

**Using Deliberate Practice to Improve Therapeutic Effectiveness**

SCOTT D. MILLER   MARK A. HUBBLE
DARYL CHOW

---

A companion workbook for Better Results

# The Field Guide to BETTER RESULTS

Evidence Based Exercises to Improve Therapeutic Effectiveness

Edited by
SCOTT D. MILLER, DARYL CHOW,
SAM MALINS, and MARK A. HUBBLE
Foreword by BRUCE WAMPOLD

---

# CREATING IMPACT

The four pillars of private psychology practice

Kaye Frankcom, Daryl Chow,
RaeLynn Alvarez Wicklein,
Nathan Castle, Aaron Frost

www.ingramcontent.com/pod-product-compliance
Lightning Source LLC
Chambersburg PA
CBHW022028290426
44109CB00014B/787